EDUCATIONAL
PSYCHOLOGY
in Context

To our children, Aly, Lauren, and Rachel

EDUCATIONAL PSYCHOLOGY
in Context
Readings for Future Teachers

Editors
Bruce A. Marlowe • Alan S. Canestrari
Roger Williams University

SAGE Publications
Thousand Oaks ■ London ■ New Delhi

For information:

Sage Publications, Inc.
2455 Teller Road
Thousand Oaks, California 91320
E-mail: order@sagepub.com

Sage Publications Ltd.
1 Oliver's Yard
55 City Road
London EC1Y 1SP
United Kingdom

Sage Publications India Pvt. Ltd.
B-42, Panchsheel Enclave
Post Box 4109
New Delhi 110 017 India

Printed in the United States of America

Library of Congress Cataloging-in-Publication Data

Educational psychology in context: readings for future teachers / edited by Bruce A. Marlowe, Alan S. Canestrari.
      p. cm.
Includes bibliographical references and index.
ISBN 1-4129-1387-X (cloth) — ISBN 1-4129-1388-8 (pbk.)
   1. Educational psychology. I. Marlowe, Bruce A. II. Canestrari, Alan S.
LB1051.E3625 2006
370.15—dc22   2005009857

This book is printed on acid-free paper.

05   06   07   08   09   10   9   8   7   6   5   4   3   2   1

Acquisitions Editor:	Diane McDaniel
Editorial Assistant:	Marta Peimer
Production Editor:	Tracy Alpern
Proofreader:	Penelope Sippel
Typesetter:	C&M Digitals (P) Ltd.
Cover Designer:	Michelle Kenny

Contents

Acknowledgments

We have been extremely fortunate to have had the opportunity to work with hundreds of pre-service and in-service teachers in the last several years. It is really their questions and reflections about how young children and adolescents learn and develop over time that has inspired this book. There are too many students to thank each of them individually here, but we would be remiss if we did not mention a few by name. Aura Ryder, Candice McLean, Michael Parrillo, Colleen Roberts, Lori Henault, Holly Bedrosian, Richard Mason, and Caroline Fletcher continued to ask us tough, thoughtful questions throughout the course of their classroom experiences, many of which can be found throughout this manuscript.

This is our second project with Sage Publications. Diane McDaniel and Marta Peimer were particularly helpful in shepherding this book from its early inception to the final product you now hold in your hands. Our book went through an extensive pre-publication review process and we are indebted to the following scholars for their feedback: Marilyn Page, Penn State University; Robert C. DiGiulio, Johnson State College; Eric Fretz, University of Michigan; Michelle M. Riconscente, University of Maryland, College Park; Susan J. Parault, University of Maryland, College Park; Michele Gregoire Gill, University of Central Florida; Karen E. Eifler, University of Portland, Oregon; Donna Carol Browning, Mississippi State University; William Lan, Texas Tech University; and James Milton Applefield, University of North Carolina, Wilmington.

We have had extraordinary support from Jeffrey Hill, who oversaw the layout, scanning, design of figures, and word processing of the entire manuscript. His organizational skills are without parallel. Here at Roger Williams University, we are indebted to Mary Gillette and Lisa Medeiros and especially to Danielle Bento, one of our most promising pre-service teachers, for their ongoing support.

❖ CREDITS

For permission to reprint from the following, grateful acknowledgment is made to the publishers and copyright holders:

Chapter 1

From Hunter, M., Planning for effective instruction: Lesson design in *Enhancing Teaching*. Copyright © 1994, reprinted with permission of Prentice Hall, Inc. a Pearson Education Company.

Chapter 2

From Aronson, E., & Bridgeman, D., Jigsaw groups and the desegregated classroom: In pursuit of common goals in *Personality and Social Psychology Bulletin, 5*(4), 1979, pp. 438–466. Reprinted with permission from Sage Publications, Inc.

Chapter 3

From Marzano, R. J., & Marzano, M. L., The key to classroom management in *Educational Leadership, 61*(1), 2003, pp. 6–13. Reprinted by permission. The Association for Supervision and Curriculum Development is a worldwide community of educators advocating sound policies and sharing best practices to achieve the success of each learner. To learn more, visit ASCD at www.ascd.org.

Chapter 4

From Traina, R., What makes a good teacher, as first appeared in *Education Week, 18*(19), p. 34, 1999.

Chapter 5

From Skinner, B. F., "The Science of Learning and the Art of Teaching," *Harvard Educational Review, 24*(2), Spring, pp. 86–97. Copyright © 1954 by the President and Fellows of Harvard College. All rights reserved. Reprinted with permission.

Chapter 6

From Bandura, A., Ross, D., & Ross, S. A. (1961), Transmission of aggression through imitation of aggressive models in *Journal of Abnormal*

Psychology, 63, pp. 575–582. Copyright © American Psychological Association. Reprinted with permission.

Chapter 7

From Willingham, D. T., Students remember . . . what they think about in *American Educator,* Summer 2003, the quarterly journal published by the American Federation of Teachers, AFL-CIO. Reprinted with permission.

Chapter 9

From J. Piaget, The stages of intellectual development of the child in Mussen, Conger, and Kagan (Eds.), *Readings in child development and personality, 2/e.* Copyright © 1965. Reprinted with permission.

Chapter 10

From Erik H. Erikson, Eight Ages of Man, in *Childhood and Society.* Copyright © 1950, © 1963 by W. W. Norton Company, Inc., renewed © 1978, 1991 by Erik H. Erikson. Used by permission of W. W. Norton & Company, Inc.

Chapter 11

From Kohlberg, L., & Kramer, K., Continuities and discontinuities in childhood and adult moral development in *Human Development, 12,* 1969, pp. 93–120. Reprinted with permission from Karger.

Chapter 12

From Carol Gilligan, In a different voice: women's conceptions of self and morality in *Harvard Educational Review, 47*(4), pp. 481–517. Copyright © 1977 by the President and Fellows of Harvard College. All rights reserved. Reprinted with permission.

Chapter 13

From Macedo, D., English only: The tongue-tying of America in *Journal of Education, 173*(2), Spring 1991. Reprinted with permission of Trustees of Boston University and the author.

Chapter 14

From O'Neill, J., Can inclusion work? A conversation with Jim Kauffman and Mara Sapon-Shevin in *Educational Leadership*, 1994, 7–11. Reprinted by permission. The Association for Supervision and Curriculum Development is a worldwide community of educators advocating sound policies and sharing best practices to achieve the success of each learner. To learn more, visit ASCD at www.ascd.org.

Chapter 15

From Checkley, K., The first seven . . . and the eighth. A conversation with Howard Gardner in *Educational Leadership*, 55(1), 1997, pp. 8–13. Reprinted by permission. The Association for Supervision and Curriculum Development is a worldwide community of educators advocating sound policies and sharing best practices to achieve the success of each learner. To learn more, visit ASCD at www.ascd.org.

Chapter 16

From Torrance, E. P., Insights about creativity: Questioned, rejected, ridiculed. In *Educational Psychology Review, 7*, 1995, pp. 313–322, copyright © 1995, with kind permission from Springer Science and Business Media.

Chapter 17

From Kohn, A., Five reasons to stop saying "Good job!" Copyright © 2001 by Alfie Kohn. Reprinted from Young Children with the author's permission. For more information, please see www.alfiekohn.org.

Chapter 18

From Dweck, C., Caution—praise can be dangerous in *American Educator,* Spring 1999, the quarterly journal published by the American Federation of Teachers, AFL-CIO. Reprinted with permission.

Chapter 19

From Maslow, A. H., A theory of human motivation in *Motivation and Personality*, 1954. Reprinted with permission.

Chapter 20

Chapter 21

Chapter 22

Chapter 23

Chapter 24

Introduction:
Theory Into Practice

❖ WHY IS *THIS* BOOK ON THE
EDUCATIONAL PSYCHOLOGY SHELF?

We know what you are thinking. You just returned from the bookstore with an armload of books, a lot less money, and some pretty serious doubts about the real value of all these new purchases. If you are a freshman, this will soon be a familiar beginning-of-the-semester ritual. The bookstore was undoubtedly jammed with students blocking every path to the school of education section, the aisles were hardly passable, and the new arrivals cluttered the stacks from floor to ceiling. As you maneuvered, elbowed, and excused your way toward the education section you heard students complaining about the costs, and worse about how most of these purchases will be returned—maybe even before the course is over. And, there it was, the book you now have before you. *Couldn't there simply be a used text for this class, you wondered. This isn't the text the psychology professors used last semester. It's new. I hope this book is good. Maybe if I don't mark it up or write in it, I'll get a little more money when I return it.*

Well, if your professor is like us, he or she might not be that happy with the texts on the market and has searched for an alternative. We applaud your professor's choice. Like you, your professor probably surmised that virtually all of the textbooks written for coursework in educational psychology, or learning theory, are boring. We do too. That's why we wrote this book. And, we hope that you will find in this text some fresh ideas and important insights for helping prepare thoughtful, caring, and competent teachers.

In our view, most textbooks in the psychology of learning—in fact, most university textbooks in every field—deny students the opportunity to develop critical reading and writing skills, because the authors have already reduced the big ideas to easily digestible pabulum. Moreover, they simply provide the textbook author's interpretation, without allowing students to read, reflect, and think critically about what is most significant, relevant, or interesting about a particular theoretical approach or original piece of scientific research. In fact, even if you were actually motivated to read all of the material in a typical textbook, you would likely be left with only a shallow understanding of the big concepts because the author took great pains to cover these ideas in only a paragraph or two. In their attempt to cover everything, textbook authors leave students little opportunity to delve deeply into any substantive issues.

As the content demands widen, students have become responsible for knowing less and less about more and more, largely so that they may perform better on standardized, multiple-choice exit exams. As a result, the scope of the course has become broader but the power and novelty of the ideas of psychologists like Piaget, Skinner, and Erikson have become lost in a sea of bland summary. And, the texts on the market leave professors few options other than assuming a highly didactic, teacher-directed approach to instruction. That is, the organization, and the remarkable breadth of most texts, promotes practices that are antithetical to meaningful instruction: lecture, memorization, multiple-choice assessment. Finally, because of their size and scope, and their explicit reference to a variety of standards and standardized tests, most textbooks do not encourage deep reflection about the connections between research and instruction but instead foster acceptance of pre-packaged, commercially produced teaching materials.

What You Will Not Find in This Text

In our experience, the teacher education textbook market has allowed itself to be dominated by the standardized test movement: Tests—and test preparation—have become the curriculum, instead of a measurement of it. So, rather than letting the Interstate New Teacher Assessment and Support Consortium (INTASC) Standards or probable questions from the Praxis exam drive the format of each chapter, we have organized this text thematically. The textbook market's increasing emphasis on helping pre-service teachers to meet standards, and pass certification exams, obscures the importance of having students carefully examine the important ideas, *and the actual words of those who first spoke them.*

What You Will Find in This Text

Well, enough about what is wrong with other books and what you won't find in ours. For a glimpse of what you will find, take a look at the letter we recently received from one of our education students currently working in an elementary classroom.

Hi Professors:

I have some real concerns regarding the inclusion of special education students into mainstream regular education. There is a lack of modification being done for special education students, due to what I call "the wrath of the rubric." There also seems to be some alarming issues concerning the inadequate amount of communication that is happening between special educators and the regular education teachers to meet IEP obligations. These issues have been a problem in every grade I have observed, and it is obviously detrimental to the student's behavioral and academic success. What do you think?

Aura Ryder

It was this letter, and many, many others like it, that got us thinking about the need for an educational psychology book that addresses the questions real teachers in real schools ask about real kids. *How old do kids have to be before I can introduce them to abstract concepts? How do children learn the difference between wrong and right? Why do young kids have so much more trouble sharing? What should I do with kids for whom English is not their first language? What about kids with varying abilities in one classroom? Is it okay to recommend some kids for the lower tracks? Does moral reasoning develop over time? How about intelligence?*

Take another look at Aura's letter. Inclusion? Rubrics? Behavioral *and* academic success? Modifications for special education students in regular mainstream classrooms? Even this short letter provides a window into the many new challenges and questions facing today's teachers. How can teachers create instructional opportunities that reflect an understanding of how *all* children learn and develop? How can teachers adequately address the enormous diversity of today's learners and approaches to learning? How can they use a variety of formal and informal assessment strategies to support the continuous development of each learner?

These are the kinds of questions you will read about in letters from students, and former students—many of whom now have their own classrooms—from all across the United States; letters about real class-rooms in real schools. But, the answers will not come from the usual sources. As we have noted above, university textbooks traditionally summarize the views of important thinkers for you. In this book, you will actually read what some of the most notable educators, psycholo-gists, and researchers think and have had to say about these issues and then *you* will be asked to think critically about what *you* believe.

❖ WHY IS EDUCATIONAL PSYCHOLOGY
    ESSENTIAL FOR TEACHERS?

Think for a moment. Where do stressed-out teachers go to get advice about how to deal with kids, usually unruly ones? Yes, it is the teachers' room. We are not saying that there may not be some really valuable advice or lessons learned in that venue. But, in a moment of weakness, what "junk" might teachers carry away when they ask the question: *Why don't the kids get it?* Perhaps the kind of junk you have heard many times before. We believe that it is the business of teachers to see that kids get it. But, when they don't, here's what is usually offered as explanation—*The kids are slow learners,* or *have poor motiva-tion,* or *short attention spans.* As Schon (1987) notes, "These are ways of describing what Clifford Geertz has called *junk categories* to remove their not getting it from the range of things with which the teacher would have to deal" (p. 3).

The teachers' room is a place where absolution is granted, where the answers to the "not getting it" questions are forgiven, displaced, rationalized away; here comfort can be restored. But, where can real answers be found? Well, we used to know back when *we* were in a teacher preparation program. Once, professors and mentors in the field encouraged preparing teachers to be reflective, to inform their practice with a deep understanding of how children learn and develop. Once, action-research models guided teachers in the field and students at the graduate level were encouraged to use what was discovered in their action research to address practical issues of teaching and learning. Textbooks and testing has done much to co-opt teachers and steer them away from models that might supply the real answers to why kids don't "get it." We propose a return to this earlier, reflective practitioner model like the one in Figure 1.

Figure 1   The Reflective Practitioner Feedback Model

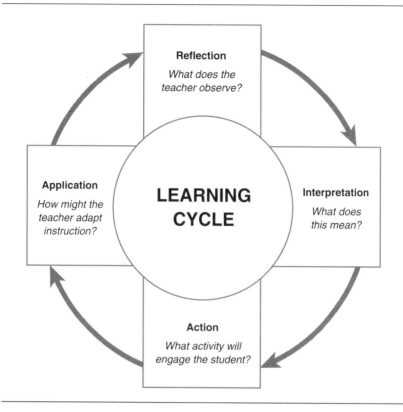

Teachers who are reflective practitioners use this framework to design and develop learning plans, select materials and resources for their students, deliver instruction and interpret student responses to new learning, and re-teach, redirect, or adapt their instruction accordingly. Their practice is informed by formal study, and by personal and collegial experiences. This dynamic relationship between theory and practice is not an additive phenomenon but rather a synergistic interplay that reflects the constant back and forth between the teacher's theories about learning and what is really happening in the classroom. The notion of the reflective practitioner is based on a feedback loop, a reflection *in action* model where theory and experience continue to inform and shape each other.

So, how can teachers put action into the reflective practitioner model? Consider this letter from the field:

Professor Canestrari:

I am currently halfway through my student teaching process. Although I have learned a lot about teaching and classroom management, I am still very confused about how to motivate my fourth-grade students. Specifically, my class is very high energy; however, they cannot seem to channel that energy into being productive and following directions. I know that an easy and quick solution to this problem is to create some sort of point system where the students are rewarded for doing what I want them to do. The problem with this is that I am opposed to trying to control the class by dangling a carrot in front of them in order to get them to do exactly what I want. How can I get the class to follow directions and pay attention without using some type of reward system?

Colleen Roberts

Here is another.

Dr. Marlowe:

I am a second-year teacher who has a class of 27 students. I have one full-time aide; however, my class is extremely slow this year and I am therefore constantly trying to get them to catch up. To complicate matters even more, I have one student who requires me to give him all my attention (he acts up, doesn't do work, etc.), which takes me away from the rest of my class. His parents have also reprimanded me on several occasions for singling him out in class. Another teacher has offered to take the student and place him in her class, but I am not sure if that is the best idea. If I remove this one student from my class, does that reflect negatively on my ability to teach? Or, will the removal of one student send a negative image of me to the rest of my class?

Pam Rivers

What does research say about motivation? How might teacher experience inform the answer to the question, *How can we motivate unmotivated students?* We can imagine the "junk" responses that Colleen and Pam might get in the teachers' room—*My patience ran out years ago, I have stopped trying, I just keep them in their seats and demand that they be quiet so that the other kids can learn.* On the other hand, we can encourage our students to do some reading, to start thinking about what teacher behaviors contribute to student achievement and success and then to start a list of critical questions that perhaps could be the focus of some future action research in the classroom. Perhaps this may even uncover some surprising results. One source for a model that teachers can use in their own classrooms is *Action Research: A Guide for the Teacher Researcher* by Geoffrey Mills (2000). Take a look at the model from Mills in Figure 2.

This model provides a way for teachers to engage in systematic inquiry that can help them improve their teaching in a way that is more likely to ensure that kids "get it." What other kinds of data can teachers use to inform their instruction? Questions like this are a central focus of our text. In fact, as you make your way through the readings, think about how your experience, your reflections about the readings, and the comments of your peers and professors can further inform how you think about student learning and development, how students are really motivated, and how they might reach their potential in your classrooms.

Figure 2   The Dialectic Action Research Spiral

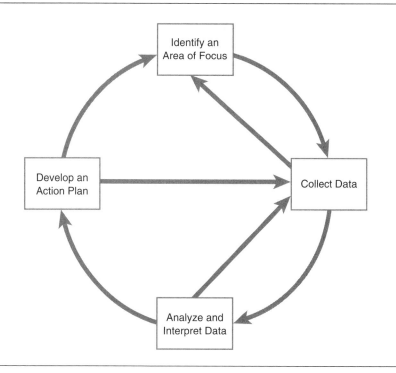

SOURCE: Mills, p. 20.

How This Text Is Organized, and Why It Is Challenging

The book lends itself to Socratic dialogue, to debate, and to discussion, and we hope that is how your instructor uses it. Listening to lectures about what your *professor* thinks is most important about the views of notable educators and psychologists is not what we have in mind; that's why we provided their original words, so that *you* may arrive at your own conclusions by reading actively, making further investigations, and initiating conversations in your university classrooms with your professor and your peers. We introduce each reading with a *Letter from the Field*, like the ones you read above from Aura Ryder, Colleen Roberts, and Pam Rivers. Immediately following each letter is a piece of original research or commentary written by a leading psychologist, cognitive scientist, or educator whose published work has helped to form part of the very foundation of the field of educational psychology.

In our view, understanding cannot be gleaned from reading research summaries or paraphrased accounts. This means the book will likely be both much more interesting *and* much more challenging than other psychology texts with which you are familiar. So, here are a few tips.

Read With a Purpose

Some of the pieces in this anthology are original research, complete with statistical analyses, graphs, and tables summarizing numerical data. Others are simply more challenging than a traditional textbook summary because of the writing style required in academic journals. Don't get hung up with the jargon, the statistics, or even the formal tone. Instead, look for the main points, which are often best explained in the text rather than in tables. Where there is straightforward reporting of numerical data (such as averages, frequency distributions, grade point score differences, etc.), try to use the data to trace the overall logic of the analysis—ignore the statistical technicalities and skip what you do not understand for now. Read the raw numbers in the tables: Do they add up? Do they seem to support the arguments of the author or authors?

When you begin to grasp the overall picture, take notes, make a rough flow chart of the author's argument, construct a table, draw a web—do whatever you must to summarize the central arguments and the evidence that supports them. Be sure to take careful notes of words and concepts that appear particularly important but with which you are unfamiliar. Work around them as well as you can until you get more clarity. It is unlikely that a single word or phrase will bring you to a complete halt. Just remember to read with a purpose. Ask yourself these questions:

- What is the author's purpose?
- What questions does the author pose?
- How do the author's answers to these questions add to the knowledge base about this topic? In what way?
- Are the author's conclusions justified?
- Is the work valuable?
- How does the study help support my views/answer my questions about this topic?

When you do get confused and/or frustrated (and you will, on occasion), keep in mind the following: *Reading scholarly work is not a spectator sport.* Simply reading most of what is found in academic journals will not lead to understanding. Instead, think about your work as a problem-solving task, as opposed to reading for pleasure. To get a handle on most academic articles requires frequent flipping forward and backward through the pages, underlining, making margin notes and connections to your own experience, writing questions, drawing diagrams, and taking frequent breaks! If you expect to understand challenging essays by simply reading carefully from the beginning to the end you will be sorely disappointed.

Read With a Critical Eye

If you believe there is obvious error, nonsense, stupidity, faulty assumptions, or flawed reasoning make note of it (and then continue to move on with the job of understanding). Once you understand the article, then try to piece together where and how you believe the author might have gone astray. Be suspicious. What are the author's assumptions? Are they valid? Can the conclusions make sense if the assumptions are false? Does the author answer the question she or he poses? For those of you without a strong background in statistics, reading the work of authors who use quantitative research methods may present a challenge, but keep the following in mind: None of the authors in this anthology rely on complex statistics to make their arguments about how children learn and develop. If you are interested in learning more about the work and want to pursue understanding of how the use of statistics might support the authors' views, see your professor about supplemental materials that can assist you in "decoding" the results section, or take a course in statistics. We suggest for example, Gerald Bracey's *Bail Me Out: Handling Difficult Data and Tough Questions About Public Schools* (2000). But, remember, you can, if you are persistent and thoughtful, understand these pieces even with no background whatsoever in statistics.

Take a Stand

Read with an eye toward taking a position. Do you agree with what the author says? Why? Does it square with your experience? Is it consistent with your beliefs about how children learn? Were the authors' views true in an earlier age, but no longer relevant? How does the author's argument address or help inform the questions raised by the letter that introduced it? Does the work of authors who have long since passed away stand up to modern criticism? What new information, perhaps unavailable to the author at the time of his or her life, might change his or her position?

Throughout this text, our focus is on how maturation, experience, and, perhaps most important, *teaching* influence the unfolding development of children's abilities. The role of culture, motivation, intelligence, and socioeconomic status each receive attention, and in readings that we think are unique, we also offer novel thinking about creativity, and social and affective components of learning.

Using Scholarly Work to Inform Instruction

How exactly should students approach these admittedly difficult pieces to help them prepare for tomorrow's classrooms? Incidentally, by itself, using neon-colored highlight pens does little to inform meaning and practice. Instead, we propose that you use an approach to critical reading, such as the example from B. F. Skinner (1968, p. 10) that we have provided in Figure 3, so that you might be prepared to interact with your professor and classmates.

❖ A FINAL THOUGHT

Before turning to Part I, where you will read a variety of scholarly opinions about how learning occurs, think about the kinds of questions

Figure 3   A Critical Reading Model

The Science of Learning and the Art of Teaching

See Prof's notes on Thorndike ←

What is the Law of Effect? →

Recent improvements in the conditions which control behavior in the field of learning are of two principal sorts. The Law of Effect has been taken seriously; we have made sure that effects *do* occur and that they occur under conditions which are optimal for producing the changes called learning. Once we have arranged the particular type of consequence called a rein-forcement, our techniques permit us to shape up the behavior of an organism almost at will. It has become a routine exercise to demonstrate this in classes in elementary psychology by conditioning such an organism as a pigeon. Simply by presenting food to a hungry pigeon at the right time, it is possible to shape up three or four well-defined responses in a single dem-onstration period—such responses as turning around, pacing the floor in the pattern of a figure-8, standing still in a corner of the demonstration apparatus, stretching the neck, or stamping the foot. Extremely complex perfor-mances may be reached through successive stages in the shaping process, the contingencies of reinforcement being changed progressively in the direction of the required behavior. The results are often quite dramatic. In such a demonstration one can *see* learning take place. A significant change in behavior is often obvious as the result of a single reinforcement.

What does he mean by "shape"? →

How is this related to reinforcement schedules? →

Is this really the same as learning? →

Is training a response the same as teaching?

Behaviorist definition of learning ←

teachers might ask about this topic. Are teachers necessary for learning to occur? At what age does real learning begin? Is learning to walk the same kind of process as learning to read? What do you imagine are new teachers' biggest concerns?

Our anthology is organized around the following essential ques-tions: How does learning occur? What role does maturation play in learning? How should student diversity affect teaching practice? What factors influence student motivation? What do good assessments look like? Each chapter follows the same format: Foreshadowing some of the important issues, a letter from the field will introduce each reading. Following the reading, you will find a series of questions that asks *you* to interpret the big ideas that are offered and to make connections between the views of the authors and the concerns raised by the letter that preceded it.

References

Bracey, G. (2000). *Bail me out: Handling difficult data and tough questions about public schools.* Thousand Oaks, CA: Corwin.

Mills, G. (2000). *Action research: A guide for the teacher researcher.* Upper Saddle River, NJ: Prentice Hall.

Schon, D. (1987, April). *Educating the reflective practitioner.* Paper presented to the American Educational Research Association, Washington, DC.

Skinner, B. F. (1968). *The technology of teaching.* New York: Appleton-Century-Crofts.

PART I

Real Classrooms

1

❖ ❖ ❖

Dear Professor Canestrari:

I absolutely loved last night's class. I thought that Matt and Meredith did a great job with their inquiry demonstration lesson on child labor. I thought that they were really well prepared and they worked so effortlessly together. They knew what they wanted to accomplish, they asked us the right questions, they had great visuals by Lewis Hine and Jacob Riis, but above all, they really made us think. The lesson was really engaging. Your follow-up modeling with the puzzling Samoset, Kensington Stone, and Kwakiutl situations further reinforced my understanding about how we can promote inquiry in our classrooms. I think I'm getting a handle on getting kids to speculate. But my practicum cooperating teacher says that there are times when I have to be more explicit and when more instruction is necessary. What do you think? Have you any suggestions how about how I can approach this? I'm pretty sure how the inquiry lessons are going to go in my unit on commercial fishing in Rhode Island but what about more explicit lessons? I'm not quite sure about how to combine the two. Is there a way to combine them? Can we talk about this?

Carol Feinstein

❖ HOW WOULD YOU RESPOND?

Think about what makes teachers engaging. What skills do they possess? How do they communicate? What models of instruction might be useful to enhance teaching and learning? What are the component parts of a lesson? How do teachers sequence these components? How do effective teachers get student attention to begin a lesson? How do teachers model problem-solving behaviors? How can teachers assure that students will master new subject matter and essential skills? Keep these questions in mind as you read "Planning for Effective Instruction: Lesson Design" by Madeline Hunter and Doug Russell. What questions do you have about direct teaching? How can you help extend the discussion of these ideas in class? Finally, how would you respond to Carol Feinstein?

❖ PLANNING FOR EFFECTIVE INSTRUCTION: LESSON DESIGN

Madeline Hunter and Doug Russell

Skill in planning is acknowledged to be one of the most influential factors in successful teaching. Should there be a system to this planning or does one hope for a burst of inspiration from which effective instruction automatically will flow? While teacher educators are all for inspiration, we agree with Edison, that well-directed "planning perspiration" *plus* inspiration will work wonders in increasing learners' successful achievement. We believe that a systematic consideration of seven elements, which research has shown to be influential in learning and which therefore should be deliberately *included* or *excluded* in the plan for instruction, will make a great deal of difference in learners' success or lack of it.

It is assumed that *before* a teacher begins to plan for a particular day's teaching, the following decisions, which make effective instruction probable, will have been made:

1.   Within each general content or process area, the teacher will have determined the particular strand for immediate diagnosing and teaching. For example, in the general content area of reading, the teacher might diagnose and teach to either students responding to a piece of literature or identifying main theme or separating fact from opinion or increasing decoding skills. In a process area, the learning could be metacognition, brainstorming, or the generation of meaning in terms of a student's own experience; that is, what the student already knows.

2.   The teacher will have identified a major target objective in the strand and have diagnosed students' achievement in relation to that objective. For example, the teacher will identify students' ability to

respond to literature, determine which students can identify main theme, separate fact from opinion, or use beginning consonants to decode words. When a teacher determines which students need to learn a particular content, process, or appreciation, learning opportunities to accomplish that particular objective need to be planned.

3. On the basis of a diagnosis, the teacher will have selected the specific objective for the total group's or the subgroup's subsequent instruction. ("The learners will write their responses to the story, indicating the feelings it evoked" or "The learners will generate meaning in relation to self" or "The learners will select the main idea and underline it" or "The learners will place an F by each statement that is a fact and an O by each that is an opinion.")

Only after these three determinations (specific content, students' entry behaviors, target objectives) have been made is the teacher ready to *plan* for tomorrow's learning opportunity—regardless of whether the plan is implemented by direct input from the teacher, by materials, by computer, or by the students themselves in discovery or cooperative learning. Elements in a planning sequence are necessary for *every* mode of learning, not just direct instruction.

For each instructional session, the teacher must consider the following seven elements separately to determine whether or not each element is relevant for the particular content or process objective, for *these* students in *this* situation. Thus, a decision has to be made as to whether that element should be included, excluded, or combined with another element.

If the element is included, how to effectively sequence and integrate it in an artistic "flow" of instruction is the essence of the planning task.

When *designing* lessons, the teacher needs to consider the element in a certain order since each element is derived from and has a relationship to previous elements. Also a decision must be made about inclusion or exclusion of each element in the final design. When the design is *implemented* in teaching, the sequence of the elements included is determined by the professional judgment of the teacher.

1. What Instructional Input Is Needed?

All lesson design begins with articulation of an instructional objective. It specifies the perceivable student behavior that validates achievement—the *precise content or process or skill* that is to be the learning outcome.

To plan the instructional input needed to achieve the target objective, the teacher must determine what information (new or already possessed) the student needs in order to accomplish the intended outcome. Students should not be expected to achieve an objective without having the opportunity to learn that which is essential in order for them to succeed. Task analysis is the process by which the teacher identifies the component learnings or skills essential to the accomplishment of an objective.

Once the necessary information, process, or skill has been identified, the teacher needs to select the means for "getting it in students' heads." Will it be done by discovery, inquiry, teacher presentation, book, film, record, filmstrip, field trip, diagram, picture, real objects, demonstration? Will it be done individually, collaboratively, or in a larger group? The possibilities are legion, and there is no one that is always best.

Examples

- The teacher explains.
- A film is used to give information or demonstrate an activity.
- Students use library resources.
- Students discover the information by doing laboratory experiments or field observations.

In a lesson designed to increase fluency or to develop automaticity, often no input is needed. The input has occurred in previous lessons.

2. What Type of Modeling Will Be Most Effective?

It is facilitating for students not only to know about, but to see or hear, examples of an acceptable finished product (story, poem, model, diagram, graph) or observe a person's actions or articulated decisions in performing a task (how to identify the main idea, weave, determine ways of thinking or making decisions while fulfilling the assignment).

It is important that the visual input of *modeling* be accompanied by the verbal input of *labeling* the critical elements of what is happening (or has happened) so that students are focused on essentials rather than being distracted by transitory or nonrelevant factors in the process or product.

Examples

- "I am going to use my thumb to work the clay in here like this so the tail has a firm foundation where it is joined to the body of the animal. In that way, it's less likely to break off in the kiln."
- "While I do this problem, I'll tell you what I'm thinking as I work."
- "Notice that this story has a provocative introductory paragraph that catches your interest by the first question the author asks."

In lessons designed to produce divergent thinking or creativity, the teacher usually should not model because students will tend to imitate. The modeling should have occurred in previous lessons so that students have acquired a repertoire of alternatives from which they synthesize an outcome satisfying to them.

3. How Will I Check for Understanding?

The teacher needs to know at what point students possess the information and/or skill necessary to achieve the instructional objective. The following are some ways of ascertaining this.

Sampling

Sampling means posing questions to the total group, allowing them time to think, and then calling on class members representative of strata of the group (most able, average, least able). This process focuses everyone on the generation of an answer and develops student readiness to hear an affirmation or challenge of his/her answer. Note that at the beginning of learning, correct answers are most enabling. Therefore, it is recommended that the teacher at first call on able students to avoid incorrect answers, which can "pollute" learning.

Examples

State the question or give the direction, then give thinking time before naming a student to respond:

- "Be ready to summarize the results of _____"
- "What do you believe were the reasons that Washington was a great leader? I'll give you a minute to think."
- "How would you estimate the answer?"
- "What operation would you use and why?"

Signaled Responses

Each member of the group makes a response, using a signal. For example, students show their selection of the first, second, third, or fourth alternative by showing that number of fingers, put a pencil straight up for "don't call on me for this question," make a "c" with a hand when examples are correct or an "i" when incorrect. Math operations, first letters of words, and punctuation all can be hand-signaled. Nodding or shaking of heads, use of counting sticks, and pointing to a place in the book or to parts in a diagram or to objects are samples of the many signals that can validate learning, or lack of it, for each member of the group.

Examples

- "Nod your head if you agree. Shake your head if you don't."
- "Signal whether you add, subtract, multiply, or divide, by making that sign with your fingers."
- "Show a c with your fingers if what I say is correct; and i if incorrect. Don't do anything if you're not sure."
- "Raise your hand when you are ready to answer this question."
- "On your microscope, point to _____."

Group Choral Response

After the teacher presents a question to the total group and gives thinking time, the strength of a choral response can indicate the general degree of student accuracy and comfort with the learning. However, this method usually does not give information about individuals.

Individual Private Response

A brief written or whispered-to-teacher response makes students accountable for demonstrating possession of, or progress toward, achievement of the needed information or skills.

Examples

- "Write the names of the three important categories we have discussed and one member of each."
- "Do the first part of this problem on your paper."
- "As I walk around, be ready to tell me your topic and the main idea of your paper."

4. How Will I Design Guided/Monitored Practice?

The beginning stages of learning are critical in the determination of future successful performance. Initial errors can "set" and be difficult to eradicate. Consequently, students' initial attempts in new learning should be carefully monitored and, when necessary, guided so they are accurate and successful. Teachers need to practice with the total group or circulate among students to make sure instruction has "taken" before "turning students loose" to practice independently (with no help available). With teacher guidance, the student needs to perform all (or enough) of the task so that clarification or remediation can occur immediately should it be needed. In that way, the teacher is assured that students will subsequently perform the task correctly without assistance rather than be practicing errors when working by themselves.

5. What Independent Practice Will Cement the Learning?

Once students can perform with a minimal amount of errors, difficulty, or confusion, they are ready to develop fluency, along with increased accuracy, by practicing without the supervision and guidance of the teacher. Only at that point can students be given an assignment to practice the new skill or process with little or no teacher direction.

Teachers, like doctors, are successful only when the student no longer needs them. All teaching has as its purpose to make the student as independent as possible. When lessons are carefully planned, student independence becomes much more probable. It is important that in independent work, the student does what already has been practiced rather than some new, related, or "inverted" endeavor.

An "inverted" assignment is one where a skill is taught and its reciprocal is practiced. It is as if you taught a child how to untie shoes and take them off and then assigned the practice of putting them on and tying them, or you taught addition and then assigned a practice sheet of subtraction. The same situation is created by teaching students to solve word problems and then asking them to generate word problems, teaching punctuation of written sentences and assigning creation of sentences requiring that punctuation, teaching how to recognize a topic sentence and then requiring generation of topic sentences.

6. Should the Students Be Aware of the Objective and Its Value?

This element of an effective lesson involves communicating to students what they will learn during the instruction and why that accomplishment is important, useful, and relevant to their present and/or future life situations. It is not the pedantic, "At the end of today's lesson you will be able to _____."

Examples

- "You were slowed down yesterday because you had trouble with _____. Today we are going to practice in order that you develop more speed and accuracy."
- "We are going to work on the correct form of letter writing so that you can write for the materials you need in your social studies project."
- "Today you are going to practice ways of participating in a discussion so each of you gets turns and you also learn from other people's ideas."
- "You are going to be surprised to find out what happened after Columbus returned and the difference his voyage made to ways of thinking."

Note that the objective as *stated to the student* is not as it is stated in the teacher's plan book: "The learner will use correct form in writing a letter"; "The learner will list the results of Columbus voyage and explain their significance."

Usually, students will learn more efficiently if they know what the learning will be and why it is important in their lives. There are times, however, when the objective should not be known because it will distract them or turn them off. ("Today you are going to learn the difference between colons and semicolons" could elicit "Who cares?")

7. What Anticipatory Set Will Focus Students on the Objective?

"Anticipatory set" results from a brief activity that occurs at the beginning of the lesson or when students are mentally "shifting" gears from one activity to the next. The purpose of an anticipatory set is to elicit students' attending behavior, focus them on the content of the ensuing instruction, and develop a mental readiness (or "set") for it. The "set" may (but doesn't need to) include a review of previous learning if it *will help the student achieve today's objective*, but not routine review of old material. The set also may give the teacher some diagnostic data needed for teaching the current objective.

An anticipatory activity should continue only long enough to get students "ready, set to go," so that the major portion of instructional time is available for the accomplishment of the current objective.

Examples

Examples of activities that produce anticipatory set are having students

- Give synonyms for overused words, when the current objective is improvement in descriptive writing
- Create word problems to go with a numeral problem on the chalkboard, when the current objective is meaningful computation practice
- Review the main ideas of yesterday's lesson, which will be extended today
- State ways a skill might be useful in daily life, when the objective is to develop fluency with that skill
- Practice speedy answers to multiplication facts for a quick review before today's math lesson on two-place multiplication

An anticipatory set is *not* needed if students are already alert and "ready to go" because yesterday's teaching built a bridge or transition to today's lesson.

Summary

Not all the seven elements just described will be included in every lesson. It may take several lessons before students are ready for guided and/or independent practice. Also, *mere presence of an element in a lesson does not guarantee quality teaching.* A teacher may use an anticipatory set that spreads rather than focuses students' attention ("Think of your favorite food; today we are going to talk about cereals"). Input may be done ineffectively. The modeling may be distracting ("I will cut this chocolate cupcake in fourths"). The seven elements are guides in *planning* for creative and effective lessons. They are not mandates!

Simply "knowing" the seven elements of planning for effective instruction will not ensure that those elements are implemented effectively. *Also,* simply having a "knack with kids" will not ensure the elements that promote successful learning will be included in instructional planning. Both the science and the art of teaching are essential. It is the belief of the writer, however, that deliberate consideration of these seven elements, which can promote effective instruction, constitutes the launching pad for planning effective and artistic teaching (using any model of teaching with *any* type of student) to achieve greater student achievement of *any* objective or goal.

2

❖   ❖   ❖

Dear Professor Marlowe:

When we left your class last semester I remember you saying that we ought to keep in touch and that if we also had any questions in the future that we should not hesitate to e-mail you. Well, here is your wish come true. I'm working at Bridgeton Middle with Mrs. Maceli. Dr. Marlowe, you can't imagine the yelling that is going on. "Sit down!" "Be quiet!" "Do your work!" "OK, Staci, that is the third time I've written your name on the board. You are to stay after school today." "I'm not staying!" When I say that a positive learning atmosphere doesn't exist, I mean it is a constant battle. Even worse, there are kids that are very quiet, unassuming, and maybe a little, or a lot afraid of some of the other kids and the teacher. I am trying to stay calm. I'm trying to think of ways to develop a more positive and productive learning environment but I'm really struggling. What can I do? Even if I can't do much in Mrs. Maceli's class, I do not want this to be my future. Is there a way to build more of a sense of community? Is there a way to get kids to develop self-control without threatening them all the time?

Kate Rogers

❖   HOW WOULD YOU RESPOND?

What are the advantages to cooperative learning? What is the best way to group students? What skills may students acquire in cooperative groups in addition to content learning? What challenges does cooperative learning present to teachers and students? How might the use of cooperative learning enhance classroom community? How might cooperative learning address social problems in society at large? Keep these questions in mind as you read "Jigsaw Groups and the Desegregated Classroom: In Pursuit of Common Goals" by Elliot Aronson and Diane Bridgeman. What questions do you have about cooperative learning? How can you help extend the discussion of these ideas in class? Finally, how would you respond to Kate Rogers?

❖ JIGSAW GROUPS AND THE DESEGREGATED
CLASSROOM: IN PURSUIT OF COMMON GOALS

Elliot Aronson and Diane Bridgeman

The desegregated classroom has not produced many of the positive results initially expected by social scientists some 25 years ago. It is argued that one of the major reasons for this failure is the overemphasis on competitiveness at the expense of interdependence in the classroom. In short, students in most classrooms very rarely cooperate with each other in pursuit of common goals. In this article, we describe a program of research in which elementary school students are "forced" to spend part of their classroom time mastering material in an interdependent structure. The results indicate that such structured interdependence increases the self-esteem, the morale, the interpersonal attraction, and the empathy of students across ethnic and racial divisions, and also improves the academic performance of minority students without hampering the performance of the ethnic majority.

There were high hopes when the Supreme Court outlawed school segregation a quarter of a century ago. If black and white children could share classrooms and become friends, it was thought that perhaps they could develop relatively free of racial prejudice and some of the problems that accompany prejudice. The case that brought about the court's landmark decision was that of *Brown v. Board of Education*; the decision reversed the 1896 ruling (*Plessy v. Ferguson*) that held that it was permissible to segregate racially, as long as equal facilities were provided for both races. In the *Brown* case, the court held that psychologically there could be no such thing as "separate but equal." The mere fact of separation implied to the minority group in question that its members were inferior to those of the majority.

The *Brown* decision was not only a humane interpretation of the Constitution, it was also the beginning of a profound and exciting social experiment. As Stephan (1978) has recently pointed out, the testimony of social psychologists in the *Brown* case, as well as in previous similar cases in state supreme courts, suggested strongly that desegregation would not only reduce prejudice but also increase the self-esteem of minority groups and improve their academic performance. Of course the social psychologists who testified never meant to imply that such benefits would accrue automatically. Certain preconditions would have to be met. These preconditions were most articulately stated by Allport in his classic, *The Nature of Prejudice,* published the same year as the Supreme Court decision:

> Prejudice . . . may be reduced by equal status contact between majority and minority groups in the pursuit of common goals. The effect is greatly enhanced if this contact is sanctioned by institutional supports (i.e., by law, custom or local atmosphere), and provided it is of a sort that leads to the perception of common interests and common humanity between members of the two groups. (Allport, 1954, p. 281)

The Effects of Desegregation

A quarter of a century after desegregation was begun, an assessment of its effectiveness is not encouraging. One of the most careful and thoroughgoing longitudinal studies of desegregation was the Riverside project conducted by Gerard and Miller (1975). They found that long after the schools were desegregated, black, white, and Mexican-American children tended not to integrate but to hang together in their own ethnic clusters. Moreover, anxiety increased and remained high long after desegregation occurred. These trends are echoed in several other studies. Indeed, the most careful, scholarly reviews of the research show few if any benefits (see St. John, 1975; Stephan, 1978). For example, according to Stephan's review, there is no single study that shows a significant increase in the self-esteem of minority children following desegregation; in fact, in fully 25 percent of the studies, desegregation is followed by a significant decrease in the self-esteem of young minority children.

Moreover, Stephan reports that desegregation reduced the prejudice of whites toward blacks in only 13 percent of the school systems studied. The prejudice of blacks toward whites increased in about as many cases as it decreased. Similarly, studies of the effects of desegregation on the academic performance of minority children present a mixed and highly variable picture.

What went wrong? Let us return to Allport's prediction: Equal status contact in pursuit of common goals, sanctioned by authority, will produce beneficial effects. We will look at each of these three factors separately.

Sanction by Authority

In some school districts there was clear acceptance and enforcement of the ruling by responsible authority. In others the acceptance was not as clear. In still others (especially in the early years) local authorities were in open defiance of the law. Pettigrew (1961) has shown that desegregation proceeded more smoothly and with less violence in those localities where local authorities sanctioned integration. But such variables as self-esteem and the reduction of prejudice do not necessarily change for the better even where authority clearly sanctions desegregation. While sanction by authority may be necessary, it is clearly not a sufficient condition.

Equal Status Contact

The definition of equal status is a trifle slippery. In the case of school desegregation, we would claim that there is equal status on the grounds that all children in the fifth grade (for example) have the same "occupational" status; that is, they are all fifth grade students. On the other hand, if the teacher is prejudiced against blacks, he may treat them less fairly than he treats whites, thus lowering their perceived status in the classroom (see Gerard and Miller, 1975). Moreover, if, because of an inferior education (prior to desegregation) or because of language difficulties, black or Mexican-American students perform poorly in the classroom, this could also lower their status among their peers. An interesting complication was introduced by Cohen (1972). While Allport (1954) predicted that positive interactions will result if cooperative equal status is achieved, expectation theory, as developed by Cohen, holds that even in such an environment biased expectations by both whites and blacks may lead to sustained white dominance. Cohen reasoned that both of these groups accepted the premise that the majority group's competence results in dominance and superior achievement. She suggested that alternatives be created to reverse these often unconscious expectations. According to Cohen, at least a temporary exchange of majority and minority roles is therefore required as a prelude to equal status. In one study (Cohen and Roper, 1972), black children were instructed in building radios and in how to teach this skill to others. Then a group of white children and the newly trained black children viewed a film of themselves building the radios. This was followed by some of the black children teaching the whites how to construct radios while others taught a black administrator. Then all the children came together in small groups. Equal status interactions were found in the groups where black children had taught whites how to construct the radios. The other group, however, demonstrated the usual white dominance. We will return to this point in a moment.

In Pursuit of Common Goals

Children vie with one another for good grades and the respect of the teacher. This occurs not only during the quizzes and exams but also in the informal give and take of the classroom, where children typically learn to raise their hands (often frantically) in response to questions from the teacher, groan when someone else is called upon, and revel in the failure of their classmates. This pervasive competitive atmosphere unwittingly leads the children to view one another as foes to be heckled and vanquished. In a newly desegregated school, all other things being equal, this atmosphere could exacerbate whatever prejudice existed prior to desegregation.

A dramatic example of dysfunctional competition was demonstrated by Sherif et al. (1961) in the classic "Robber's Cave" experiment. In this field experiment, the investigators encouraged intergroup competition between two teams of boys at a summer camp; this created fertile ground for anger and hostility even in previously benign, noncompetitive circumstances—like watching a movie. Positive relations between the groups were ultimately achieved only after both groups were required to work cooperatively to solve a common problem.

It is our contention that the competitive process interacts with "equal status contact." That is to say, whatever differences in ability that existed between minority children and white children prior to desegregation are emphasized by the competitive structure of the learning environment; furthermore, since segregated school facilities are rarely equal, minority children frequently enter the newly desegregated school at a distinct disadvantage, which is made more salient by the competitive atmosphere.

It was this reasoning that led Aronson and his colleagues (1975, 1978a) to develop the hypothesis that interdependent learning environments would establish the conditions necessary for the increase in self-esteem and performance and the decrease in prejudice that were expected to occur as a function of desegregation. Toward this end they developed a highly structured method of interdependent learning and systematically tested its effects in a number of elementary school classrooms. The aim of this research program was not merely to compare the effects of cooperation and competition in a classroom setting. This had been ably demonstrated by other investigators dating as early as Deutsch's (1949) experiment. Rather, the intent was to devise a cooperative classroom structure that could be utilized easily by classroom teachers on a long-term sustained basis and to evaluate the effects of this intervention via a well-controlled series of field experiments. In short, this project is an action research program aimed at developing and evaluating a classroom atmosphere that can be sustained by the classroom teachers long after the researchers have packed up their questionnaires and returned to the more cozy environment of the social psychological laboratory.

The method is described in detail elsewhere (Aronson et al., 1978a). Briefly, students are placed in six-person learning groups. The day's lesson is divided into six paragraphs such that each student has one segment of the written material. Each student has a unique and vital part of the information, which, like the pieces of a jigsaw puzzle, must be put together before any of the students can learn the whole picture. The individual must learn his own section and teach it to the other members of the group. The reader will note that in this method each child spends part of her time in the role of expert. Thus, the method incorporates Cohen's findings (previously discussed) within the context of an equal status contact situation.

Working with this "jigsaw" technique, children gradually learn that the old competitive behavior is no longer appropriate. Rather, in order to learn all of the material (and thus perform well on a quiz), each child must begin to listen to the others, ask appropriate questions, and in other ways contribute to the group. The process makes it possible for children to pay attention to one another and begin to appreciate each other as potentially valuable resources. It is important to emphasize that the motivation of the students is not necessarily altruistic; rather, it is primarily self-interest, which, in this case, happens also to produce outcomes that are beneficial to others.

Other Cooperative Techniques

In recent years a few research teams utilizing rather different techniques for structuring cooperative behavior have produced an array of data consistent with those resulting from the jigsaw technique. For example, Cook and his colleagues (1978) have shown that interracial cooperative groups in the laboratory underwent a significant improvement in attitudes about people of other races. In subsequent field experiments, Cook and his colleagues found that interdependent groups produced more improved attitudes toward members of previously disliked racial groups than was present in noninterdependent groups. It should be noted, however, that no evidence for generalization was found; that is, the positive change was limited to the specific members of the interdependent group and did not extend to the racial group as a whole.

Johnson and Johnson (1975) have developed the "Learning Together" model, which is a general and varied approach to interdependent classroom learning. Basically, Johnson and Johnson have found evidence for greater cross-ethnic friendship ratings, greater self-esteem, and higher motivation in their cooperative groups than in control conditions. They have also found increases in academic performance.

In a different vein, Slavin (1978) and DeVries, Edwards, and Slavin (1978) have developed two highly structured techniques that combine within-group cooperation with across-group competition. These techniques, "Teams Games and Tournaments" (TGT) and "Student Teams Achievement Divisions" (STAD), have consistently produced beneficial results in lower class, multi-racial classrooms. Basically, in TGT and STAD, children form heterogeneous five-person teams; each member of a team is given a reasonably good opportunity to do well by dint of the fact that she competes against a member of a different team with similar skills to her own. Her individual performance contributes to her team's score. The results are in the same ball park as jigsaw: Children participating in TGT and STAD groups show a greater increase in sociometric, cross-racial friendship choices and more observed cross-racial interactions than control conditions. They also show more satisfaction with school than the controls do. Similarly, TGT and STAD produce greater learning effectiveness among racial minorities than do the control groups.

It is interesting to note that the basic results of TGT and STAD are similar to those of the jigsaw technique in spite of one major difference in procedure: While the jigsaw technique makes an overt attempt to minimize competition, TGT and STAD actually promote competitiveness and utilize it across teams—within the context of intrateam cooperation. We believe that this difference is more apparent than real. In most classrooms where jigsaw has been utilized, the students are in jigsaw groups for less than two hours per day. The rest of the class time is spent in a myriad of process activities, many of which are competitive in nature. Thus, what seems important in both techniques is that *some* specific time is structured around cooperativeness. Whether the beneficial results are produced *in spite* of a surrounding atmosphere of competitiveness or because of it is the task of future research to determine.

Conclusions

We are not suggesting that jigsaw learning or any other cooperative method constitutes the solution to our interethnic problems. What we have shown is that beneficial effects occur as a result of structuring the social psychological aspects of classroom learning so that children spend at least a portion of their time in pursuit of common goals. These effects are in accordance with predictions made by social scientists in their testimony favoring desegregating schools some 25 years ago. It is important to emphasize the fact that the jigsaw method has proved effective even if it is employed for as little as 20 percent of a child's time in the classroom. Moreover, other techniques have produced beneficial results even when interdependent learning was purposely accompanied by competitive activities. Thus, the data do not indicate the desirability of either placing a serious limit on classroom competition or interfering with individually guided education. Interdependent learning can and does coexist easily with almost any other method used by teachers in the classroom.

References

Aronson, E., Stephan, C., Sikes, J., Blaney, N., and Snapp, M. *The Jigsaw Classroom.* Beverly Hills: Sage Publications, 1978. (a)

Aronson, E., Bridgeman, D. L., and Geffner, R. The effects of a cooperative classroom structure on students' behavior and attitudes. In D. Bar-Tal and L. Saxe (eds.), *Social Psychology of Education: Theory and Research.* Washington, D.C.: Hemisphere, 1978. (b)

Blaney, N. T., Stephan, C., Rosenfield, D., Aronson, E., and Sikes, J. Interdependence in the classroom: A field study. *Journal of Educational Psychology,* 1977, 69, 139–146.

Bridgeman, D. L. Enhanced role taking through cooperative interdependence: A field study. *Child Development,* 1981, 52, 1231–1238.

Chandler, M. J. Egocentrism and antisocial behavior: The assessment and training of social perspective-taking skills. *Developmental Psychology,* 1973, 9, 326–332.

Cohen, E. Interracial interaction disability. *Human Relations,* 1972, 25(1), 9–24.

Cohen, E., and Roper, S. Modification of interracial interaction disability: An application of status characteristics theory. *American Sociological Review,* 1972, 6, 643–657.

Cook, S. W. Interpersonal and attitudinal outcomes in cooperating interracial groups. Journal of Research and Development in Education, 1978.

Covington, M. V., and Beery, R. G. *Self-Worth and School Learning.* New York: Holt, Rinehart & Winston, 1976.

Deutsch, M. An experimental study of the effects of cooperation and competition upon group process. *Human Relations,* 1949, 2, 199–231.

Devries, D. L., Edwards, K. J., AND Slavin, R. E. Bi-racial learning teams and race relations in the classroom: Four field experiments on Teams-Games-Tournament. *Journal of Educational Psychology,* 1978.

Franks, D. D., and Marolla, J. Efficacious action and social approval as interacting dimensions of self-esteem: A tentative formulation through construct validation. *Sociometry,* 1976, 39, 324–341.

Geffner, R. A. The effects of interdependent learning on self-esteem, interethnic relations, and intra-ethnic attitudes of elementary school children: A field experiment. Unpublished Doctoral Thesis, University of California, Santa Cruz, 1978.

Gerard, H., and Miller, N. *School Desegregation.* New York: Plenum. 1975.

Johnson, D. W., and Johnson, R. T. *Learning Together and Alone.* Englewood Cliffs, NJ: Prentice-Hall, 1975.

Lucker, G. W., Rosenfield, D., Sikes, J., and Aronson, E. Performance in the interdependent classroom: A field study. *American Educational Research Journal,* 1977, 13, 115–123.

Pettigrew, T. Social psychology and desegregation research. *American Psychologist,* 1961, 15, 61–71.

Purkey, W. W. *Self-Concept and School Achievement.* Englewood Cliffs, N.J.: Prentice-Hall, 1970.

Sherif, M.. Harvey, O. J., White, J., Hood, W., and Sherif, C. *Intergroup Conflict and Cooperation: The Robber's Cave Experiment.* Norman, Okla.: University of Oklahoma Institute of Intergroup Relations, 1961.

Slavin, R. E. Student teams and achievement divisions. *Journal of Research and Development in Education,* in press.

Stephan, C., Pressner, N. R., Kennedy, J. C. and Aronson, E. Attributions to success and failure in cooperative, competitive and interdependent interactions. European *Journal of Social Psychology,* 1978, 8, 269–274.

Stephan, W. G. School desegregation: An evaluation of predictions made in Brown v. Board of Education. *Psychological Bulletin,* 1978, 85, 217–238.

St. John, N. *School Desegregation: Outcomes for Children.* New York: John Wiley and Sons, 1975.

3

❖ ❖ ❖

Dear Professor Marlowe:

I was thinking about that last class the other morning on my way to student teaching. The small seminar format you ran was so comfortable that by the end of the semester everyone seemed like family. Really, that last class was like one of those farewells when people leave the warm embrace of summer camp. I know we discussed it in class that last night too, but the way people felt at ease really allowed so much more risk taking, and question asking, and, well . . . learning.

I wish I could say the same about the third-grade class where they placed me for student teaching. The cooperating teacher is all about threatening the kids, raising her voice, and speaking in this saccharine voice whenever they do something she likes. It all seems so fake and inauthentic whenever she's talking with the kids. And it seems like it's either the punitive voice or the sickly sweet one. There's never just normal talking.

Yesterday she said, "You have to communicate that you mean business. Don't let them see you smile for at least the first 3 weeks. And, when they do what you want, praise away so that they know what they're doing is OK. That's how they learn what is acceptable behavior and what is not." Don't smile? Is she serious? Maybe I've got this all wrong, but don't I want the kids to be comfortable rather than afraid? Shouldn't they feel safe? Anyway, those were the questions I was thinking about (but kept to myself) the entire time she was giving me her tips for successful classrooms.

Here's what's really bothering me though. I just nodded with this stupid grin on my face when she was giving me these "important pointers," but after a kid refused to do something I asked him to do, I'm now wondering if she's right. Maybe they see me as a pushover. Maybe I'm too nice.

Maybe the kids do need to know who's boss first and then I can make the class a comfortable place to learn. Do I need to be strict first, and worry about community later? Kids are resilient, right? What do you think about all of this? How do you make kids feel safe, like the class is inviting, but not have the kids treat you disrespectfully? I want them to feel comfortable like we all did in your class, but how do you make that happen?

Melanie Johnson

❖ HOW WOULD YOU RESPOND?

What's your definition of classroom management? Is it the same as discipline? Do you think students today are less well behaved than they were in the past? How can teachers foster an attitude of positive self-control? Should teachers post rules in their classrooms? Who should develop them? When is punishment OK? How about corporal punishment—is this appropriate in the classroom? What do you think are the relative advantages and challenges to using measures like school uniforms, prayer, and metal detectors, for example, in an attempt to promote positive behavior? Keep these questions in mind as you read "The Key to Classroom Management" by Robert J. and Jana S. Marzano. What questions do you have about classroom management? How can you help extend the discussion about these ideas in class? Finally, how would you respond to Melanie Johnson?

❖ THE KEY TO CLASSROOM MANAGEMENT

Robert J. Marzano and Jana S. Marzano

Today, we know more about teaching than we ever have before. Research has shown us that teachers' actions in their classrooms have twice the impact on student achievement as do school policies regarding curriculum, assessment, staff collegiality, and community involvement (Marzano, 2003a). We also know that one of the classroom teacher's most important jobs is managing the classroom effectively.

A comprehensive literature review by Wang, Haertel, and Walberg (1993) amply demonstrates the importance of effective classroom management. These researchers analyzed 86 chapters from annual research reviews, 44 handbook chapters, 20 government and commissioned reports, and 11 journal articles to produce a list of 228 variables affecting student achievement. They combined the results of these analyses with the findings from 134 separate meta-analyses. Of all the variables, classroom management had the largest effect on student achievement. This makes intuitive sense—students cannot learn in a chaotic, poorly managed classroom.

Research not only supports the importance of classroom management, but it also sheds light on the dynamics of classroom management. Stage and Quiroz's meta-analysis (1997) shows the importance of there being a balance between teacher actions that provide clear consequences for unacceptable behavior and teacher actions that recognize and reward acceptable behavior. Other researchers (Emmer, Evertson, & Worsham, 2003; Evertson, Emmer, & Worsham, 2003) have identified important components of classroom management, including beginning the school year with a positive emphasis on management; arranging the room in a way conducive to effective management; and identifying and implementing rules and operating procedures.

In a recent meta-analysis of more than 100 studies (Marzano, 2003b), we found that the quality of teacher-student relationships is the keystone for all other aspects of classroom management. In fact, our meta-analysis indicates that on average, teachers who had high-quality relationships with their students had 31 percent fewer discipline problems, rule violations, and related problems over a year's time than did teachers who did not have high-quality relationships with their students.

What are the characteristics of effective teacher-student relationships? Let's first consider what they are not. Effective teacher-student relationships have nothing to do with the teacher's personality or even with whether the students view the teacher as a friend. Rather, the most effective teacher-student relationships are characterized by specific teacher behaviors: exhibiting appropriate levels of dominance; exhibiting appropriate levels of cooperation; and being aware of high-needs students.

Appropriate Levels of Dominance

Wubbels and his colleagues (Wubbels, Brekelmans, van Tartwijk, & Admiral, 1999; Wubbels & Levy, 1993) identify appropriate dominance as an important characteristic of effective teacher-student relationships. In contrast to the more negative connotation of the term dominance as forceful control or command over others, they define dominance as the teacher's ability to provide clear purpose and strong guidance regarding both academics and student behavior. Studies indicate that when asked about their preferences for teacher behavior, students typically express a desire for this type of teacher-student interaction. For example, in a study that involved interviews with more than 700 students in grades 4–7, students articulated a clear preference for strong teacher guidance and control rather than more permissive types of teacher behavior (Chiu & Tulley, 1997). Teachers can exhibit appropriate dominance by establishing clear behavior expectations and learning goals and by exhibiting assertive behavior.

Establish Clear Expectations and Consequences

Teachers can establish clear expectations for behavior in two ways: by establishing clear rules and procedures, and by providing consequences for student behavior.

The seminal research of the 1980s (Emmer, 1984; Emmer, Sanford, Evertson, Clements, & Martin, 1981; Evertson & Emmer, 1982) points to the importance of establishing rules and procedures for general classroom behavior, group work, seat work, transitions and interruptions, use of materials and equipment, and beginning and ending the period or the day. Ideally, the class should establish these rules and procedures through discussion and mutual consent by teacher and students (Glasser, 1969, 1990).

Along with well-designed and clearly communicated rules and procedures, the teacher must acknowledge students' behavior, reinforcing acceptable behavior and providing negative consequences for unacceptable behavior. Stage and Quiroz's research (1997) is instructive. They found that teachers build effective relationships through such strategies as the following:

- Using a wide variety of verbal and physical reactions to students' misbehavior, such as moving closer to offending students and using a physical cue, such as a finger to the lips, to point out inappropriate behavior.
- Cuing the class about expected behaviors through prearranged signals, such as raising a hand to indicate that all students should take their seats.

- Providing tangible recognition of appropriate behavior—with tokens or chits, for example.
- Employing group contingency policies that hold the entire group responsible for behavioral expectations.
- Employing home contingency techniques that involve rewards and sanctions at home.

Establish Clear Learning Goals

Teachers can also exhibit appropriate levels of dominance by providing clarity about the content and expectations of an upcoming instructional unit. Important teacher actions to achieve this end include

- Establishing and communicating learning goals at the beginning of a unit of instruction.
- Providing feedback on those goals.
- Continually and systematically re-visiting the goals.
- Providing summative feedback regarding the goals.

The use of rubrics can help teachers establish clear goals. To illustrate, assume that a teacher has identified the learning goal "understanding and using fractions" as important for a given unit. That teacher might present students with the following rubric:

4 points. You understand the characteristics of fractions along with the different types. You can accurately describe how fractions are related to decimals and percentages. You can convert fractions to decimals and can explain how and why the process works. You can use fractions to understand and solve different types of problems.

3 points. You understand the basic characteristics of fractions. You know how fractions are related to decimals and percentages. You can convert fractions to decimals.

2 points. You have a basic understanding of the following, but have some small misunderstandings about one or more: the characteristics of fractions; the relationships among fractions, decimals, and percentages; how to convert fractions to decimals.

1 point. You have some major problems or misunderstandings with one or more of the following: the characteristics of fractions; the relationships among fractions, decimals, and percentages; how to convert fractions to decimals.

0 points. You may have heard of the following before, but you do not understand what they mean: the characteristics of fractions; the relationships among fractions, decimals, and percentages; how to convert fractions to decimals.

The clarity of purpose provided by this rubric communicates to students that their teacher can provide proper guidance and direction in academic content.

Exhibit Assertive Behavior

Teachers can also communicate appropriate levels of dominance by exhibiting assertive behavior. According to Emmer and colleagues, assertive behavior is "the ability to stand up for one's legitimate rights in ways that make it less likely that others will ignore or circumvent them" (2003, p. 146).

Assertive behavior differs significantly from both passive behavior and aggressive behavior. These researchers explain that teachers display assertive behavior in the classroom when they

- Use assertive body language by maintaining an erect posture, facing the offending student but keeping enough distance so as not to appear threatening and matching the facial expression with the content of the message being presented to students.
- Use an appropriate tone of voice, speaking clearly and deliberately in a pitch that is slightly but not greatly elevated from normal classroom speech, avoiding any display of emotions in the voice.
- Persist until students respond with the appropriate behavior. Do not ignore an inappropriate behavior; do not be diverted by a student denying, arguing, or blaming, but listen to legitimate explanations.

Appropriate Levels of Cooperation

Cooperation is characterized by a concern for the needs and opinions of others. Although not the antithesis of dominance, cooperation certainly occupies a different realm. Whereas dominance focuses on the teacher as the driving force in the classroom, cooperation focuses on the students and teacher functioning as a team. The interaction of these two dynamics—dominance and cooperation—is a central force in effective teacher-student relationships. Several strategies can foster appropriate levels of cooperation.

Provide Flexible Learning Goals

Just as teachers can communicate appropriate levels of dominance by providing clear learning goals, they can also convey appropriate levels of cooperation by providing flexible learning goals. Giving students the opportunity to set their own objectives at the beginning of a unit or asking students what they would like to learn conveys a sense of cooperation. Assume, for example, that a teacher has identified the topic of fractions as the focus of a unit of instruction and has provided students with a rubric. The teacher could then ask students to identify some aspect of fractions or a related topic that they would particularly like to study. Giving students this kind of choice, in addition to increasing their understanding of the topic, conveys the message that the teacher cares about and tries to accommodate students' interests.

Take a Personal Interest in Students

Probably the most obvious way to communicate appropriate levels of cooperation is to take a personal interest in each student in the class. As McCombs and Whisler (1997) note, all students appreciate personal attention from the teacher. Although busy teachers—particularly those at the secondary level—do not have the time for extensive interaction with all students, some teacher actions can communicate personal interest and concern without taking up much time. Teachers can

- Talk informally with students before, during, and after class about their interests.
- Greet students outside of school—for instance, at extracurricular events or at the store.
- Single out a few students each day in the lunchroom and talk with them.
- Be aware of and comment on important events in students' lives, such as participation in sports, drama, or other extracurricular activities.
- Compliment students on important achievements in and outside of school.
- Meet students at the door as they come into class; greet each one by name.

Use Equitable and Positive Classroom Behaviors

Programs like Teacher Expectations and Student Achievement emphasize the importance of the subtle ways in which teachers can communicate their interest in students (Kerman, Kimball, & Martin, 1980). This program recommends many practical strategies that emphasize equitable and positive classroom interactions with all students. Teachers should, for example,

- Make eye contact with each student. Teachers can make eye contact by scanning the entire room as they speak and by freely moving about all sections of the room.
- Deliberately move toward and stand close to each student during the class period. Make sure that the seating arrangement allows the teacher and students clear and easy ways to move around the room.
- Attribute the ownership of ideas to the students who initiated them. For instance, in a discussion a teacher might say, "Cecilia just added to Aida's idea by saying that . . ."
- Allow and encourage all students to participate in class discussions and interactions. Make sure to call on students who do not commonly participate, not just those who respond most frequently.
- Provide appropriate wait time for all students to respond to questions, regardless of their past performance or your perception of their abilities.

Awareness of High-Needs Students

Classroom teachers meet daily with a broad cross-section of students. In general, 12–22 percent of all students in school suffer from mental, emotional, or behavioral disorders, and relatively few receive mental health services (Adelman & Taylor, 2002). The Association of School Counselors notes that 18 percent of students have special needs and require extraordinary interventions and treatments that go beyond the typical resources available to the classroom (Dunn & Baker, 2002).

Although the classroom teacher is certainly not in a position to directly address such severe problems, teachers with effective classroom management skills are aware of high-needs students and have a repertoire of specific techniques for meeting some of their needs (Marzano, 2003b). Figure 3.1 summarizes five categories of high-needs students and suggests classroom strategies for each category and subcategory.

- *Passive* students fall into two subcategories: those who fear *relationships* and those who fear *failure.* Teachers can build strong relationships with these students by refraining from criticism, rewarding small successes, and creating a classroom climate in which students feel safe from aggressive people.

- The category of *aggressive* students comprises three subcategories: *hostile, oppositional,* and *covert.* Hostile students often have poor anger control, low capacity for empathy, and an inability to see the consequences of their actions. Oppositional students exhibit milder forms of behavior problems, but they consistently resist following rules, argue with adults, use harsh language, and tend to annoy others. Students in the covert subcategory may be quite pleasant at times, but they are often nearby when trouble starts and they never quite do what authority figures ask of them. Strategies for helping aggressive students include creating behavior contracts and providing immediate rewards and consequences. Most of all, teachers must keep in mind that aggressive students, although they may appear highly resistant to behavior change, are still children who are experiencing a significant amount of fear and pain.

- Students with *attention* problems fall into two categories: *hyperactive* and *inattentive.* These students may respond well when teachers contract with them to manage behaviors; teach them basic concentration, study, and thinking skills; help them divide tasks into manageable parts; reward their successes; and assign them a peer tutor.

- Students in the *perfectionist* category are driven to succeed at unattainable levels. They are self-critical, have low self-esteem, and feel inferior. Teachers can often help these students by encouraging them to develop more realistic standards, helping them to accept mistakes, and giving them opportunities to tutor other students.

- *Socially inept* students have difficulty making and keeping friends. They may stand too close and touch others in annoying ways, talk too much, and misread others' comments. Teachers can help these students by counseling them about social behaviors.

School may be the only place where many students who face extreme challenges can get their needs addressed. The reality of today's

Figure 3.1   Categories of High-Needs Students

Category	Definitions & Source	Characteristics	Suggestions
Passive	Behavior that avoids the domination of others or the pain of negative experiences. The child attempts to protect self from criticism, ridicule, or rejection, possibly reacting to abuse and neglect. Can have a biochemical basis, such as anxiety.	**Fear of relationships:** Avoids connection with others, is shy, doesn't initiate conversations, attempts to be invisible. **Fear of failure:** Gives up easily, is convinced he or she can't succeed, is easily frustrated, uses negative self-talk.	Provide safe adult and peer interactions and protection from aggressive people. Provide assertiveness and positive self-talk training. Reward small successes quickly. Withhold criticism.
Aggressive	Behavior that overpowers, dominates, harms, or controls others without regard for their well-being. The child has often taken aggressive people as role models. Has had minimal or in-effective limits set on behavior. Is possibly reacting to abuse and neglect. Condition may have a biochemical basis, such as depression.	**Hostile:** Rages, threatens, or intimidates others. Can be verbally or physically abusive to people, animals, or objects. **Oppositional:** Does opposite of what is asked. Demands that others agree or give in. Resists verbally or nonverbally. **Covert:** Appears to agree but then does the opposite of what is asked. Often acts innocent while setting up problems for others.	Describe the student's behavior clearly. Contract with the student to reward corrected behavior and set up consequences for uncorrected behavior. Be consistent and provide immediate rewards and consequences. Encourage and acknowledge extracurricular activities in and out of school. Give student responsibilities to help teacher or other students to foster successful experiences.
Attention problems	Behavior that demonstrates either motor or attentional difficulties resulting from a neurological disorder. The child's symptoms may be exacerbated by family or social stressors or	**Hyperactive:** Has difficulty with motor control, both physically and verbally. Fidgets, leaves seat frequently, interrupts, talks excessively. **Inattentive:** Has difficulty staying	Contract with the student to manage behaviors. Teach basic concentration, study, and thinking skills. Separate student in a quiet work area. Help the student list each step of a task. Reward

Category	Definitions & Source	Characteristics	Suggestions
	biochemical conditions, such as anxiety, depression, or bipolar disorders.	focused and following through on projects. Has difficulty with listening, remembering, and organizing.	successes; assign a peer tutor.
Perfectionist	Behavior that is geared toward avoiding the embarrassment and assumed shame of making mistakes. The child fears what will happen if errors are discovered. Has unrealistically high expectations of self. Has possibly received criticism or lack of acceptance while making mistakes during the process of learning.	Tends to focus too much on the small details of projects. Will avoid projects if unsure of outcome. Focuses on results and not relationships. Is self-critical.	Ask the student to make mistakes on purpose, then show acceptance. Have the student tutor other students.
Socially inept	Behavior that is based on the misinterpretation of nonverbal signals of others. The child misunderstands facial expressions and body language. Hasn't received adequate training in these areas and has poor role modeling.	Attempts to make friends but is inept and unsuccessful. Is forced to be alone. Is often teased for unusual behavior, appearance, or lack of social skills.	Teach the student to keep the appropriate physical distance from others. Teach the meaning of facial expressions, such as anger and hurt. Make suggestions regarding hygiene, dress, mannerisms, and posture.

SOURCE: Marzano, R. J. (2003). *What works in schools: Translating research into action* (pp. 104–105). Alexandria, VA: ASCD.

schools often demands that classroom teachers address these severe issues, even though this task is not always considered a part of their regular job.

In a study of classroom strategies (see Brophy, 1996; Brophy & McCaslin, 1992), researchers examined how effective classroom teachers interacted with specific types of students. The study found that the most effective classroom managers did not treat all students the same; they tended to employ different strategies with different types of students. In contrast, ineffective classroom managers did not appear sensitive to the diverse needs of students. Although Brophy did not couch his findings in terms of teacher-student relationships, the link is clear. An awareness of the five general categories of high-needs students and appropriate actions for each can help teachers build strong relationships with diverse students.

Don't Leave Relationships to Chance

Teacher-student relationships provide an essential foundation for effective classroom management-and classroom management is a key to high student achievement. Teacher-student relationships should not be left to chance or dictated by the personalities of those involved. Instead, by using strategies supported by research, teachers can influence the dynamics of their classrooms and build strong teacher-student relationships that will support student learning.

References

Adelman, H. S., & Taylor, L. (2002). School counselors and school reform: New directions. *Professional School Counseling, 5*(4), 235–248.

Brophy, J. E. (1996). *Teaching problem students.* New York: Guilford.

Brophy, J. E., & McCaslin, N. (1992). Teachers' reports of how they perceive and cope with problem students. *Elementary School Journal, 93*, 3–68.

Chiu, L. H., & Tulley, M. (1997). Student preferences of teacher discipline styles. *Journal of Instructional Psychology, 24*(3), 168–175.

Dunn, N. A., & Baker, S. B. (2002). Readiness to serve students with disabilities: A survey of elementary school counselors. *Professional School Counselors, 5*(4), 277–284.

Emmer, E. T. (1984). *Classroom management: Research and implications.* (R & D Report No. 6178). Austin, TX: Research and Development Center for Teacher Education, University of Texas. (ERIC Document Reproduction Service No. ED251448)

Emmer, E. T., Evertson, C. M., & Worsham, M. E. (2003). *Classroom management for secondary teachers* (6th ed.). Boston: Allyn and Bacon.

Emmer, E. T., Sanford, J. P., Evertson, C. M., Clements, B. S., & Martin, J. (1981). *The classroom management improvement study: An experiment in elementary school classrooms.* (R & D Report No. 6050). Austin, TX: Research and

Development Center for Teacher Education, University of Texas. (ERIC Document Reproduction Service No. ED226452)

Evertson, C. M., & Emmer, E. T. (1982). Preventive classroom management. In D. Duke (Ed.), *Helping teachers manage classrooms* (pp. 2–31). Alexandria, VA: ASCD.

Evertson, C. M., Emmer, E. T., & Worsham, M. E. (2003). Classroom management for elementary teachers (6th ed.). Boston: Allyn and Bacon.

Glasser, W. (1969). Schools without failure. New York: Harper and Row.

Glasser, W. (1990). The quality school: Managing students without coercion. New York: Harper and Row.

Kerman, S., Kimball, T., & Martin, M. (1980). *Teacher expectations and student achievement*. Bloomington, IN: Phi Delta Kappan.

Marzano, R. J. (2003a). *What works in schools*. Alexandria, VA: ASCD.

Marzano, R. J. (with Marzano, J. S., & Pickering, D. J.). (2003b). *Classroom management that works*. Alexandria, VA: ASCD.

McCombs, B. L., & Whisler, J. S. (1997). *The learner-centered classroom and school*. San Francisco: Jossey-Bass.

Stage, S. A., & Quiroz, D. R. (1997). A meta-analysis of interventions to decrease disruptive classroom behavior in public education settings. *School Psychology Review, 26*(3), 333–368.

Wang, M. C., Haertel, G. D., & Walberg, H. J. (1993). Toward a knowledge base for school learning. *Review of Educational Research, 63*(3), 249–294.

Wubbels, T., Brekelmans, M., van Tartwijk, J., & Admiral, W. (1999). Interpersonal relationships between teachers and students in the classroom. In H. C. Waxman & H. J. Walberg (Eds.), *New directions for teaching practice and research* (pp. 151–170). Berkeley, CA: McCutchan.

Wubbels, T., & Levy, J. (1993). *Do you know what you look like? Interpersonal relationships in education*. London: Falmer Press.

4

Dear Dr. Canestrari:

I've been working at Kennedy High School now for just under a year. I've had the opportunity to see a ton of teachers because they signed all of us new folks into this mentoring program where we have to spend time observing our colleagues. Most of them are pretty good, although some of them are just awful. One of my colleagues is widely recognized as the best teacher in the school. I've always been a little bit skeptical about the awarding of such titles . . . until I spent the day shadowing him yesterday. Do you know Pat Stevens? He's the department chair in social studies and he's really sensational. The kids hang on his every word, he's dynamic, engaging and he really looks like he's having fun too.

Here's the funny thing though. When I try to be more specific, even to myself, I can't quite put my finger on exactly what makes him so good. I mean, I get what he's doing in terms of how he gets kids to participate. His language is clear and precise, he's energetic . . . but there's more to it than just his skills. At least that's the way it seems. I want to be as good as this guy, but I want to know what it is that makes him so good. And, he really is that good too. I just sometimes get the feeling that even if I did everything he does, even in the same way, it wouldn't quite be the same.

Pat Stevens really is great, but listing all the things he does right doesn't seem to capture it for me. I don't know. What do you think makes a great teacher?

Jean LeMoyne

❖ HOW WOULD YOU RESPOND?

What do you think are the defining characteristics of a good teacher? Do all good teachers possess the same skills? Is it possible to learn how to be a great teacher or is this something people are born knowing how to do well? Think about teachers you had during your K through 12 experience. What qualities did the memorable teachers possess? What combination of characteristics do you think makes the best teachers? Keep these questions in mind as you read "What Makes a Good Teacher?" by Richard P. Traina. What questions do you have about the characteristics of good teachers? How can you extend the discussion of these ideas in class? Finally, how would you respond to Jean LeMoyne?

❖ WHAT MAKES A GOOD TEACHER?

Richard P. Traina

At every level of education, there is a recurrent question: What constitutes good teaching? Some years ago, I embarked on an interesting bit of research in pursuit of an answer to that query. As a historian, I decided to explore the autobiographies of prominent Americans from the 19th and 20th centuries (some 125 of them). As these people—men and women of different social, economic, geographic, religious, and racial backgrounds—recounted their educational experiences, what did they have to say about teachers whom they valued?

The single most notable discovery was the extraordinarily consistent pattern in the description of the good teacher. I guess I would have to say good and *memorable* teacher. There were three characteristics that were described time and again—to an astonishing degree: competence in the subject matter, caring deeply about students and their success, and character, distinctive character. These attributes were evident regardless of the level of education or the subject matter being taught.

A command of subject matter, such that students picked up on the teacher's excitement about it, was fundamental. Where there was ease on the part of the teacher "moving around the subject," a dexterity of explanation and explication, students could feel the teacher's command of the material. That confidence was a root cause of a student's respect for the teacher, opening the student up for learning—making the student more engaged. Autobiographers frequently cited teachers whose keen understanding of the subject matter caused students to see the world differently.

The second characteristic seemed equally important: caring deeply about each student and about that student's accomplishment and growth. In this instance, it began with the teacher recognizing the student as an individual who brings particular experiences, interests, enthusiasms, and fears to the classroom. It was the teacher taking time to acknowledge a student's life outside the classroom, inquiring about the family's welfare or the student's participation in an extracurricular activity. It moved to an insistence that the student take pride in his or her work—stretching each person to a level of performance that surprised and delighted the student.

The third attribute, distinctive character, is the most elusive one, and it gives flavor or texture to the other two. (It is likely the attribute that contributes most to making a good teacher also a memorable teacher.) In almost all cases, there was something distinctive about the character of the effective teacher recalled in these autobiographies. It could be an unaffected eccentricity, a handicap or tragedy overcome, an unabashed passion for the subject, or a way of demonstrating concern for the student (although throwing chalk at or hugging a student are both outside of the "communication lexicon" these days). In any event, there was a palpable energy that suffused the competent and caring teacher, some mark-making quality.

I cannot emphasize enough how powerful this combination of attributes was reported to be. The autobiographers believed that their lives were changed by such teachers and professors. It should not be surprising that a vital bond through all levels of education should be the good teacher—the competent and caring "character."

Questions for Reflection

Look back at the letters and readings in **Part I: Real Classrooms**. Consider the following questions as you begin formulating *your own ideas* about how to apply theories of learning into planned instructional practice.

1. Consider the connections between lesson design and classroom management. How might the ways in which a teacher structures her or his lessons contribute to or detract from socially appropriate behaviors? What would Madeline Hunter and the Marzanos say about this?

2. Can force of personality alone inspire student learning? What might Richard Traina say about Madeline Hunter's emphasis on lesson structure? If one follows Hunter's model, but does not possess the traits Traina describes would you consider this person to be a good teacher?

3. How would a teacher introduce cooperative learning to students who have had little experience working with their peers? How can one evaluate a particular teacher's effectiveness if during an observation all the students are working in groups and the teacher is not providing any direct instruction?

4. How might teachers incorporate Hunter's lesson components into the kind of cooperative learning formats Aronson suggests?

❖ YOUR OWN IDEAS

What ideas seem most important to you as you reflect about teaching and learning in real classrooms? What do you think is most important for new teachers to consider? What further questions did the authors raise for you in Part I that have not been adequately answered? Use the space below for your reflections.

_____

_____

_____

_____

_____

_____

_____

_____

_____

_____

_____

_____

_____

_____

_____

_____

_____

_____

Suggested Readings

Aronson, E. (2000). *Nobody left to hate: Teaching compassion after Columbine*. New York: Worth.

Bruner, J. S. (1966). *Toward a theory of instruction*. New York: Norton.

Canestrari, A. S., & Marlowe, B. A. (2004). *Educational foundations: An anthology of critical readings*. Thousand Oaks, CA: Sage.

Coles, R. (1990, September). Teachers who made a difference. *Instructor*, 58–59.

DiGiulio, R. C. (2004). *Great teaching: What matters most in helping students succeed*. Thousand Oaks, CA: Corwin.

Johnson, D. W., & Johnson, R. (1999). *Learning together and alone: Cooperation, competition, and individualization* (5th ed.). Boston: Allyn & Bacon.

Kobrin, D. (1992). *In there with the kids*. Boston: Houghton Mifflin.

Kohn, A. (2000). *Beyond discipline: From compliance to community*. Upper Saddle River, NJ: Prentice Hall.

Marlowe, B. A., & Page, M. L. (2005). *Creating and sustaining the constructivist classroom* (2nd ed.). Thousand Oaks, CA: Corwin.

Noddings, N. (1995). Teaching themes of care. *Phi Delta Kappan, 76*, 675–679.

Perrone, V. (1994). How to engage students in learning. *Educational Leadership, 51*(5), 11–13.

PART II

How Does Learning Occur?

5

Dear Dr. Marlowe:

Quick question. I don't want to harp on my cooperating teacher's style too much, but she thinks kids actually learn academic skills better when they get rewarded for it. Everything is a competition for her affection, or for points, or stickers, or more recess time, or getting your name on the "Student of the Day" chart. Last week students were asked to write a short paragraph that finishes the prompt, "On a windy day, I . . ." When the kids were done writing, she asked for volunteers. After each kid who volunteered read their piece, she instructed them to pick up a ticket (kids turn these in for prizes at the end of the week) and also to add two stars to the behavior chart. It's dizzying. There are rewards for everything!

When I told the cooperating teacher that my education courses raised questions about using rewards for learning, she said something like, "Psychology classes are interesting, but this is the real world. Kids need immediate feedback to learn. When they get something they like, they know they did what you asked correctly. That's how you learned when you were an infant and your mom praised you for eating your food, or gave you an M&M or praise later on when you were toilet trained, or for being nice to your siblings, or riding a bike. That's just how we all learn. We try something, and if we get good feedback we know we did it right. That's why we give grades, so children know how they are doing. Otherwise, they just don't understand when they're doing something correctly and when they need to improve."

Dr. Marlowe, any advice you could offer would be great.

Michael Lopes

❖ HOW WOULD YOU RESPOND?

Does competition promote learning? How about rewards for good behavior or time on task? Michael's teacher believes that kids learn best when the expectations are clear and when teacher feedback is immediate and positive. Can learning occur another way, or is reinforcement always necessary? Think about student behavior in the classroom. Will students sit still, do their work, and act respectfully in the absence of rewards? And, what about academic behaviors, like reading or learning to solve complex mathematics problems? Must teachers provide incentives for students to stay engaged? Can critical thinking and abstract reasoning be developed more easily if students are praised or given other positive feedback when they are moving in the right direction toward meeting these objectives? Are grades simply a more mature version of M&Ms? What kinds of evidence could help answer these difficult questions? Is there a way you could test out the hypothesis that student learning is more efficient when it is rewarded? Keep these questions in mind as you read "The Science of Learning and the Art of Teaching" by B. F. Skinner. What questions do *you* have about learning and rewards? How can you help extend the discussion of these ideas in class? Finally, how would you respond to Michael Lopes?

❖ THE SCIENCE OF LEARNING
    AND THE ART OF TEACHING

B. F. Skinner

Some promising advances have recently been made in the field of learning. Special techniques have been designed to arrange what are called "contingencies of reinforcement"—the relations which prevail between behavior on the one hand and the consequences of that behavior on the other—with the result that a much more effective control of behavior has been achieved. It has long been argued that an organism learns mainly by producing changes in its environment, but it is only recently that these changes have been carefully manipulated. In traditional devices for the study of learning—in the serial maze, for example, or in the T-maze, the problem box, or the familiar discrimination apparatus— the effects produced by the organism's behavior are left to many fluctuating circumstances. There is many a slip between the turn-to-the-right and the food-cup at the end of the alley. It is not surprising that techniques of this sort have yielded only very rough data from which the uniformities demanded by an experimental science can be extracted only by averaging many cases. In none of this work has the behavior of the individual organism been predicted in more than a statistical sense. The learning processes which are the presumed object of such research are reached only though a series of inferences. Current preoccupation with deductive systems reflects this state of the science.

Recent improvements in the conditions which control behavior in the field of learning are of two principal sorts. The Law of Effect has been taken seriously; we have made sure that effects *do* occur and that they occur under conditions which are optimal for producing the changes called learning. Once we have arranged the particular type of consequence called a reinforcement, our techniques permit us to shape up the behavior of an organism almost at will. It has become a routine exercise to demonstrate this in classes in elementary psychology by conditioning such an organism as a pigeon. Simply by presenting food to a hungry pigeon at the right time, it is possible to shape up three or four well-defined responses in a single demonstration period—such responses as turning around, pacing the floor in the pattern of a figure-8, standing still in a corner of the demonstration apparatus, stretching the neck, or stamping the foot. Extremely complex performances may be reached through successive stages in the shaping process, the contingencies of reinforcement being changed progressively in the direction of the required behavior. The results are often quite dramatic. In such a demonstration one can *see* learning take place. A significant change in behavior is often obvious as the result of a single reinforcement.

A second important advance in technique permits us to maintain behavior in given states of strength for long periods of time. Reinforcements continue to be important, of course, long after an organism has learned *how* to do something, long after it has acquired behavior. They are necessary to maintain the behavior in strength. Of special interest is the effect of various schedules of intermittent reinforcement. Most important types of schedules have now been investigated, and the effects of schedules in general have been reduced to a few principles. On the theoretical side we now have a fairly good idea of why a given schedule produces its appropriate performance. On the practical side we have learned how to maintain any given level of activity for daily periods limited only by the physical exhaustion of the organism and from day to day without substantial change throughout its life. Many of these effects would be traditionally assigned to the field of motivation, although the principal operation is simply the arrangement of contingencies of reinforcement.

These new methods of shaping behavior and of maintaining it in strength are a great improvement over the traditional practices of professional animal trainers, and it is not surprising that our laboratory results are already being applied to the production of performing animals for commercial purposes. In a more academic environment they have been used for demonstration purposes which extend far beyond an interest in learning as such. For example, it is not too difficult to arrange the complex contingencies which produce many types of social behavior. Competition is exemplified by two pigeons playing a modified game of ping-pong. The pigeons drive the ball back and forth across a small table by pecking at it. When the ball gets by one pigeon, the other is reinforced. The task of constructing such a "social relation" is probably completely our of reach of the traditional animal trainer. It requires a carefully designed program of gradually changing contingencies and the skillful use of schedules to maintain the behavior in strength. Each pigeon is separately prepared for its part in the total performance, and the "social relation" is then arbitrarily constructed. The sequence of events leading up to this stable state are excellent material for the study of the factors important in nonsynthetic social behavior. It is instructive to consider how a similar series of contingencies could arise in the case of the human organism through the evolution of cultural patterns.

Co-operation can also be set up, perhaps more easily than competition. We have trained two pigeons to co-ordinate their behavior in a co-operative endeavor with a precision which equals that of the most skilled human dances. In a more serious vein these techniques have permitted us to explore the complexities of the individual organism and to analyze some of the serial or co-ordinate behaviors involved in attention, problem solving, various types of self-control, and the subsidiary system of responses within a single organism called "personalities." Some of these are exemplified in what we call multiple schedules of reinforcement. In general, a given schedule has an effect upon the rate at which a response is emitted. Changes in the rate from moment to moment show a pattern typical of the schedule. The pattern may be as simple as a constant rate of responding at a given value, it may be a gradually accelerating rate between certain extremes, it may be an abrupt change from not responding at all to a given stable high rate, and so on. It has been shown that the performance characteristic of a given schedule can be brought under the control of a particular stimulus and that different performances can be brought under the control of different stimuli in the same organism. At a recent meeting of the American Psychological Association, C. B. Ferster and I demonstrated a pigeon whose behavior showed the pattern typical of "fixed-interval" reinforcement in the presence of one stimulus and, alternately, the pattern typical of the very different schedule called "fixed ratio" in the presence of a second stimulus. In the laboratory we have been able to obtain performances appropriate to *nine* different schedules in the presence of appropriate stimuli in random alternation. When Stimulus 1 is present, the pigeon executes the performance appropriate to Schedule 1. When Stimulus 2 is present, the pigeon executes the performance appropriate to Schedule 2. And so on. This result is important because it makes the extrapolation of our laboratory results to daily life much more plausible. We are all constantly shifting from schedule to schedule as our immediate environment changes, but the dynamics of the control exercised by reinforcement remain essentially unchanged.

It is also possible to construct very complex *sequences* of schedules. It is not easy to describe these in a few words, but two or three examples may be mentioned. In one experiment the pigeon generates a performance appropriate to Schedule A where the reinforcement is simply the production of the stimulus characteristic of Schedule B, to which the pigeon then responds appropriately. Under a third stimulus, the bird yields a performance appropriate to Schedule C where the reinforcement in this case is simply the production of the stimulus characteristic of Schedule D, to which the bird then responds appropriately. In a special case, fist investigated by L. B. Wyckoff, Jr., the organism responds to one stimulus where the reinforcement consists of the *clarification* of the stimulus controlling another response. The first response becomes, so to speak, an objective form of "paying attention" to the second stimulus. In one important version of this experiment, as yet unpublished, we could say that the pigeon is telling us whether it is "paying attention" to the *shape* of a spot of light or to its *color*.

One of the most dramatic applications of these techniques has recently been made in the Harvard Psychological Laboratories by Floyd Ratliff and Donald S. Blough, who have skillfully used multiple and serial schedules of reinforcement to study complex perceptual processes in the infrahuman organism. They have achieved a sort of psychophysics without verbal instruction. In a recent experiment by

Blough, for example, a pigeon draws a detailed dark-adaptation curve showing the characteristic breaks of rod and cone vision. The curve is recorded continuously in a single experimental period and is quite comparable with the curves of human subjects. The pigeon behaves in a way which, in the human case, we would not hesitate to describe by saying that it adjusts a very faint patch of light until it can just be seen.

In all this work, the species of the organism has made surprisingly little difference. It is true that the organisms studied have all been vertebrates, but they still cover a wide range. Comparable results have been obtained with pigeons, rats, dogs, monkeys, human children, and most recently, by the author in collaboration with Ogden R. Lindsley, human psychotic subjects. In spite of great phylogenetic differences, all these organisms show amazingly similar properties of the learning process. It should be emphasized that this has been achieved by analyzing the effects of reinforcement and by designing techniques which manipulate reinforcement with considerable precision. Only in this way can the behavior of the individual organism be brought under such precise control. It is also important to note that through a gradual advance to complex interrelations among responses, the same degree of rigor is being extended to behavior which would usually be assigned to such fields as perception, thinking, and personality dynamics.

From this exciting prospect of an advancing science of learning, it is a great shock to turn to that branch of technology which is most directly concerned with the learning process—education. Let us consider, for example, the teaching of arithmetic in the lower grades. The school is concerned with imparting to the child a large number of responses of a special sort. The responses are all verbal. They consist of speaking and writing certain words, figures and signs which, to put it roughly, refer to numbers and to arithmetic operations. The first task is to shape up these responses—to get the child to pronounce and to write responses correctly, but the principal task is to bring this behavior under many sorts of stimulus control. This is what happens when the child learns to count, to recite tables, to count while ticking off the items in an assemblage of objects, to respond to spoken or written numbers by saying "odd," "even," "prime," and so on. Over and above this elaborate repertoire of numerical behavior, most of which is often dismissed as the product of rote learning, the teaching of arithmetic looks forward to these complex serial arrangements of responses involved in transposing, clearing fractions, and so on, which modify the order or pattern of the original material so that the response called a solution is eventually made possible.

Now, how is this extremely complicated verbal response set up? In the first place, what reinforcements are used? Fifty years ago the answer would have been clear. At that time educational control was still frankly aversive. The child read numbers, copied numbers, memorized tables, and performed operations upon numbers to escape the threat of the birch rod or cane. Some positive reinforcements were perhaps eventually derived from the increased efficiency of the child in the field of arithmetic, and in rare cases some automatic reinforcement may have resulted from the sheer manipulation of the medium—from the solution of problems or the discovery of the intricacies of the number system. But for the immediate purposes of education the child acted to avoid or escape punishment. It was part of the reform movement known as progressive education to make the positive consequences more immediately effective, but anyone who visits the lower grades of the average school today will observe that a change has been made, not from aversive to positive control, but from one form of aversive stimulation to another. The child at his desk, filling in his workbook, is behaving primarily to escape from the threat of a series of minor aversive events— the teacher's displeasure, the criticism or ridicule of his classmates, an ignominious showing in a competition, low marks, a trip to the office "to be talked to" by the principal, or a word to the parent who may still resort to the birch rod. In this welter of aversive consequences, getting the right answer is in itself an insignificant event, any effect of which is lost amid the anxieties, the boredom, and the aggressions which are the inevitable by-products of aversive control.

Secondly, we have to ask how the contingencies of reinforcement are arranged. When is a numerical operation reinforced as "right"? Eventually, of course, the pupil may be able to check his own answers and achieve some sort of automatic reinforcement, but in the early stages the reinforcement of being right is usually accorded by the teacher. The contingencies she provides are far from optimal. It can easily be demonstrated that, unless explicit mediating behavior has been set up, the lapse of only a few seconds between response and reinforcement destroys most of the effect. In a typical classroom, nevertheless, long periods of time customarily elapse. The teacher may walk up and down the aisle, for example, while the class is working on a sheet of problems, pausing here and there to say right or wrong. Many seconds or minutes intervene between the child's response and the teacher's reinforcement. In many cases—for example, when papers are taken home to be corrected—as much as 24 hours may intervene. It is surprising that this system has any effect whatsoever.

A third notable shortcoming is the lack of a skillful program which moves forward through a series of progressive approximations to the final complex behavior desired. A long series of contingencies is necessary to bring the organism into the possession of mathematical behavior more efficiently. But the teacher is seldom able to reinforce at each step in such a series because she cannot deal with the pupil's responses one at a time. It is usually necessary to reinforce the behavior in blocks of responses—as in correcting a worksheet or page from a workbook. The responses within such a block must not be interrelated. The answer to one problem must not depend upon the answer to another. The number of stages through which one may progressively approach a complex pattern of behavior is therefore small, and the task so much the more difficult. Even the most modern workbook in beginning arithmetic is far from exemplifying an efficient program for shaping up mathematical behavior.

Perhaps the most serious criticism of the current classroom is the relative infrequency of reinforcement. Since the pupil is usually dependent upon the teacher for being right, and since many pupils are usually dependent upon the same teacher, the total number of contingencies which may be arranged during, say, the first four years is of the order of only a few thousand. But a very rough estimate suggests that efficient mathematical behavior at this level requires something of the order of 25,000 contingencies. We may suppose that even in the brighter student a given contingency must be arranged several times to place the behavior well in hand. The responses to be set up are not simply the various items in tables of addition, subtraction, multiplication and division; we have also to consider the alternative forms in which each item may be stated. To the learning of such material we should add hundreds of responses concerned with factoring, identifying primes, memorizing series, using short-cut techniques of calculation, constructing and using geometric representations or number forms, and so on. Over and above all this, the whole mathematical repertoire must be brought under the control of concrete problems of considerable variety. Perhaps 50,000 contingencies is a more conservative estimate. In this frame of reference the daily assignment in arithmetic seems pitifully meagre.

The result of all this is, of course, well known. Even our best schools are under criticism for their inefficiency in the teaching of drill subjects such as arithmetic. The condition in the average school is a matter of widespread national concern. Modern children simply do not learn arithmetic quickly or well. Nor is the result simply incompetence. The very subjects in which modern techniques are weakest are those in which failure is most conspicuous, and in the wake of an ever-growing incompetence come the anxieties, uncertainties, and aggressions which in their turn present other problems to the school. Most pupils soon claim the asylum of not being "ready" for arithmetic at a given level or, eventually, of not having a mathematical mind. Such explanations are readily seized upon by defensive teachers and parents. Few pupils ever reach the stage at which automatic reinforcements follow as the natural consequences of mathematical behavior. On the contrary, the figures and symbols of mathematics have become standard emotional stimuli. The glimpse of a column of figures, not to say an algebraic symbol or an integral sign, is likely to set off—not mathematical behavior—but a reaction of anxiety, guilt, or fear.

The teacher is usually no happier about this than the pupil. Denied the opportunity to control via the birch rod, quite at sea as to the mode of operation of the few techniques at her disposal, she spends as little time as possible on drill subjects and eagerly subscribes to philosophies of education which emphasize material of greater inherent interest. A confession of weakness is her extraordinary concern lest the child be taught something unnecessary. The repertoire to be imparted is carefully reduced to an essential minimum. In the field of spelling, for example, a great deal of time and energy has gone into discovering just those words which the young child is going to use, as if it were a crime to waste one's educational power in teaching an unnecessary word. Eventually, weakness of technique emerges in the disguise of a reformulation of the aims of education. Skills are minimized in favor of vague achievements—educating for democracy, educating the whole child, educating for life, and so on. And there the matter ends; for, unfortunately, these philosophies do not in turn suggest improvements in techniques. They offer little or no help in the design of better classroom practices.

There would be no point in urging these objections if improvement were impossible. But the advances which have recently been made in our control of the learning process suggest a thorough revision of classroom practices, and, fortunately, they tell us how the revision can be brought about. This is not, of course, the first time that the results of an experimental science have been brought to bear upon the practical problems of education. The modern classroom does not, however, offer much evidence that research in the field of learning has been respected or used. This condition is no doubt partly due to the limitations of earlier research. But it has been encouraged by a too hasty conclusion that the laboratory study of learning is inherently limited because it cannot take into account the realities of the classroom. In the light of our increasing knowledge of the learning process we should, instead, insist upon dealing with those realities and forcing a substantial change in them. Education is perhaps the most important branch of scientific technology. It deeply affects the lives of all of us. We can no longer allow the exigencies of a practical situation to suppress the tremendous improvements which are within reach. The practical situation must be changed.

There are certain questions which have to be answered in turning to the study of any new organism. What behavior is to be set up? What reinforcers are at hand? What responses are available in embarking upon a program of progressive approximation which will lead to the final form of the behavior? How can reinforcements be most efficiently scheduled to maintain the behavior in strength? These questions are all relevant in considering the problem of the child in the lower grades.

In the first place, what reinforcements are available? What does the school have in its possession which will reinforce a child? We may look first to the material to be learned, for it is possible that this will provide considerable automatic reinforcement. Children play for hours with mechanical toys, paints, scissors and paper, noise-makers, puzzles—in short, with almost anything which feeds back significant changes in the environment and is reasonably free of aversive properties. The sheer control of nature is itself reinforcing. This effect is not evident in the modern school because it is masked by the emotional responses generated by aversive control. It is true that automatic reinforcement from the manipulation of the environment is probably only a mild reinforcer and may need to be carefully husbanded, but one of the most striking principles to emerge from recent research is that the net amount of reinforcement is of little significance. A very slight reinforcement may be tremendously effective in controlling behavior if it is wisely used.

If the natural reinforcements inherent in the subject matter is not enough, other reinforcers must be employed. Even in school the child is occasionally permitted to do "what he wants to do," and access to reinforcements of the behavior to be established. Those who advocate competition as a useful social motive may wish to use the reinforcements which follow from excelling others, although there is the difficulty that in this case the reinforcement of one child is necessarily aversive to another. Next in order we might place the good will and affection of the teacher, and only when that has failed need we turn to the use of aversive stimulation.

In the second place, how are these reinforcements to be made contingent upon the desired behavior? There are two considerations here—the gradual elaboration of extremely complex patterns of behavior and the maintenance of the behavior in strengths at each stage. The whole process of becoming competent in any field must be divided into a very large number of very small steps, and reinforcement must be contingent upon the accomplishment of each step. This solution to the problem of creating a complex repertoire of behavior also solves the problem of maintaining the behavior in strength. We could, of course, resort to the techniques of scheduling already developed in the study of other organisms but in the present state of our knowledge of educational practices, scheduling appears to be most efficiently arranged through the design of the material to be learned. By making each successive step as small as possible, the frequency of reinforcement can be raised to a maximum, while the possibly aversive consequences of being wrong are reduced to a minimum. Other ways of designing material would yield other programs of reinforcement. Any supplementary reinforcement would probably have to be scheduled in the more traditional way.

These requirements are not excessive, but they are probably incompatible with the current realities of the classroom. In the experimental study of learning it has been found that the contingencies of reinforcement which are most efficient in controlling the organism cannot be arranged through the personal meditation of the experimenter. An organism is affected by subtle details of contingencies which are beyond the capacity of the human organism to arrange. Mechanical and electrical devices must be used. Mechanical help is also demanded by the sheer number of contingencies which may be used efficiently in a single experimental session. We have recorded many millions of responses from a single organism during thousands of experimental hours. Personal arrangement of the contingencies and personal observation of the results are quite unthinkable. Now, the human organism is, if anything, more sensitive to precise contingencies than the other organisms we have studied. We have every reason to expect, therefore, that the most effective control of human learning will require instrumental aid. The simple fact is that, as a mere reinforcing mechanism, the teacher is out of date.

6

Dear Dr. Canestrari:

I wanted to send you a quick e-mail, because I saw something yesterday that was hilarious. These two boys were pretending to play ice hockey on the playground. They had sticks and a tennis ball, but no other equipment, and they went back and forth taking shots and passing the ball around. Then, right in the middle of the back and forth, as if on cue, the kids dropped their sticks, and pretended to fight. It was exactly like watching a game on television: They threw down their imaginary gloves, grabbed each other's shirts, locked arms, and then sort of circled around in place. It almost looked like a dance routine they had practiced together for weeks. Really, really funny. How'd they learn to do this? I mean, the kids are in kindergarten, and they can't be more than 5 years old!

Lucas Bennet

❖ HOW WOULD YOU RESPOND?

The school play yard is one of those places where teachers can stand off to the side and blend into the scenery without kids really noticing them too much. It is a perfect environment for just plain observing. Are all behaviors the result of direct instruction or might some behaviors be the result of what psychologists call *incidental learning*, like the mock ice hockey brawl? If adults are behaving this way, why can't kids? If adults let kids watch an NHL hockey game, isn't this reason enough for kids to skate, handle and shoot the puck, and, even, fight? What sorts of adult behaviors are children most likely to imitate, and why? Keep these questions in mind as you read the "Transmission of Aggression Through Imitation of Aggressive Models" by Albert Bandura, Dorothea Ross, and Sheila A. Ross. What questions do *you* have about social learning? How can you help extend the discussion of these ideas in class? Finally, how would you respond to Lucas Bennet?

❖ TRANSMISSION OF AGGRESSION THROUGH
   IMITATION OF AGGRESSIVE MODELS

Albert Bandura, Dorothea Ross, and Sheila A. Ross

A previous study, designed to account for the phenomenon of identification in terms of incidental learning, demonstrated that children readily imitated behavior exhibited by an adult model in the presence of the model (Bandura & Huston, 1961). A series of experiments by Blake (1958) and others (Grosser, Polansky, & Lippitt, 1951; Rosenblith, 1959; Schachter & Hall, 1952) have likewise shown that mere observation of a model has a facilitating effect on subjects' reactions in the immediate social influence setting.

While these studies provide convincing evidence for the influence and control exerted on others by the behavior of a model, a more crucial test of imitative learning involves the generalization of imitative response patterns in new settings in which the model is absent.

In the experiment reported in this paper children were exposed to aggressive and nonaggressive adult models and were then tested on the amount of imitative learning in a new situation in the absence of the model. According to the prediction, subjects exposed to aggressive models would reproduce aggressive acts resembling those of their models and would differ in this respect both from subjects who observed nonaggressive models and from those who had no prior exposure to any models. This hypothesis assumed that subjects had learned imitative habits as a result of prior reinforcement, and these tendencies would generalize to some extent to adult experimenters (Miller & Dollard, 1941).

It was further predicted that observation of subdued nonaggressive models would have generalized inhibiting effect on the subjects' subsequent behavior, and this effect would be reflected in a difference between the nonaggressive and the control groups, with subjects in the latter group displaying significantly more aggression.

Hypotheses were also advanced concerning the influence of the sex of model and sex of subjects on imitation. Fauls and Smith (1956) have shown that preschool children perceive their parents as having distinct preferences regarding sex appropriate modes of behavior for their children. Their findings, as well as informal observation, suggest that parents reward imitation of sex appropriate behavior and discourage or punish sex inappropriate imitative responses, e.g., a male child is unlikely to receive much reward for performing female appropriate activities, such as cooking, or for adopting other aspects of the maternal role, but these same behaviors are typically welcomed if performed by females. As a result of differing reinforcement histories, tendencies to imitate male and female models thus acquire differential habit strength. One would expect, on this basis, subjects to imitate the behavior of a same-sex model to a greater degree than a model of the opposite sex.

Since aggression, however, is a highly masculine-typed behavior, boys should be more predisposed than girls toward imitating aggression, the difference being most marked for subjects exposed to the male aggressive model.

Method

Subjects

The subjects were 36 boys and 36 girls enrolled in the Stanford University Nursery School. They ranged in age from 37 to 69 months, with a mean age of 52 months.

Two adults, a male and a female, served in the role of model, and one female experimenter conducted the study for all 72 children.

Experimental Design

Subjects were divided into eight experimental groups of six subjects each and a control group consisting of 24 subjects. Half the experimental subjects were exposed to aggressive models and half were exposed to models that were subdued and nonaggressive in their behavior. These groups were further subdivided into male and female subjects. Half the subjects in the aggressive and nonaggressive conditions observed same-sex models, while the remaining subjects in each group viewed models of the opposite sex. The control group had no prior exposure to the adult models and was tested only in the generalization situation.

It seemed reasonable to expect that the subjects' level of aggressiveness would be positively related to the readiness with which they imitated aggressive modes of behavior. Therefore, in order to increase the precision of treatment comparisons, subjects in the experimental and control groups were matched individually on the basis of ratings of their aggressive behavior in social interactions in the nursery school.

The subjects were rated on four five-point rating scales by the experimenter and a nursery school teacher, both of whom were well acquainted with the children. These scales measured the extent to which subjects displayed physical aggression, verbal aggression, aggression toward inanimate objects, and aggressive inhibition. The latter scale, which dealt with the subjects' tendency to inhibit aggressive reactions in the face of high instigation, provided a measure of aggression anxiety.

Fifty-one subjects were rated independently by both judges so as to permit an assessment of interrater agreement. The reliability of the composite aggression score, estimated by means of the Pearson product-moment correlation, was .89.

The composite score was obtained by summing the ratings on the four aggression scales; on the basis of these scores, subjects were arranged in triplets and assigned at random to one of two treatment conditions or to the control group.

Experimental Conditions

In the first step in the procedure subjects were brought individually by the experimenter to the experimental room and the model who was in the hallway outside the room, was invited by the experimenter to come and join in the game. The experimenter then escorted the subject to one corner of the room, which was structured as the subject's play area. After seating the child at a small table, the experimenter demonstrated how the subject could design pictures with potato prints and picture stickers provided. The potato prints included a variety of geometrical forms; the stickers were attractive multicolor pictures of animals, flowers, and Western figures to be pasted on a pastoral scene. These activities were selected since they had been established, by previous studies in the nursery school, as having high interest value for the children.

After having settled the subject in his corner, the experimenter escorted the model to the opposite corner of the room which contained a small table and chair, a tinker toy set, a mallet, and a 5-foot inflated

Bobo doll. The experimenter explained that these were the materials provided for the model to play with and, after the model was seated, the experimenter left the experimental room.

With subjects in the *nonaggressive condition*, the model assembled the tinker toys in a quiet subdued manner totally ignoring the Bobo doll.

In contrast, with subjects in the *aggressive condition*, the model began by assembling the tinker toys but after approximately a minute had elapsed, the model turned to the Bobo doll and spent the remainder of the period aggressing toward it.

Imitative learning can be clearly demonstrated if a model performs sufficiently novel patterns of responses which are unlikely to occur independently of the observation of the behavior of a model and if a subject reproduces these behaviors in substantially identical form. For this reason, in addition to punching the Bobo doll, a response that is likely to be performed by children independently of a demonstration, the model exhibited distinctive aggressive acts which were to be scored as imitative responses. The model laid the Bobo doll on its side, sat on it and punched it repeatedly in the nose. The model then raised the Bobo doll, picked up the mallet and struck the doll on the head. Following the mallet aggression, the model tossed the doll up in the air aggressively and kicked it about the room. This sequence of physically aggressive acts was repeated approximately three times, interspersed with verbally aggressive responses such as, "Sock him in the nose . . . ," "Hit him down . . . ," "Throw him in the air . . . ," "Kick him . . . ," "Pow . . . ," and two nonaggressive comments, "He keeps coming back for more" and "He sure is a tough fella."

Thus in the exposure situation, subjects were provided with a diverting task which occupied their attention while at the same time insured observation of the model's behavior in the absence of any instructions to observe or to learn the responses in question. Since subjects could not perform the model's aggressive behavior, any learning that occurred was purely on an observational or covert basis.

At the end of 10 minutes, the experimenter entered the room, informed the subject that he would now go to another game room, and bid the model goodbye.

Aggression Arousal

Subjects were tested for the amount of imitative learning in a different experimental room that was set off from the main nursery school building. The two experimental situations were thus clearly differentiated;

in fact, many subjects were under the impression that they were no longer on the nursery school grounds.

Prior to the test for imitation, however, all subjects, experimental and control, were subjected to mild aggression arousal to insure that they were under some degree of instigation to aggression. The arousal experience was included for two main reasons. In the first place, observation of aggressive behavior exhibited by others tends to reduce the probability of aggression on the part of the observer (Rosenbaum & deCharms, 1960). Consequently, subjects in the aggressive condition, in relation both to the nonaggressive and control groups, would be under weaker instigation following exposure to the models. Second, if subjects in the nonaggressive condition expressed little aggression in the face of appropriate instigation, the presence of an inhibitory process would seem to be indicated.

Following the exposure experience, therefore, the experimenter brought the subject to an anteroom that contained these relatively attractive toys: a fire engine, a locomotive, a jet fighter plane, a cable car, a colorful spinning top, and a doll set complete with wardrobe, doll carriage, and baby crib. The experimenter explained that the toys were for the subject to play with but, as soon as the subject became sufficiently involved with the play material (usually in about 2 minutes), the experimenter remarked that these were her very best toys, that she did not let just anyone play with them, and that she had decided to reserve these toys for the other children. However, the subject could play with any of the toys that were in the next room. The experimenter and the subject then entered the adjoining experimental room.

It was necessary for the experimenter to remain in the room during the experimental session; otherwise a number of the children would either refuse to remain alone or would leave before the termination of the session. However, in order to minimize any influence her presence might have on the subject's behavior, the experimenter remained as inconspicuous as possible by busying herself with paper work at a desk in the far corner of the room and avoiding any interaction with the child.

Test for Delayed Imitation

The experimental room contained a variety of toys including some that could be used in imitative or nonimitative aggression, and others that tended to elicit predominantly nonaggressive forms of behavior. The aggressive toys included a 3-foot Bobo doll, a mallet and peg board, two dart guns, and a tether ball with a face painted on it which hung from the ceiling. The nonaggressive toys, on the other hand, included a tea set, crayons and coloring paper, a ball, two dolls, three bears, cars and trucks, and plastic farm animals.

In order to eliminate any variation in behavior due to mere placement of the toys in the room, the play material was arranged in a fixed order for each of the sessions.

The subject spent 20 minutes in this experiments room during which time his behavior was rated in terms of predetermined response categories by judges who observed the session though a one-way mirror in an adjoining observation room. The 20-minute session was divided into 5-second intervals by means of an electric interval timer, thus yielding a total number of 240 response units for each subject.

The male model scored the experimental sessions for all 72 children. Except for the cases in which he served as the model, he did not have knowledge of the subjects' group assignments. In order to provide an estimate of interscorer agreement, the performance of half the subjects were also scored independently by second observer. Thus one or the other of the two observers usually had no knowledge of the conditions to which the subjects were assigned. Since, however, all but two of the subjects in the aggressive condition performed the models' novel aggressive responses while subjects in the other conditions only rarely exhibited such reactions, subjects who were exposed to the aggressive models could be readily identified through the distinctive behavior.

The responses scored involved highly specific concrete classes of behavior and yielded high interscorer reliabilities, the product-moment coefficients being in the .90s.

Response Measures

Three measures of imitation were obtained:

Imitation of physical aggression: This category included acts of striking the Bobo doll with the mallet, sitting on the doll and punching it in the nose, kicking the doll, and tossing it in the air.

Imitative verbal aggression: Subject repeats the phrases, "Sock him," "Hit him down," "Kick him," "Throw him in the air," or "Pow."

Imitative nonaggressive verbal responses: Subject repeats, "He keeps coming back for more," or "He sure is a tough fella."

During the pretest, a number of the subjects imitated the essential components of the model's behavior but did not perform the complete act, or they directed the imitative aggressive response to some object other than the Bobo doll. Two responses of this type were therefore scored and were interpreted as partially imitative behavior.

Mallet aggression: Subject strikes objects other than the Bobo doll aggressively with the mallet.

Sits on Bobo doll: Subject lays the Bobo doll on its side and sits on it, but does not aggress toward it.

The following additional nonimitative aggressive responses were scored:

Punches Bobo doll: Subject strikes, slaps, or pushes the doll aggressively.

Nonimitative physical and verbal aggression: This category included physically aggressive acts directed toward objects other than the Bobo doll and any hostile remarks except for those in the verbal imitation category; e.g., "Shoot the Bobo," "Cut him," "Stupid ball," "Knock over people," "Horses fighting, biting."

Aggressive gun play: Subject shoots darts or aims the guns and fires imaginary shots at objects in the room.

Ratings were also made of the number of behavior units in which subjects played nonaggressively or sat quietly and did not play with any of the material at all.

Results

Complete Imitation of Models' Behavior

Subjects in the aggression condition reproduced a good deal of physical and verbal aggressive behavior resembling that of the models, and their mean scores differed markedly from those of subjects in the nonaggressive and control groups who exhibited virtually no imitative aggression.

Since there were only a few scores for subjects in the nonaggressive and control conditions (approximately 70% of the subjects had zero scores), and the assumption of homogeneity of variance could not be made, the Friedman two-way analysis of variance by ranks was employed to test the significance of the obtained differences.

The prediction that exposure of subjects to aggressive models increases the probability of aggressive behavior is clearly confirmed. The main effect of treatment conditions is highly significant both for physical and verbal imitative aggression. Comparison of pairs of scores by the sign test shows that the obtained over-all differences were due almost entirely to the aggression displayed by subjects who had been exposed to the aggressive models. Their scores were significantly higher than those of either the nonaggressive or control groups, which did not differ from each.

Imitation was not confined to the model's aggressive responses. Approximately one-third of the subjects in the aggressive condition also repeated the model's nonaggressive verbal responses while none of the subjects in either the nonaggressive or control groups made such remarks.

Discussion

Much current research on social learning is focused on the shaping of new behavior through rewarding and punishing consequences. Unless responses are emitted, however, they cannot be influenced. The results of this study provide strong evidence that observation of cues produced by the behavior of others is one effective means of eliciting certain forms of responses for which the original probability is very low or zero. Indeed, social imitation may hasten or short-cut the acquisition of new behaviors without the necessity of reinforcing successive approximations as suggested by Skinner (1953).

Thus subjects given an opportunity to observe aggressive models later reproduced a good deal of physical and verbal aggression (as well as nonaggressive responses) substantially identical with that of the model. In contrast, subjects who were exposed to nonaggressive models and those who had no previous exposure to any models only rarely performed such responses.

To the extent that observation of adult models displaying aggression communicates permissiveness for aggressive behavior, such exposure may serve to weaken inhibitory responses and thereby to increase the probability of aggressive reactions to subsequent frustrations. The fact, however, that subjects expressed their aggression in ways that clearly resembled the novel patterns exhibited by models provides striking evidence for the occurrence of learning by imitation.

The trends in the data yielded by the present study suggest an alternative explanation. In the case of a highly masculine-typed behavior such as physical aggression, there is a tendency for both male and female subjects to imitate the male model to a greater degree than the female model. On the other hand, in the case of verbal aggression, which is less clearly sex linked, the greatest amount of imitation occurs in relation to the same-sex model. These trends together with the finding that boys in relation to girls are in general more imitative of physical aggression but do not differ in imitation of verbal aggression, suggest that subjects may be differentially affected by the sex of the model but that predictions must take into account the degree to which the behavior in question is sex-typed.

Summary

Twenty-four preschool children were assigned to each of three conditions. One experimental group observed aggressive adult models; a second observed inhibited nonaggressive models; while subjects in a control group had no prior exposure to the models. Half the subjects in the experimental conditions observed same-sex models and half viewed models of the opposite sex. Subjects were then tested for the amount of imitative as well as nonimitative aggression performed in a new situation in the absence of the models.

Comparison of the subjects' behavior in the generalization situation revealed that subjects exposed to aggressive models reproduced a good deal of aggression resembling that of the models, and that their mean scores differed markedly from those of subjects in the nonaggressive and control groups. Subjects in the aggressive condition also exhibited significantly more partially imitative and nonimitative aggressive behavior and were generally less inhibited in their behavior than subjects in the nonaggressive condition.

Imitation was found to be differentially influenced by the sex of the model with boys showing more aggression than girls following exposure to the male model, the difference being particularly marked on highly masculine-typed behavior.

Subjects who observed the nonaggressive models, especially the subdued male model, were generally less aggressive than their controls.

The implications of the findings based on this experiment and related studies for the psychoanalytic theory of identification with the aggressor were discussed.

References

Bandura, A. Relationship of family patterns to behavior disorders. Progress Report, 1960, Stanford University, Project No. M-1734, United States Public Health Service.

Bandura, A., & Huston, Aletha C. Identification as a process of incidental learning. *J. abnorm. soc. Psychol.*, 1961, 63, 311–318.

Bandura, A., & Walters, R. H. *Adolescent aggrersion.* New York: Ronald, 1959.

Blake, R. R. The other person in the situation. In R. Tagiuri & L. Petrullo (Eds.), *Person perception and interpersonal behavior.* Stanford, Calif: Stanford Univer. Press, 1958. Pp. 229–242.

Fauls, Lydia B., & Smith, W. D. Sex-role learning of five-year olds. *J. genet. Psychol.*, 1956, 89, 105–117.

Freud, Anna. *The ego and the mechanisms of defense.* New York: International Univer. Press, 1946.

Grosser, D., Polansky, N., & Lippit, R. A laboratory study of behavior contagion. *Hum. Relat.*, 1951, 4, 115–142.

Lindquist, E. F. *Design and analysis of experiments.* Boston: Houghton Mifflin, 1956.

Logan, F., Olmsted, O. L., Rosner, B. S., Shwartz, R. D., & Stevens, C. M. *Behavior theory and social science.* New Haven: Yale Univer. Press, 1955.

Maccoby, Elanor E. Role-taking in childhood and its consequences for social learning. *Child Develpm.*, 1959, 30, 239–252.

Miller, N. F., & Dollard, J. *Social learning and imitation.* New Haven: Yale Univer. Press, 1941.

Mowrer, O. H. (Ed.) Identification: A link between learning theory and psychotherapy. In, *Learning theory and personality dynamics.* New York: Ronald, 1950. Pp. 69–94.

Rosenbaum, M. E., & Dercharms, R. Direct and vicarious reduction of hostility. *J. abnorm. soc. Psychol.*, 1960, 60, 105–111.

Rosenblith, Judy F. Learning by imitation in kindergarten children. *Child Develpm.*, 1959, 30, 69–80.

Schacter S., & Hall, R. Group-derived restraints and audience persuasion. *Hum. Relat.*, 1952, 5, 397–406.

Skinner, B. F. *Science and human behavior.* New York: Macmillan, 1953.

7

❖ ❖ ❖

Dear Dr. Canestrari:

Teaching is so much more work than I imagined it would be. I am absolutely exhausted, but I've got a question for you that has really been bugging me as this first semester starts to come to a close. Here it is: How do you know when kids have really learned something? I do all the things we talked about (frequent review, repeated visits to a subject from different angles, lots of opportunities for kids to apply what they learn), but I'm still bothered. I can't tell if the kids are really learning or simply remembering for the test. Are memory and learning the same thing? And, what if they can't remember new information at a later date, did they really learn it in the first place? Also, if they don't remember stuff we're doing now in a month, or next semester, or next year, then, should I bother? For example, we just finished a unit on the American Revolution. I just know these kids did this last year, but for so many of them it's as if they're reading and talking about this era in American history for the first time. Maybe what their teacher did last year was a complete waste of time? Is what I'm doing now a waste of time if they won't remember it next year? I wonder about skill learning too, not just the content. If the kids can recite their multiplication tables, does that mean they really understand it? I want them to learn and understand, and remember, but not just so they can do well on the tests. I want what we talk about to really stick. What's the best way for this to happen? What makes information meaningful enough for kids to understand it when it's presented but also to remember it later too?

Stephen McMahon

❖ HOW WOULD YOU RESPOND?

What makes something interesting, provocative, or meaningful enough for it to be retained over time? Why do people sometimes say about particular events, "I will never forget when . . . ?" Why are some skills, like riding a bike, never forgotten once learned? In contrast, why do we often feel as if we will never be able to remember certain kinds of information? How do teacher behaviors affect memory and learning? Are there particular instructional approaches that facilitate memory? What can teachers do to help students retain information and skills? Keep these questions in mind as you read "Students Remember . . . What They Think About" by Daniel T. Willingham. What questions do *you* have about memory and learning? How can you help extend the discussion of these ideas in class? Finally, how would you respond to Stephen McMahon?

❖ STUDENTS REMEMBER . . . WHAT THEY THINK ABOUT

Daniel T. Willingham

How does the mind work—and especially how does it learn? Teachers make assumptions all day long about how students best comprehend, remember, and create. These assumptions—and the teaching decisions that result—are based on a mix of theories learned in teacher education, trial and error, craft knowledge, and gut instinct. Such gut knowledge often serves us well. But is there anything sturdier to rely on?

Cognitive science is an interdisciplinary field of researchers from psychology, neuroscience, linguistics, philosophy, computer science, and anthropology who seek to understand the mind. In this [reading], we will consider findings from this field that are strong and clear enough to merit classroom application.

Issue: The teacher presents a strong, coherent lesson in which a set of significant facts is clearly connected to a reasonable conclusion. But, at test time, the students show no understanding of the connections. Some students parrot back the conclusion, but no facts. Others spit back memorized facts, but don't see how they fit together. Though the lesson wasn't taught in a rote way, it seems like rote knowledge is what the students took in. Why do well-integrated, coherent lessons often come back to us in a less meaningful, fragmented form? Can cognitive science help explain why this result is so common—and offer ideas about how to avoid it?

Response: Rote knowledge is devoid of all meaning. The knowledge that these students appear to be regurgitating is probably not rote knowledge. It is probably "shallow" knowledge: The students' knowledge has meaning (unlike rote knowledge), in that the students understand each isolated part, but their knowledge lacks the deeper meaning that comes from understanding the relationship among the parts. For reasons noted below, this is a common problem in the early stages of learning about a new topic. But it also has another remediable source, which is the focus of this column.

Cognitive science has shown that what ends up in a learner's memory is not simply the material presented—it is the product of what the learner thought about when he or she encountered the material. This principle illuminates one important origin of shallow knowledge and also suggests how to help students develop deep and interconnected knowledge.

Let's start with an example of shallow knowledge. Suppose that you are teaching a high school class unit on World War II and develop a lesson on the Japanese attack on Pearl Harbor. Many facts might be included in such a lesson: (a) Japan had aspirations to be a regional power; (b) Japan was engaged in a protracted war with China; (c) because they were at war, European countries could not protect their colonies in the South Pacific; and (d) the attack on Pearl Harbor resulted in a declaration of war on Japan by the United States. The overarching point of this lesson might be to show that the attack on Pearl Harbor was a strategic mistake for the Japanese, given their war aims. (See Figure 7.1 for a diagram of the lesson.)

We can see two ways that this meaningful lesson might end up as shallow knowledge in the student's mind. The student might commit to memory some or all of these four facts. But knowing these facts without understanding how they relate to one another and can be integrated to support the conclusion leaves the facts isolated; they are not without meaning, but neither are they as rich as they might be. The student has the trees, but no view of the forest.

Alternatively, the student might commit to memory the conclusion, "The attack on Pearl Harbor, although militarily a successful battle for Japan, was ultimately detrimental to its long-range war plans." But

Figure 7.1   Lesson Diagram

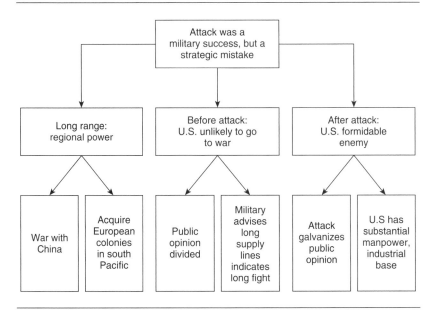

memorizing this conclusion without understanding the reasoning behind it and knowing the supporting facts is empty. It isn't rote—the student knows Japan initiated and won a battle at the place called Pearl Harbor. But the knowledge certainly is "shallow"—it has no connections. We have all had students memorize phrases from class or a textbook more or less word-for-word, and although what the student says is accurate, we can't help but wonder whether he or she really understands the ideas those words represent. Let's dig deeper.

Memory Is as Thinking Does

When students parrot back a teacher's or the textbook's words, they are, of course, drawing on memory. Thus, the question of why students end up with shallow knowledge is really a question about the workings of memory. Needless to say, determining what ends up in memory and in what form is a complex question, but *there is one factor that trumps most others in determining what is remembered: what* you *think about when you encounter the material.* The fact that the material you are dealing with has meaning does not guarantee that the meaning will be remembered. If you think about that meaning, the meaning *will* reside in memory. If you don't, it won't. For example, if I teach about Pearl Harbor, some sailing enthusiasts may starting thinking about the ships of the era and pay minimal attention to the rest of the class—just a few minutes after the bell rings they won't remember much about the causes and consequences of Pearl Harbor. Memory is as thinking does.

A classic experiment illustrating this principle was conducted by Thomas Hyde and James Jenkins in 1969. It examined how one thinks about material and the effect of that thinking on memory. Subjects in their experiment listened to a list of words at a rate of one word every two seconds. Different groups of subjects were to perform different tasks upon hearing each word. Some were to rate each word as to whether it made them think of pleasant or unpleasant things, whereas others were asked to count the number of times the letter *E* appeared in the word. Rating the pleasantness forces the subject to think about the word's meaning; the word *garbage* is unpleasant because of what it means— what it is associated with in one's memory. Counting *E* s, on the other hand, forces one to think about the spelling of the word, but not its meaning. Thus, the experimenters manipulated what subjects thought about when they encountered each word. Subjects were not told that their memory for the words would later be tested; they thought they were merely to make the pleasantness or the *E*-counting judgment.

One other detail of the experiment is especially important. The word list actually consisted of 12 pairs of very highly associated words, such as doctor-nurse, although this fact was not pointed out to any of the subjects. The order in which the words were read was random (except that related words were not allowed to be next to one another in the list).

The results are shown in Figure 7.2. First look at the left side of the chart, which shows the mean number of words recalled. Memory was much better when subjects made the pleasantness ratings. Thinking about the meaning of material is especially helpful to Memory. This finding is consistent across hundreds of other experiments.

The right side of the figure shows a measure of clustering—the extent to which subjects paired the associated words as they tried to remember them. When a subject recalled a word (e.g., *doctor*), what percentage of the time was the next word recalled the highly associated one (*nurse*)? As the figure shows, subjects who thought about the word's meaning (i.e., rated pleasantness) not only remembered more words, they tended to remember the related words together, even though the related words did not appear together in the list. The subjects who counted *E* s did not tend to remember related words together.

Figure 7.2   Thinking About Meaning Helps Memory

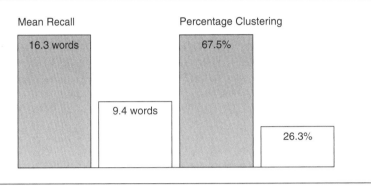

These results forcefully make the point that meaningful structure that is in the environment may or may not end up being stored in memory. In the Hyde and Jenkins experiment, the fact that some of the words were related in meaning was largely lost on the subjects who counted *E*s because thinking about *E*s did not encourage the subjects to process meaning. Subjects who made the pleasantness ratings tended to group the words together by meaning as they recalled them. Whatever subjects thought about when they heard the words (which, teachers will note, depends on what they were *asked* to think about) was what ended up in memory.

In the Hyde and Jenkins experiment, the "what they think about" principle is divided into thinking about meaning versus not thinking about meaning. Other experiments show that even if one thinks about meaning, the particular *aspect* of the meaning that one considers will be stored in memory, and other aspects of meaning will not. For example, in one experiment (Barclay et al., 1974), subjects were presented with words to remember in the context of a sentence. The sentence biased subjects to think of one or another feature of the to-be-remembered word: For example, some subjects read "The man lifted the *piano*," which encouraged thinking about the fact that pianos are heavy. Other subjects read "The man tuned the *piano*," which encouraged considering that pianos produce music. In the next phase of the experiment subjects were told that their memory for some of the nouns in the sentences would be tested and that for each sentence they would get a hint. For *piano*, some subjects were given the hint, "something heavy." If they had read the sentence about lifting the piano, this hint matched the feature they had thought about, but if they read the sentence about tuning the piano, the hint didn't match. (Other subjects saw a hint that matched the piano tuning sentence; that hint was "something with a nice sound.")

The results showed that subjects remembered about three times as many words when the hint for the test matched what subjects had thought about when they first read the word. Again, the point is that what is stored in memory is quite specific to what you think about when you encounter the material. It is not the case that if you think about *piano,* then *piano* and all of its features are stored in memory. You might think about its music-producing qualities, its weight, its cost, and so on. Or you might not focus on the referent at all, but rather on the physical properties of the word itself, as when Hyde and Jenkins asked subjects to count *E* s. In each case, what you think about is what you remember.

So what does this have to do with shallow knowledge? It shows where shallow knowledge might come from. Meaning that is in the environment won't end up in memory if students don't think about it. Students with shallow knowledge have apparently thought about the material in a shallow way. This conclusion reframes the question we might ask: Why would students think about the material in a shallow way, given that we didn't present it to them that way? Obviously, a student would learn only isolated facts or unsupported conclusions if that is what the teacher taught, but I find it difficult to believe that this is a common practice. The notion that education should emphasize meaning is deeply ingrained in our system and has been for a generation or more. There cannot be many teachers who ask their students to learn facts without concern for a larger picture. So how do students end up with shallow knowledge? There are several possible answers.

1. As noted at the beginning of this article, in one form, shallow knowledge is simply a step on the way to deep knowledge. Consider again the hierarchical diagram shown in Figure 7.1. I argued that shallow knowledge could either be memorization of the conclusion (top of the hierarchy) without knowing the facts that back it up (bottom of the hierarchy), or memorization of the facts without integrating them into a conclusion. Clearly the sort of deep knowledge we want our students to have is objectively harder to obtain than shallow knowledge, because knowledge of the facts *and* knowledge of the conclusion *and* knowledge of their interrelationships are prerequisite to it. We want students to know how the different levels of hierarchy relate to one another; it's not enough to have memorized each level in isolation of the others.

That connected knowledge will inevitably be the last thing that the student acquires. Thus, some students' knowledge will be shallow simply because they are not far enough along yet.

2. Other students may effectively quit learning before they reach the deep understanding that is our goal for them. A student may learn the facts about Pearl Harbor and think "All right, I've learned a lot about this stuff." The student is correct (so far as it goes) and simply doesn't realize that there is yet more to do.

3. Students' perception of what they are supposed to learn—and what it means to learn—may contribute to shallow knowledge. A student may seek to memorize definitions and pat phrases word-for-word from the book because the student *knows* that this information is correct and cannot be contested. When I was in eighth grade, we were given a list of vocabulary terms that we were to define and then study in preparation for a weekly test. A friend defined "cherub" as "an angel of the second order." My friends and I teased him because his definition missed what we thought was the key aspect of the word—that a cherub is small, chubby, and rosy-cheeked. He was unmoved and kept repeating "that's what the dictionary said." He liked the fact that his answer was uncontestable. Students may memorize exactly what the teacher or textbook says in order to be certain that they are *correct*, and worry less about the extent to which they understand.

4. Despite what was offered to students in the teacher's lesson, the students attended to (thought about) something different—and that's what they remembered.

What Does This Mean for Teachers?

This fundamental principle of memory—memory is as thinking does—yields a clear strategy to encourage deep, meaningful knowledge. If students think about the meaning of material, meaning will end up in memory. How can teachers be sure that students are thinking about meaning?

Obviously there is no one way to ensure that students think about the meaning of material. A compelling story may be appropriate for one lesson, whereas a carefully designed laboratory project works for a second, and a well-structured group discussion for a third. One possible common misconception is that learners can only understand meaning if they themselves construct the meaning in a physically active way. A moment's reflection should tell us that "listening" does not imply passivity or shallowness. We have all been to "active, participatory" workshops that felt like a waste of time, and we have been to lectures where we "just listened" that were gripping and informative. Constructing meaning is a matter of being *mentally* engaged; being physically engaged might help at times, but it is not necessary.

How can we ensure that students are mentally engaged? While there is still more to learn about applying this research on thinking and memory to teaching, several key principles have emerged to guide teachers in developing assignments, classroom activities, and assessments.

- **Anticipate what your lesson will lead students to think about.** The direct relationship between thought and memory is so important that it could be used as a self-check for a teacher preparing virtually any assignment: *Always try to anticipate what students will be thinking when they are doing the assignment.* Doing so may make it clear that some assignments designed with one purpose in mind will achieve another. For example, a teacher once told me that, as part of a unit on the Underground Railroad, he had his students bake biscuits so that they would appreciate what escaped slaves ate most nights. He asked what I thought of the assignment and my reply was that his students will remember baking biscuits. In other words, his students probably thought for 30 seconds about the relation of the baking to the course material, and then spent 30 minutes thinking about measuring flour, mixing dough, and so on.

Another example comes from my recent observation of my nephew as he completed a book report. The teacher asked the students to draw a poster that depicted all of the events of the book. The purpose of the assignment was to have students think of the book as a whole, and to consider how the separate events related to one another. This purpose got lost in the execution. My nephew spent a lot more time thinking about how to draw a good castle than he did about the plot of the book.

- **Use discovery learning carefully.** The principle above—anticipate the students' thoughts—also illuminates the use and misuse of discovery learning. There is little doubt that students remember material they generate themselves better than material that is handed to them. This "generation effect," as it is called (Slamecka & Graf, 1978), is indeed powerful, and it is due, in part, to forcing the learner to think about the meaning of material (although other techniques can do that as well).

Part of the effect does seem to be unique to the actual generation of the answer, over and above thinking about meaning. One might suppose, therefore, that discovery learning should be employed whenever possible. However, given that memory follows thought, one thing is clear: *Students will remember incorrect "discoveries" just as well as correct ones.*

Considerable care must be taken to ensure that the path of students' thoughts will be a profitable one. For example, advocates of discovery learning often point out that children learn to use some computer software rapidly and effectively merely by "playing around with it." That may be true, but that learning environment is also quite structured in that profitless actions are immediately discouraged by the system not working. In effect, the system is so structured that profitless discoveries are impossible; but few classroom activities can achieve this kind of structure. How much anatomy will students learn by "playing around" with frog dissection? Can one anticipate the thoughts of students who dissect frogs with little direction? Although discovery learning may be powerful in highly structured contexts that make the correct discovery virtually inevitable, in others it is likely to prove unproductive.

- **Design reading assignments that require students to actively process the text.** Many concrete strategies have been suggested for helping students to get more out of reading that likely have some or all of their effect by making readers think about the meaning of what they are reading. *Techniques such as writing outlines, self-examination during learning, review questions, and previews can encourage or require students to integrate the material and to thereby process (i.e., think about) the meaning.* These different techniques are more or less effective in different situations, perhaps due to the specific materials being studied (e.g., McDaniel & Einstein, 1989); general principles guiding when each technique should be used have not been forthcoming. Nevertheless, although one technique or another may be more effective for a given lesson or group of students, using any strategy that encourages the processing of meaning is almost always better than not using one.

- **Design lessons so that students can't avoid thinking about the lesson's goal.** On a more positive note, the "memory is as thinking does" principle can yield steps teachers can take to help students develop deep, interconnected knowledge: *Lessons should be directed so that students are very likely to think (or can't help but think) about the goal of the lesson.* The goal of the Underground Railroad lesson was not really about biscuits—it was to encourage students to consider the experience of escaped slaves. Therefore, a more effective starting point for that lesson would be to ask students leading questions that encourage consideration of what escaped slaves' experiences would be like, which might include questions of how they would obtain food, and what the constraints were on the food they could get (inexpensive, cooked rapidly, etc.). My nephew would have gotten more out of his book report project if it had emphasized what the teacher was really interested in (the connection among the book's events), perhaps by having the students label the events and connections among them (e.g., this event moves the character towards his goal; this event causes that event) and de-emphasizing the students' artistic contribution by having them use clip art or simply writing the events in words.

- **Design tests that lead students to think about and integrate the most important material.** The "memory is as thinking does" principle may also be applied to methods of assessing student knowledge: *Like lessons, study guides for texts should be developed that force students to think about the goals of the lessons being assessed.* For better or worse, some students expend their greatest effort to understand material as they prepare for an examination. Even if you would rather see such students motivated by a passion to learn, you can use the students' motivation to earn a good grade to ensure that they are getting the most out of your lessons. Announcing the general topics to be covered on an exam leaves the specifics of what to learn up to the student. Even if the teacher emphasizes that deep understanding will be tested, the student may misconstrue what is deep or, as noted earlier, the student may quit once some facts have been memorized, believing that he or she has already done quite a bit of studying. Suppose, however, that the teacher provides a list of integrative questions for the students to study from, such as "Describe why the attack on Pearl Harbor was a strategic mistake by Japan, given its war aims." Suppose further that the students know that the examination will consist of five questions from the 30-question list that they have been given, with an essay to be written on each of the five questions. Students will very likely restrict their studying to the 30 question list, but that might be just fine with the teacher if he or she feels that any student who can answer those 30 questions has mastered the material. This method of testing has the advantage of ensuring that while students are highly motivated, they think about the deepest meaning of the material that the teacher intended.

In summary, in the early stages of learning, students may display "shallow" learning. These students have acquired bits of knowledge that aren't well-integrated into a larger picture. Research tells us that deep, connected knowledge can be encouraged by getting students to think about the interrelation of the various pieces of knowledge that they have acquired. Cognitive science has not progressed to the point that it can issue prescriptions of exactly how that can be achieved—that job is very much in the hands of experienced teachers. But in considering how to encourage students to acquire meaningful knowledge, teachers will do well to keep the "memory is as thinking does" principle in mind.

References

Barclay, J. R., Bransford, J. D., Franks, J. J., McCarrel, N. S., & Nitsch, K. (1974). Comprehension and semantic flexibility. *Journal of Verbal Learning & Verbal Behavior, 13*, 471–481.

Hyde, T. S., & Jenkins, J. J. (1969). Differential effects of incidental tasks on the organization of recall of a list of highly associated words. *Journal of Experimental Psychology, 82*, 472–481.

McDaniel, M. A., & Einstein, G. O. (1989). Material-appropriate processing: A contextualist approach to reading and studying strategies. *Educational Psychology Review, 1*, 113–145.

Slamecka, N. J., & Graf, P. (1978). The generation effect: Delineation of a phenomenon. *Journal of Experimental Psychology: Human Learning & Memory, 4*, 592–604.

8

Dear Dr. Marlowe:

What's the best way for teachers to really connect with kids so that they connect with learning in an emotional way? I want to be the kind of teacher I had when I was in second grade. That's when I fell in love with reading and I know it's because of the kind of relationship my second-grade teacher established with each of us in that class, but somehow also with books and stories and learning. I still remember my second-grade teacher like it was yesterday and I'm sure it's because of how she tied the emotional and intellectual components of learning together. I'm not sure how she did this, but I am sure that's the kind of effect I want to have on my students.

Rachel Lauren

❖ HOW WOULD YOU RESPOND?

Rachel Lauren raises some good questions. What is the relationship between emotion and learning? Why do schools focus so heavily on the intellectual, cognitive components of learning and spend so little time exploring the affective, emotional connections to learning? How can teachers create a classroom atmosphere that promotes emotional investment in learning? Keep these questions in mind as you read the piece by Darlene L. Witte-Townsend and Anne E. Hill. What questions do you have about the relationship between intellectual and affective components of learning? How might you extend the discussion of these ideas in class? Finally, how would you respond to Rachel Lauren?

❖ TOWARD A PEDAGOGY OF DEPTH IN EVERYDAY
CLASSROOMS: EXPLORING RELATIONAL CONSCIOUSNESS
AMONG TEACHERS AND YOUNG CHILDREN

Darlene L. Witte-Townsend and Anne E. Hill

Furthering Pedagogical Depth in Classrooms

Children arrive at school on their first day already having important knowledge. In order for continued learning to be possible they
must sense connections between what they already know and the new
experiences that their teachers and classrooms provide. New awareness and new language must continually unfold for them within a flow
of feeling, thinking, wondering, and saying, and this flow establishes
an emerging context for thinking as well as for unfolding awareness.
Within classrooms, *what* is known is as significant as *how* it is known,
and the quality of the interaction between the teacher and child, and
between a child and the group is as powerful as the ideas that are
explored. Young children and their teachers flourish in classrooms
where relations such as these are nurtured, despite longstanding traditions that continually attempt to move them toward the separation
of knowing from feeling. In the worlds of young children, an overly
strong focus on such dualism may not enhance learning (Dennison,
2004; Miall & Kuiken, 2004): Teachers must allow for the flow of awareness and connection as the ground of meaning.

Why does it matter how children experience the making of meaning? Why is it important for teachers to be aware of the complex relations between knowing, thinking, and feeling? We are teachers of many
years experience working in real classrooms, and over the years the
children have taught us that that these relations are fundamental to
learning. They open the possibilities for learning to take place. Nell
Noddings (Noddings & Shore, 1984) observes that in classrooms, where
an attitude of caring or "educational caritas" (p. 157) is encouraged,
there exists a heightened intellectual as well as moral sensitivity.
Educational caritas allows shared connections to become shared vision
because during interaction, something more than interaction emerges.
From within the ongoing flow of classroom relations we engage the
making of meaning, as well as the making of what is meaningful. As

Levin (1988) suggests, for human beings, *seeing* meaning is a transcendent as well as a physical capacity.

Classrooms are places of extreme busyness, yet in the midst of intense activity, teachers and children look for and find ways to extend, explore, and express their connections with each other. Teachers do this not only through language, but also through the positioning of their bodies in relation to the children's, through the movement of their hands, a look, or even just a glance. Teachers do this through the tone of their voices, through the rhythm of the flow of words, and through silences, those moments of pause in the flow that catch and hold children's attention and allow for thoughtfulness before moving on. Teachers and children communicate through the embodied, the spoken and the unspoken, the active and the still. Knowing how to connect with children this way develops out of teachers' personal and professional knowledge and experience, and requires the continual exercise of sensitive awareness.

Pedagogical Struggle and Awareness
Within and Across Educational Communities

Our limitations as human beings, however, preclude full awareness of our perceptions and knowledge. We cannot fully attend to our own memories of childhood experiences, or even of teaching habits and skills applied with such frequency that they no longer require conscious attention. Polanyi (1962) suggests that our humanness also means that we are unable to say all that we know. As teachers, we can't describe all that our awareness encompasses. We continually struggle to *get* the messages the children send us; in our classrooms and in the world beyond we struggle to say, do, and be what we know; we struggle to see and be seen; we struggle to hear and be heard. As professionals, we do not even share common understandings for the terms and expressions used in the discourse of our teaching practice. The difficulty of creating shared meaning is addressed by Ralph Waldo Emerson (1981) when he reminds us that we are not able to know everything and that what we see is incomplete. He says, "The visible creation is the terminus of the circumference of the invisible world" (p. 25). Dewey (1938) likewise seems to understand this principle, and relates it to the complexity of teachers' worlds. He describes an "opposition between the idea that education is development from within and that it is formation from without" (p. 17). An opposition of ideas sustains the discourse within a broad range of constituents who are invested in education but do not see the process of learning and education in the same way; this opposition of ideas is also to be found between communities of educators and the legislative bodies who mandate policies and structures such as the No Child Left Behind Act of 2000 (PL 107–110).

Across this range of educational constituencies, discourse that relates to the formations of learning is expressed in endless conversations. To extend this ongoing conversation, we propose a pedagogy that allows for a depth of awareness and the enhancing of connectedness on the part of both teachers and children; we urge a pedagogy that honors depth in relations between teachers and children, and we are not satisfied with test-driven educational practices that do not allow children to learn within a context that *wholistically* supports their needs. Despite external pressure to conform to a single vision we remain willing to question what we think we see. Emerson urged us to not be satisfied with a "paltry idea of experience" that limits knowledge to that which is visible to our everyday awareness (Cavell, 1981, p. 126). Meanwhile, teachers in everyday classrooms draw upon their professional and personal knowledge, and attempt to form and reform their classroom practice in relation to children's needs. In the shifts from theories to texts, from mandates to teaching and learning, teachers and children also engage each other. Their potential for engagement in these complex realms is an aspect of what Hay and Nye (1998) describe as "a universal human awareness" (p. 4). How does this level of awareness begin? Do the conditions teachers need for their own learning really differ significantly from the conditions children need? The professional knowledge of teachers about pedagogical relationship often begins in much the same way as when a child learns to transform knowledge of sound and letter into knowledge about text and meaning as it occurs in the following story:

Two first grade girls sat side by side composing letters to "Dear Frog" after the class had listened to many *Frog and Toad* stories (Lobel, 1976). They knew that Frog or Toad would answer their letters the next day. While one of the girls wrote, she sang the words of her story to herself, and her voice slipped over the sounds of the words as she worked. After a few minutes she stopped singing and she began to speak the words carefully as she wrote them, first separating the sounds and then putting them back together. A text began to form on the paper as she worked, and her friend helped with the spelling. She wrote,

Dear Frog,
   Where do you live? I want to know if you can come to school and see the world. Come to my birthday. (Hill, 1996, p. 77; Witte-Townsend & Hill, in press)

The teacher who observed this interaction held this experience in her memory. She treasured the wonder of learning something about how children learn to read and write. She was thrilled to become aware of the seen and unseen depths as this child shared her awareness of the difference between the world outside school and the world of school. The child did what the teacher herself had done with the children since the first day of school: She invited them into her newfound world; she extended an invitation to establish a relationship; and, she also extended her knowledge of the phonetic code, the sound and rhythm, and the meaning of communicating through text.

Here, the teacher's learning about the child's process, and child's reaching out into unknown worlds reveals a pedagogical relationship in which each is aware of something more than the print itself, something more than the presence of another person, and something more than the phonetic decoding of letter combinations (Witte, 1993). The lingering nearness of the teacher, the shift in the child's voice from singing to speaking, and the silent waiting of the teacher come together in a whole that is more than the parts. The consciousness of the experience for each is, "different from and transcend[s] everyday awareness, which is potentially present in all human beings" (Hay, 2000, p. 10). Hay's notion of the "relational consciousness" (p. 37) provides a language for expressing the transcendent quality of an everyday awareness of the known and thus to glimpse what is otherwise unspoken, and remains, the "invisible world."

In classrooms, moments of relational consciousness occur when teachers and children together create moments of shared meaning; for example, when the letters on the board or in a book, or the words on a page acquire, for the child, a transcendence of form and meaning emerges. "I get it!" they say. It is this elusive but universal quality of consciousness that drives learning in classrooms. It drives children's learning. It also drives the professional and personal reflection of educators and legislators: We seek to understand better why a child is able to learn.

We also seek solutions to the challenges faced when children do not learn. For example, in another first grade classroom, a child developed a routine of putting his head down on the desk and hiding his eyes as soon as he came into the classroom every morning. This began despite the teacher's use of accepted teaching practices that encourage children to attend, to participate, and to complete tasks. Puzzled by his withdrawal, the teacher decided to take him aside for a while each day to play with letters, words, and stories. She decided to do this because it was all she could think of; she had already done all that she had been taught to do in these situations and she could not bear to have a child in her class give up. For months, her everyday awareness of teaching practices and personal, past experiences had been sufficient for other children in the class, but this one boy seemed to require something more. At first, the child did not respond to her efforts; instead, he kept his head on his arms and watched while she "played" with the letters on the table. It was during the 3rd session, as she changed one word into another, "ran" to "pan" and "pan" to "man," that he leaned forward and picked up a letter. His eyes twinkled, and he asked, "What would happen if we put this letter here?" (Witte-Townsend & Hill, in press; Witte, 1993). As Vygotsky (1986) advised, the teacher extended the child's knowledge by sustaining the pedagogical relationship in order to help the child reach beyond that with which he was familiar. Through her sensitive awareness of the child, she extended his awareness. Because of the shift in his body, the question that lifted the tone of his voice, and the light that sparkled in his eyes, the teacher knew that there had been a change and his being was engaged. A meaningful connection was made and a relationship was established. The child and the teacher transcended the everyday limits of their vision: The child saw potential and power in letters, and the teacher saw potential and power in the child.

To go beyond the everyday awareness of our vision, teachers and teacher educators need to understand relational awareness as it differs from and moves beyond everyday awareness: The power of relational awareness lies in the pedagogical relationships that emerge. Children recognize and acknowledge this. They show their awareness in small but important ways, as did a child who approached a principal with a gift, a few beads on a piece of wool, tied at the ends to make a loop. "This is for you," she said, offering it up. "It's a friendship necklace. You're the best principal." Thanks and smiles followed, marking renewed pedagogical potential.

Learning to Reconcile the Visible and the Invisible

In school communities where Noddings' notion of educational caritas is practiced, teachers and administrators create an atmosphere in which children assist in the creation of the whole school community. It begins with teachers who extend themselves, seek depth in their practice, and "go beyond superficialities and become involved with the other person" (Noddings & Shore, 1984, p. 157). When acts of relational awareness such as kindness and caring for each other become part of the culture of the school, the teachers and children tell each other about their shared world. Together, they become something more for each other than they were, and they change the quality of their world. They become "beacons that help illuminate the moral universe" (Paley, 1999, p. 129).

The teacher's story of the child whose eyes lit up when he asked, "What would happen if . . ." is an example of Paley's (1999) metaphor of beacons that illuminate a moral universe—teacher and child engaged in a pedagogical relationship that empowered and connected both. Teachers often say, "Their eyes just light up!" It is as if, in moment of awareness, a light goes on. To act in kind and caring ways, to go beyond the superficialities, to look and listen for power and potential in our students, to be aware of the light in the eyes of a child, all these are qualities of a relational consciousness and prepare the way for a pedagogy of depth (Witte-Townsend & Hill, in press). Hay and Nye say that this "universal human awareness" is a spiritual sensibility and that it is inseparable from the physical, cognitive, emotional, and affective aspects of being human (1998, p. 9). When children and their teachers extend and accept invitations to enter unfamiliar worlds, possibilities are created for boundaries of awareness to dissolve and reform, and for the spaces to emerge in which both may go beyond the accustomed awareness in order to learn a little more. When children first begin school, they learn about many kinds of boundaries and markers that affect the flow of light from one person or idea to another: They learn the physical boundaries of classroom and playground as well as those of language and behavior. The classroom story that follows may act as a metaphor for children's developing awareness of the boundaries for learning in schools. The child's teacher says,

In my kindergarten class, I made name tags to use for games and activities such as printing. Each tag was stuck to the chalkboard so they could be moved as I used them. During center time on the 4th day of school I noticed that Mervin was moving the tags into a cluster on one side of the board. I was annoyed! I put them there for a reason. I wanted them there. Why was he moving them? Then, to make things worse, a little girl, Emily, joined him. I thought I'd better move fast if I wanted my organization to remain. But just as

I took a step, Mervin picked up a piece of chalk and began to draw a circle around the cluster of names. Mervin and Emily, two heads close together, red and ebony, stood gazing at their work. They became the foreground in a frame of what I suddenly saw as our class. We were a community already, at least as far as they were concerned. The community had an inside and an outside. We were all inside, connected by the placement of names inside the boundary drawn by Mervin. I picked up my camera and snapped a picture; a sense of something significant prompted me to take the photograph. I kept it for years. To me it was a child's interpretation of a classroom community, a child's gesture intended to express a thought, a feeling, an awareness of something not yet formed in language. (A. Hill, personal communication, 1996)

In these small gestures a kind of learning that cannot be packaged or mandated is visible. The buoy that marks the depth is the light in the children's eyes, the circumference of the invisible world of learning. For children, this depth often occurs between the visible and the invisible, where adults cannot always see.

The children who invite Frog to share their world, who gift their principal with a knobby bit of damp, finger-stained, bead-strung wool tied in a loop, or who ask questions like, "What would happen if . . . ?" remind us not to abandon the pedagogical sensitivity and depth that brings the spark of light to their eyes, despite the pressure to have them produce higher test scores. When teachers respond to the light in their eyes and to the beacons of their stories and acts of kindness, they are responding also to a plea made by Maxine Greene to "make an intensified effort to break through the frames of custom and to touch the consciousness of those we teach" (2000, p. 56). Such moments of relation can be irrevocably weighed down by legislation and costly programs: Learning in everyday classrooms requires, more than anything else, the relational consciousness of child and teacher, with each enabling the other to see beyond the visible.

Becoming a Pilgrim: Seeking an Attitude of Inquiry

Members of the educational community bring frames and customs of reference to classrooms along with discussions about educational practice (Kuhn, 2000). Teachers also bring their personal and professional knowledge (Clandinin, 1985). For those occasions that require the formal presentations of our thoughts, such as lectures and essays "a frame of reference" is expected, perhaps because these frames help us as adults to orient ourselves to the whole, and they provide us with something that seems concrete to hold onto. However, while they give us a sense of organization, the difficulty is that at times these frames of reference may prevent us from seeing beyond them, and we forget that they are not real, never were real, and they are not sufficient. They provide a map of knowledge, but they are not the knowledge itself (Bateson, 1972). In the same way, established programs, laws, and customs seldom fit all the situations and dilemmas of everyday classrooms and they sometimes create more difficulties than they solve.

Educational communities continue to struggle with institutional structures, mandates, and frames of reference that do not sufficiently illuminate the being-in-the-world of teachers and children in schools. Because we lack shared experience and a shared language, do we, as Wittgenstein (1953) suggests, approach each other as strangers? Does the lack of fit between the lived meanings of our language-in-use (Austin, 1965) cause us to remain strangers? This image of strangers who speak different languages helps us to describe our educational dilemma, but it is Robert Coles, a psychiatrist and professor at Harvard University, who furthers our linguistic shift and enables us to begin to see with more clarity. He says, "we connect with one another, move in and out of one another's lives, teach and heal and affirm one another, across space and time—all of us wanderers, explorers, adventurers, stragglers and ramblers . . . but now and then as pilgrims . . ." (1990, p. 335). His insight is helpful to us because, as he explains, early in his career he often failed to have this open attitude and he fell short of embracing children's insights. In order to open his awareness and enter a more satisfying level of relational depth, he had to learn a more respectful way. He describes how he learned this as he and a young Hopi girl watched a thundercloud together.

> I awaited the end of her fixed gaze, the return earthward of her eyes . . . she took the initiative, lifted her right aim, pointed to the cloud and especially to its thunderhead part—the swollen part on the top, "the home of the noise," she told me. I'd not before thought of noise as having a home. I decided to respond in that way, comment on her way of putting things. She smiled as she said, "Noise has a home in us too." (Coles, 1990, p. 26)

Like the teacher who hesitated for a moment when her students began to rearrange the organization of nametags on the chalkboard, Coles was learning to be aware that perceptions of the same event can be different: Meaning perceived by some may not be visible to others. Like all teachers must, Coles was learning that to embrace a child's insight is to embrace the child. Merleau-Ponty (1968) also shows us that perception is a multi-dimensional field, a topography that is visible, saying that "through the reflections, shadows, levels, and horizons between . . . Like the light, these levels and dimensions, this system of lines of force, are not what we see; they are *that with which, according to which, we see . . .*" (1968, p. 128). For Coles, for Merleau-Ponty, for ourselves and the other teachers who pause before turning aside from a child, or before stepping forward to impose a frame of reference, learning about children's learning is dependent upon our ability to move past the everyday awareness of the adult world. Like the light, the children's language and actions are that with which we can see, and they reveal levels of awareness that are invisible when looked at through a single dimension of awareness. Children are capable of expressing what adults do not always recognize: That we are all part of each other. We need to learn to wait, stop to think, and respond in the child's way of thinking. We need to take on an attitude of inquiry and make it possible for ourselves to open to the possibility of depth in children's awareness and acknowledge the pedagogical implications of relational consciousness. We need to embrace our ability to know the transcendent experience of connection between ourselves, children, and the world outside, as well as with the traditions of our communities, the earth, the sky, and even with those strangers who come speaking the languages of educational ideologies that are far from our own. Is it possible for all members of the educational community, as pilgrims inquiring together, to open to a depth of awareness that will enable seeing others' worlds? Will we develop our relational consciousness, transcend our limits of vision, and begin to express these universal qualities of awareness in order to enable a pedagogy of depth to emerge from within classroom relations?

References

Austin, J. L. (1965). *How to do things with words.* (J. Urmson, Ed.). Englewood Cliffs, NJ: Prentice-Hall.

Bateson, G. (1972). *Steps to an ecology of mind.* New York: Ballantine Books.

Cavell, S. (1981). *The senses of Walden: An expanded edition.* Chicago: University of Chicago Press.

Clandinin, J. (1985). Personal practical knowledge: A study of teachers' classroom images. *Curriculum inquiry: A Journal from the Ontario Institute for Studies in Education, 15*(4), 361–385.

Coles, R. (1990). *The spiritual life of children.* Boston: Houghton Mifflin.

Dennison, P. E. (2004). *The dynamic brain.* Ventura, CA: Edu-K.

Dewey, J. (1938). *Experience & education.* New York: Collier Books.

Emerson, R. W. (1981). *Selected essays, lectures, and poems.* (Robert D. Richardson, Jr., Ed.). New York: Bantam Books.

Greene, M. (2000). Releasing the imagination: Essays on education, the arts, and social change. San Francisco: Jossey-Bass.

Hay, D. (2000). Spirituality versus individualism: Why we should nurture relational consciousness. *International Journal of Children's Spirituality, 5*(1), 37–48.

Hay, D., & Nye, R. (1998). *The spirit of the child.* London: Fount.

Hill, A. E. (1996). *Pedagogical presence: Rhythmic relation.* Unpublished doctoral dissertation, University of Alberta, Canada.

Kuhn, T. S. (2000). *The road since structure* (J. Conant & J. Haugeland, Eds.). Chicago: University of Chicago Press.

Levin, D. M. (1988). *The opening of vision: Nihilism and the postmodern situation.* London: Routledge.

Lobel, A. (1976). *Frog and toad all year.* New York: Scholastic Book Services.

Merleau-Ponty, M. (1968). *The visible and the invisible.* (C. Lefort, Ed. & A. Lingis, Trans.). Evanston, IL: Northwestern University Press.

Miall, D. S., & Kuiken, D. (2002). A feeling for fiction: Becoming what we behold. *Poetics, 30,* 221–241.

No Child Left Behind Act of 2000 (PL 107–110). Washington, DC: US Department of Education. Available from http://www.ed.gov/nclb/overview/welcome/list.jhtml

Noddings, N., & Shore, P. (1984). *Awakening the inner eye: Intuition in education.* New York: Teachers College Press.

Paley, V. G. (1999). *The kindness of children.* Boston: Harvard University Press.

Polanyi, M. (1962). *Personal knowledge: Toward a post-critical philosophy.* Chicago: University of Chicago Press.

Vygotsky, L. (1986). *Thought and language.* (A. Kozulin, Ed.). Cambridge: MIT Press.

Witte, D. L. (1993). *Children's language play and literacy development: Pedagogy in a Japanese garden.* Unpublished doctoral dissertation, University of Alberta, Canada.

Witte-Townsend, D. L., & Hill, A. E. (in press). Light-ness of being in the primary classroom: Inviting conversations of depth across educational communities. *Educational philosophy and theory.*

Wittgenstein, L. (1953). *Philosophical investigations* (G. Anscombe, Ed.). Oxford, UK: Blackwell.

Questions for Reflection

Look back at the letters and readings in **Part II: How Does Learning Occur**? Consider the following questions as you begin formulating your own ideas about how to apply theories of learning into planned instructional practice.

1. Consider the connections between Skinner's theory of operant conditioning and Bandura's social learning theory. How do the reinforcements that adults provide to children, both deliberately and unintentionally, influence their behavior?

2. When you think about the ways in which Skinner and Bandura might inform instructional practice, what is missing?

3. Willingham is clear about what must happen in classrooms for learning to endure. Can "stand-and-deliver" instruction be justified given what we know about the cognitive psychology of learning?

4. Think about Witte-Townsend's idea of relational consciousness. How does Witte-Townsend's piece help inform teachers about making the kinds of connections with students that result in the most powerful learning? What specific teacher behaviors will result in the kind of dialogue and relationships Witte-Townsend observes in the teachers and students she describes? Are other theorists that you have read about relevant here?

❖ YOUR OWN IDEAS

What ideas seem most important to you as you reflect about teaching and learning in real classrooms? What do you think is most important for new teachers to consider? What further questions did the authors raise for you in Part II that have not been adequately answered?

_____

_____

_____

_____

_____

_____

_____

_____

_____

_____

_____

_____

_____

_____

_____

_____

_____

_____

_____

Suggested Readings

Baddeley, A. (1998). *Human memory: Theory and practice.* Boston: Allyn & Bacon.

Bandura, A. (1977). *Social learning theory.* Englewood Cliffs, NJ: Prentice Hall.

Caine, R., Caine, J., Klimek, K., & McClintic, C. (2004). *12 brain/mind learning principles in action: The fieldbook for making connections, teaching, and the human brain.* Thousand Oaks, CA: Corwin.

Coles, R. (1990). *The spiritual life of children.* Boston: Houghton Mifflin.

Jensen, E. (1998). *Teaching with the brain in mind.* Alexandria, VA: Association for Supervision and Curriculum Development.

Miller, G. A. (1965). The magical number seven, plus or minus two: Some limits on our capacity for processing information. *Psychological Review, 63,* 81–97.

Piaget, J. (1963). *Origins of intelligence in children.* New York: Norton.

Premack, D. (1965). Reinforcement theory. In D. Levine (Ed.), *Nebraska symposium on motivation* (Vol. 13, pp. 123–180). Lincoln: University of Nebraska Press.

Skinner, B. F. (1950). Are theories of learning necessary? *Psychological Review, 57,* 193–216.

Vygotsky, L. (1962). *Thought and language.* Cambridge: MIT Press. (Original work published 1934)

PART III

What Role Does Maturation Play in Learning?

9

❖ ❖ ❖

Dear Dr. Marlowe:

I'm doing student teaching now in a mostly typical third-grade classroom, but the students in my class range from one just turning 8 to a boy who just turned 11. I guess he got left back a few times or something. Anyway, the kid who's 11 has his chronological age and maturity working against him. Steve often feels very different from his classmates. Outside of school his friends are older kids, keeping consistent with his age even though he's behind them in most ways academically. When I first met him, he was reading at a preschool level. Through hard work and a great deal of one-on-one work with me and with an itinerant, Steve made great strides during the course of the year, but he's still really struggling with reading. Here's the curious thing though. Even though his reading skills are lower than the other third graders in my room, his thinking seems higher. I know that doesn't make sense, but if I ask my class questions like "What would happen if . . ." they get stuck on the concrete, or they say things like "But, it's not like that now." Steve seems more able to imagine what might be and then to think about a hypothetical situation. Also, they started to do this really stupid thing in my school where they're introducing these sort of pre-algebra exercises. Kids are asked to fill in boxes like □ + 8 = 15 and some of them have multiplication too. Most of them respond by saying something like, "Hey, yesterday you said the box was 4. How can it be 7 today?" Steve's generally not better in math than the other kids, but on this sort of stuff he's the only one who seems to get it. How can that be?

Johnny Stevens

❖ HOW WOULD YOU RESPOND?

What does it mean to be "intelligent"? Does one get more intelligent as one gets older? Are older children really smarter than younger ones? How are maturation and learning connected? Why do children at younger ages have difficulty understanding abstract concepts? What happens when children are exposed to skills and concepts too early? How should teachers respond to students who lack basic skills, but whom, nevertheless, are ready to be introduced to abstract concepts? Should we wait to teach some skills until students reach a certain age? What might account for this familiar refrain in the classroom: "This is boring"? How will you respond to students who have the capacity to think in unexpected, original ways, and who may use their own models to solve problems?

Keep these questions in mind as you read "The Stages of the Intellectual Development of the Child" by Jean Piaget. What questions do *you* have about cognitive development? How can you help extend the discussion of these ideas in class? Finally, how would you respond to Johnny Stevens?

❖ THE STAGES OF THE INTELLECTUAL
    DEVELOPMENT OF THE CHILD

Jean Piaget

A consideration of the stages of the development of intelligence should be preceded by asking the question, What is intelligence? Unfortunately, we find ourselves confronted by a great number of definitions. For Claparède, intelligence is an adaptation to new situations. When a situation is new, when there are no reflexes, when there are no habits to rely on, then the subject is obliged to search for something new. That is to say, Claparède defines intelligence as groping, as feeling one's way, trial-and-error behavior. We find this trial-and-error behavior in all levels of intelligence, even at the superior level, in the form of hypothesis testing. As far as I am concerned, this definition is too vague, because trial and error occurs in the formation of habits, and also in the earliest established reflexes: when a newborn baby learns to suck.

Karl Bühler defines intelligence as an act of immediate comprehension; that is to say, an insight. Bühler's definition is also very precise, but it seems to me too narrow. I know that when a mathematician solves a problem, he ends by having an insight, but up to that moment he feels, or gropes for, his way; and to say that the trial-and-error behavior is not intelligent and that intelligence starts only when he finds the solution to the problem, seems a very narrow definition. I would, therefore, propose to define intelligence not by a static criterion, as in previous definitions, but by the direction that intelligence follows in its evolution, and then I would define intelligence as a form of equilibration, or forms of equilibration, toward which all cognitive functions lead.

But I must first define equilibration. Equilibration in my vocabulary is not an exact and automatic balance, as it would be in Gestalt theory; I define equilibration principally as a compensation for an external disturbance.

When there is an external disturbance, the subject succeeds in compensating for this by an activity. The maximum equilibration is thus the maximum of the activity, and not a state of rest. It is a mobile equilibration, and not an immobile one. So equilibration is defined as compensation; compensation is the annulling of a transformation by an inverse transformation. The compensation which intervenes in equilibration implies the fundamental idea of reversibility, and this reversibility is precisely what characterizes the operations of the intelligence. An operation is an internalized action, but it is also a reversible action. But an operation is never isolated; it is always subordinated to other operations; it is part of a more inclusive structure. Consequently, we define intelligence in terms of operations, coordination of operations.

Take, for example, an operation like addition: Addition is a material action, the action of reuniting. On the other hand, it is a reversible action, because addition may be compensated by subtraction. Yet addition leads to a structure of a whole. In the case of numbers, it will be the structure that the mathematicians call a "group." In the case of addition of classes which intervene in the logical structure it will be a more simple structure that we will call a grouping, and so on.

Consequently, the study of the stages of intelligence is first a study of the formation of operational structures. I shall define every stage by a structure of a whole, with the possibility of its integration into succeeding stages, just as it was prepared by preceding stages. Thus, I shall distinguish four great stages, or four great periods, in the development of intelligence: first, the sensori-motor period before the appearance of language; second, the period from about two to seven years of age, the pre-operational period which precedes real operations; third, the period from seven to 12 years of age, a period of concrete operations (which refers to concrete objects); and finally after 12 years of age, the period of formal operations, or propositional operations.

Sensori-Motor Stage

Before language develops, there is behavior that we can call intelligent. For example, when a baby of 12 months or more wants an object which is too far from him, but which rests on a carpet or blanket, and he pulls it to get to the object, this behavior is an act of intelligence. The child uses an intermediary, a means to get to his goal. Also, getting to an object by means of pulling a string when the object is tied to the string, or when the child uses a stick to get the object, are acts of intelligence. They demonstrate in the sensori-motor period a certain number of stages, which go from simple reflexes, from the formation of the first habits, up to the coordination of means and goals.

Remarkable in this sensori-motor stage of intelligence is that there are already structures. Sensori-motor intelligence rests mainly on actions, on movements and perceptions without language, but these actions are coordinated in a relatively stable way. They are coordinated under what we may call schemata of action. These schemata can be generalized in actions and are applicable to new situations. For example, pulling a carpet to bring an object within reach constitutes a schema which can be generalized to other situations when another object rests on a support. In other words, a schema supposes an incorporation of new situations into the previous schemata, a sort of continuous assimilation of new objects or new situations to the actions already schematized. For example, I presented to one of my children an object completely new to him—a box of cigarettes, which is not a usual toy for a baby. The child took the object, looked at it, put it in his mouth, shook it, then took it with one hand and hit it with the other hand, then rubbed it on the edge of the crib, then shook it again, and gave the impression of trying to see if there were noise. This behavior is a way of exploring the object, of trying to understand it by assimilating it to schemata already known. The child behaves in this situation as he will later in Binet's famous vocabulary test, when he defines by usage, saying, for instance, that a spoon is for eating, and so on.

But in the presence of a new object, even without knowing how to talk, the child knows how to assimilate, to incorporate this new object into each of his already developed schemata which function as practical concepts. Here is a structuring of intelligence. Most important in this structuring is the base, the point of departure of all subsequent operational constructions. At the sensori-motor level, the child constructs the schema of the permanent object.

The knowledge of the permanent object starts at this point. The child is not convinced at the beginning that when an object disappears from view, he can find it again. One can verify by tests that object permanence is not yet developed at this stage. But there is there the beginning of a subsequent fundamental idea which starts being constructed at the sensori-motor level. This is also true of the construction of the ideas of space, of time, of causality. What is being done at the sensori-motor level concerning all the foregoing ideas will constitute the substructure of the subsequent, fully achieved ideas of permanent objects, of space, of time, of causality.

In the formation of these substructures at the sensori-motor level, it is very interesting to note the beginning of a *reversibility*, not in thought, since there is not yet representation in thought, but in action itself. For example, the formation of the conception of space at the sensori-motor stage leads to an amazing decentration if one compares the conception of space at the first weeks of the development with that at one and one-half to two years of age. In the beginning there is not one space which contains all the objects, including the child's body itself; there is a multitude of spaces which are not coordinated: there are the buccal space, the tactilokinesthetic space, the visual and auditory spaces; each is separate and each is centered essentially on the body of the subject and on actions. After a few months, however, after a kind of Copernican evolution, there is a total reversal, a decentration such that space becomes homogenous, a one-and-only space that envelops the others. Then space becomes a container that envelops all objects, including the body itself; and after that, space is mainly coordinated in a structure, a coordination of positions and displacements, and these constitute what the geometricians call a "group"; that is to say, precisely a reversible system. One may move from A to B, and may come back from B to A; there is the possibility of returning, of reversibility. There is also the possibility of making detours and combinations which give a clue to what the subsequent operations will be when thought will supersede the action itself.

Pre-Operational Stage

From one and one-half to two years of age, a fundamental transformation in the evolution of intelligence takes place in the appearance of symbolic functions. Every action of intelligence consists in manipulating significations (or meanings) and whenever (or wherever) there is significations, there are on the one hand the "significants" and on the other the "significates." This is true in the sensori-motor level, but the only significants that intervene there are perceptual signs or signals (as in conditioning) which are undifferentiated in regard to the significate; for example, a perceptual cue, like distance, which will be a cue for the size of the distant object, or the apparent size of an object, which will be the cue for the distance of the object. There, perhaps, both indices are different aspects of the same reality, but they are not yet differentiated significants. At the age of one and one-half to two years a new class of significants arises, and these significants are differentiated in regard to their significates. These differentiations can be called symbolic function. The appearance of symbols in a children's game is an example of the appearance of new significants. At the sensori-motor level the games are nothing but exercises; now they become symbolic play, a play of fiction; these games consist in representing something by means of something else. Another example is the beginning of delayed imitation, an imitation that takes place not in the presence of the original object but in its absence, and which consequently constitutes a kind of symbolization or mental image.

At the same time that symbols appear, the child acquires language; that is to say, there is the acquisition of another phase of differentiated significants, verbal signals, or collective signals. This symbolic function then brings great flexibility into the field of intelligence. Intelligence up to this point refers to the immediate space which surrounds the child and to the present perceptual situation; thanks to language, and to the symbolic functions, it becomes possible to invoke objects which are not present perceptually, to reconstruct the past, or to make projects, plans for the future, to think of objects not present but very distant in space— in short, to span spatio-temporal distances much greater than before.

But this new stage, the stage of representation of thought which is superimposed on the sensori-motor stage, is not a simple extension of what was referred to at the previous level. Before being able to prolong, one must in fact reconstruct, because behavior in words is a different thing from representing something in thought. When a child knows how to move around in his house or garden by following the different successive cues around him, it does not mean that he is capable of representing or reproducing the total configuration of his house or his garden. To be able to represent, to reproduce something, one must be capable of reconstructing this group of displacements, but at a new level, that of the representation of the thought.

I recently made an amusing test with Nel Szeminska. We took children of four to five years of age who went to school by themselves and came back home by themselves, and asked them if they could trace the way to school and back for us, not in design, which would be too difficult, but like a construction game, with concrete objects. We found that they were not capable of representation; there was a kind of motor-memory, but it was not yet a representation of a whole—the group of displacements had not yet been reconstructed on the plan of the representation of thought. In other words, the operations were not yet formed. There are representations which are internalized actions; but actions still centered on the body itself, on the activity itself. These representations do not allow the objective combinations, the decentrated combinations that the operations would. The actions are centered on the body. I used to call this egocentrism; but it is better thought of as lack of reversibility of action.

At this level, the most certain sign of the absence of operations which appear at the next stage is the absence of the knowledge of conservation. In fact, an operation refers to the transformation of reality. The transformation is not of the whole, however; something constant is always untransformed. If you pour a liquid from one glass to another there is transformation; the liquid changes form, but its liquid property stays constant. So at the pre-operational level, it is significant from the point of view of the operations of intelligence that the child has not yet a knowledge of conservation. For example, in the case of liquid, when the child pours it from one bottle to the other, he thinks that the quantity of the liquid has changed. When the level of the liquid changes, the child thinks the quantity has changed—there is more or less in the second glass than in the first. And if you ask the child where the larger quantity came from, he does not answer this question. What is important for the child is that perceptually it is not the same thing any more. We find this absence of conservation in all object properties, in the length, surface, quantity, and weight of things.

This absence of conservation indicates essentially that at this stage the child reasons from the configuration. Confronted with a transformation, he does not reason from the transformation itself; he starts from the initial configuration, then sees the final configuration, compares the two but forgets the transformation, because he does not know how to reason about it. At this stage the child is still reasoning on the basis of what he sees because there is no conservation. He is able to master this problem only when the operations are formed and these operations, which we have already sensed at the sensori-motor level, are not formed until around seven to eight years of age. At that age the elementary problems of conservation are solved, because the child reasons on the basis of the transformation per se, and this requires a manipulation of the operation. The ability to pass from one stage to the other and be able to come back to the point of departure, to manipulate the reversible operations, which appears around seven to eight years of age, is limited when compared with the operations of the superior level only in the sense that they are concrete. That is to say, the child can manipulate the operations only when he manipulates the object concretely.

Stage of Concrete Operations

The first operations of the manipulation of objects, the concrete operations, deal with logical classes and with logical relations, or the number. But these operations do not deal yet with propositions, or hypotheses, which do not appear until the last stage.

Let me exemplify these concrete operations: the simplest operation is concerned with classifying objects according to their similarity and their difference. This is accomplished by including the subclasses within larger and more general classes, a process that implies inclusion. This classification, which seems very simple at first, is not acquired until around seven to eight years of age. Before that, at the pre-operational level, we do not find logical inclusion. For example, if you show a child at the pre-operational level a bouquet of flowers of which one half is daisies and the other half other flowers and you ask him if in this bouquet there are more flowers or more daisies, you are confronted with this answer, which seems extraordinary until it is analyzed: The child cannot tell you whether there are more flowers than daisies; either he reasons on the basis of the whole or of the part. He cannot understand that the part is complementary to the rest, and he says there are more daisies than flowers, or as many daisies as flowers, without understanding this inclusion of the subclass, the daisies, in the class of flowers. It is only around seven to eight years of age that a child is capable of solving a problem of inclusion.

Another system of operation that appears around seven to eight years of age is the operation of serializing; that is, to arrange objects according to their size, or their progressive weight. It is also a structure of the whole, like the classification which rests on concrete operations, since it consists of manipulating concrete objects. At this level there is also the construction of numbers, which is, too, a synthesis of classification and serration. In numbers, as in classes, we have inclusion, and also a serial order, as in serializing. These elementary operations constitute structures of wholes. There is no class without classification; there is no symmetric relation without serialization; there is not a number independent of the series of numbers. But the structures of these wholes are simple structures, groupings in the case of classes and relations, which are already groups in the case of numbers, but very elementary structures compared to subsequent structures.

Stage of Formal Operations

The last stage of development of intelligence is the stage of formal operations or propositional operations. At about eleven to twelve years of age we see great progress; the child becomes capable of reasoning not only on the basis of objects, but also on the basis of hypotheses, or of propositions.

An example which neatly shows the difference between reasoning on the basis of propositions and reasoning on the basis of concrete objects comes from Burt's tests. Burt asked children of different ages to compare the colors of the hair of three girls: Edith is fairer than Susan, Edith is darker than Lilly; who is the darkest of the three? In this question there is seriation, not of concrete objects, but of verbal statements which supposes a more complicated mental manipulation. This problem is rarely solved before the age of 12.

Here a new class of operations appears which is superimposed on the operations of logical class and number, and these operations are the propositional operations. Here, compared to the previous stage, are fundamental changes. It is not simply that these operations refer to language, and then to operations with concrete objects, but that these operations have much richer structures.

The first novelty is a combinative structure; like mathematical structures, it is a structure of a system which is superimposed on the structure of simple classifications or seriations which are not themselves systems, because they do not involve a combinative system. A combinative system permits the grouping in flexible combinations of each element of the system with any other element of that system. The logic of propositions supposes such a combinative system. If children of different ages are shown a number of colored disks and asked to combine each color with each other two by two, or three by three, we find these combinative operations are not accessible to the child at the stage of concrete operations. The child is capable of some combination, but not of all the possible combinations. After the age of 12, the child can find a method to make all the possible combinations. At the same time he acquires both the logic of mathematics and the logic of propositions, which also supposes a method of combining.

A second novelty in the operations of propositions is the appearance of a structure which constitutes a group of four transformations. Hitherto there were two reversibilities: reversibility by inversion, which consists of annulling, or canceling; and reversibility which we call reciprocity, leading not to cancellation, but to another combination. Reciprocity is what we find in the field of a relation. If A equals B, by reciprocity B equals A. If A is smaller than B, by reciprocity B is larger than A. At the level of propositional operations a new system envelops these two forms of reversibility. Here the structure combines inversion and reversibility in one single but larger and more complicated structure. It allows the acquisition of a series of fundamental operational schemata for the development of intelligence, which schemata are not possible before the constitution of this structure.

It is around the age of 12 that the child, for example, starts to understand in mathematics the knowledge of proportions, and becomes capable of reasoning by using two systems of reference at the same time. For example, if you advance the position of a board and a car moving in opposite directions, in order to understand the movement of the board in relation to the movement of the car and to other movement, you need a system of four transformations. The same is true in regard to proportions, to problems in mathematics or physics, or to other logical problems.

The four principal stages of the development of intelligence of the child progress from one stage to the other by the construction of new operational structures, and these structures constitute the fundamental instrument of the intelligence of the adult.

10

Dear Dr. Canestrari:

I was just about to give up hope, but after looking for almost 18 months I finally got a job in an eighth-grade classroom at the end of last summer . . . 3 weeks before the school year started! Anyway, it's been a little crazy from the moment I accepted the position. I can't believe it's Christmas break already. Remember when I had you in Psychology of Learning and every once in a while we'd talk about how you have to pay attention to kids' feelings too? Every once in a while? You can't imagine what eighth grade is really like. How come nobody ever told me how crazy middle school kids are? I know it sounds like an excuse, but I've got to tell you these kids have a lot more on their minds right now than colonial America, pre-algebra, and diagramming sentences. The questions I over-hear all the time—"Do you think J Lo is a loser?" "How come nobody likes me?" "Why is everyone staring at me?" "Do I have too much make-up on?" "You think Cindy likes me?"—It's like one giant communal identity crisis being played out every single day. And it has nothing to do with school! How can you fight against the hormones and get these kids to stop thinking about who they are, who likes them, what groups they want to be identified with? Really, they have no interest, no mental energy for anything but thinking about themselves. I feel like I'm always swimming upstream.

Got any suggestions?

Jacki Carter

❖ HOW WOULD YOU RESPOND?

What do children and young adults worry about most? Do the kinds of issues that students worry about depend on how old they are? How can teachers help students successfully resolve what Erikson calls "crises"? How can teachers connect their instruction to what really occupies the thinking of students at different age levels? How important is it for teachers to consider the emotional lives of their students? Why might unresolved issues present obstacles to student learning?

Keep these questions in mind as you read "Eight Ages of Man" by Erik H. Erikson. What questions do *you* have about psychosocial development? How can you help extend the discussion of these ideas in class? Finally, how would you respond to Jacki Carter?

❖ EIGHT AGES OF MAN

Erik H. Erikson

1. Basic Trust vs. Basic Mistrust

The first demonstration of social trust in the baby is the ease of his feeding, the depth of his sleep, the relaxation of his bowels. The experience of a mutual regulation of his increasingly receptive capacities with the maternal techniques of provision gradually helps him to balance the discomfort caused by the immaturity of homeostasis with which he was born. In his gradually increasing waking hours he finds that more and more adventures of the senses arouse a feeling of familiarity, of having coincided with a feeling of inner goodness. Forms of comfort, and people associated with them, become as familiar as the gnawing discomfort of the bowels. The infant's first social achievement, then, is his willingness to let the mother out of sight without undue anxiety or rage, because she has become an inner certainty as well as an outer predictability. Such consistency, continuity, and sameness of experience provide a rudimentary sense of ego identity which depends, I think, on the recognition that there is an inner population of remembered and anticipated sensations and images which are firmly correlated with the outer population of familiar and predictable things and people.

The firm establishment of enduring patterns for the solution of the nuclear conflict of basic trust versus basic mistrust in mere existence is the first task of the ego, and thus first of all a task for maternal care. But let it be said here that the amount of trust derived from earliest infantile experience does not seem to depend on absolute quantities of food or demonstrations of love, but rather on the quality of the maternal relationship. Mothers create a sense of trust in their children by that kind of administration which in its quality combines sensitive care of the baby's individual needs and a firm sense of personal trustworthiness within the trusted framework of their culture's life style. This forms the basis in the child for a sense of identity which will later combine a sense of being "all right," of being oneself, and of becoming what other people trust one will become. There are, therefore (within certain limits previously defined as the "musts" of child care), few frustrations in either this or the following stages which the growing child cannot endure if the frustration leads to the ever-renewed experience of greater sameness and stronger continuity of development, toward a final integration of the individual life cycle with some meaningful wider belongingness. Parents must not only have certain ways of guiding by prohibition and permission; they must also be able to represent to the child a deep, an almost somatic conviction that there is a meaning to what they are doing. Ultimately, children become neurotic not from frustrations, but from the lack or loss of societal meaning in these frustrations.

But even under the most favorable circumstances, this stage seems to introduce into psychic life (and become prototypical for) a sense of inner division and universal nostalgia for a paradise forfeited. It is against this powerful combination of a sense of having been deprived, of having been divided, and of having been abandoned—that basic trust must maintain itself throughout life.

2. Autonomy vs. Shame and Doubt

Shame is an emotion insufficiently studied, because in our civilization it is so early and easily absorbed by guilt. Shame supposes that one is completely exposed and conscious of being looked at: in one word, self-conscious. One is visible and not ready to be visible; which is why we dream of shame as a situation in which we are stared at in a condition of incomplete dress, in night attire, "with one's pants down." Shame is early expressed in an impulse to bury one's face, or to sink, right then and there, into the ground. But this, I think, is essentially rage turned against the self. He who is ashamed would like to force the world not to look at him, not to notice his exposure. He would like to destroy the eyes of the world. Instead he must wish for his own invisibility. This potentiality is abundantly used in the educational method of "shaming" used so exclusively by some primitive peoples. Visual shame precedes auditory guilt, which is a sense of badness to be had all by oneself when nobody watches and when everything is quiet—except the voice of the superego. Such shaming exploits an increasing sense of being small, which can develop only as the child stands up and as his awareness permits him to note the relative measures of size and power.

Too much shaming does not lead to genuine propriety but to a secret determination to try to get away with things, unseen—if, indeed, it does not result in defiant shamelessness. There is an impressive American ballad in which a murderer to be hanged on the gallows before the eyes of the community, instead of feeling duly chastened, begins to berate the onlookers, ending every salvo of defiance with the words, "God damn your eyes." Many a small child, shamed beyond endurance, may be in a chronic mood (although not in possession of either the courage or the words) to express defiance in similar terms. What I mean by this sinister reference is that there is a limit to a child's and an adult's endurance in the face of demands to consider himself, his body, and his wishes as evil and dirty, and to his belief in the infallibility of those who pass such judgment. He may be apt to turn things around, and to consider as evil only the fact that they exist: his chance will come when they are gone, or when he will go from them.

Doubt is the brother of shame. Where shame is dependent on the consciousness of being upright and exposed, doubt, so clinical observation leads me to believe, has much to do with a consciousness of having a front and a back—and especially a "behind." For this reverse area of the body, with its aggressive and libidinal focus in the sphincters and in the buttocks, cannot be seen by the child, and yet it can be dominated by the will of others. The "behind" is the small being's dark continent, and area of the body which can be magically dominated and effectively invaded by those who would attack one's power of autonomy and who would designate as evil those products of the bowels which were felt to be all right when they were being passed. This basic sense of doubt in whatever one has left behind forms a substratum for later and more verbal forms of compulsive doubting; this finds its adult expression in paranoiac fears concerning hidden persecutors and secret persecutions threatening from behind (and from within the behind).

This stage, therefore, becomes decisive for the ratio of love and hate, cooperation and willfulness, freedom of self-expression and its suppression. From a sense of self-control without loss of self-esteem comes a lasting sense of good will and pride; from a sense of loss of self-control and of foreign overcontrol comes a lasting propensity for doubt and shame.

3. Initiative vs. Guilt

There is in every child at every stage a new miracle of vigorous unfolding, which constitutes a new hope and a new responsibility for all. Such is the sense and the pervading quality of initiative. The criteria for all these senses and qualities are the same: a crisis, more or less beset with fumbling and fear, is resolved, in that the child suddenly seems to "grow together" both in his person and in his body. He appears "more himself," more loving, relaxed and brighter in his judgment, more activated and activating. He is in free possession of a surplus of energy which permits him to forget failures quickly and to approach what seems desirable (even if it also seems uncertain and even dangerous) with undiminished and more accurate direction. Initiative adds to autonomy the quality of undertaking, planning and "attacking" a task for the sake of being active and on the move, where before self-will, more often than not, inspired acts of defiance or, at any rate, protested independence.

I know that the very word "initiative" to many, has an American, and industrial connotation. Yet, initiative is a necessary part of every act, and man needs a sense of initiative for whatever he learns and does, from fruit-gathering to a system of enterprise.

The ambulatory stage and that of infantile genitality add to the inventory of basic social modalities that of "making," first in the sense of "being on the make." There is no simpler, stronger word for it; it suggests pleasure in attack and conquest. In the boy, the emphasis remains on phallic-intrusive modes; in the girl it turns to modes of "catching" in more aggressive forms of snatching or in the milder form of making oneself attractive and endearing.

The danger of this stage is a sense of guilt over the goals contemplated and the acts initiated in one's exuberant enjoyment of new locomotor and mental power: acts of aggressive manipulation and coercion which soon go far beyond the executive capacity of organism and mind and therefore call for an energetic halt on one's contemplated initiative.

While autonomy concentrates on keeping potential rivals out, and therefore can lead to jealous rage most often directed against encroachments by younger siblings, initiative brings with it anticipatory rivalry with those who have been there first and may, therefore, occupy with their superior equipment the field toward which one's initiative is directed. Infantile jealousy and rivalry, those often embittered and yet essentially futile attempts at demarcating a sphere of unquestioned privilege, now come to a climax in a final contest for a favored position with the mother; the usual failure leads to resignation, guilt, and anxiety.

4. Industry vs. Inferiority

Thus the inner stage seems all set for "entrance into life," except that life must first be school life, whether school is field or jungle or classroom. The child must forget past hopes and wishes, while his exuberant imagination is tamed and harnessed to the laws of impersonal things—even the three R's. For before the child, psychologically already a rudimentary parent, can become a biological parent, he must begin to be a worker and potential provider. With the oncoming latency period, the normally advanced child forgets, or rather sublimates, the necessity to "make" people by direct attack or to become papa and mama in a hurry: he now learns to win recognition by producing things. He has mastered the ambulatory field and the organ modes. He has experienced a sense of finality regarding the fact that there is no workable future within the womb of his family, and thus becomes ready to apply himself to given skills and tasks, which go far beyond the mere playful expression of his organ modes or the pleasure in the function of his limbs. He develops a sense of industry—i.e., he adjusts himself to the inorganic laws of the tool world. He can become an eager and absorbed unit of a productive situation. To bring a productive situation to completion is an aim which gradually supersedes the whims and wishes of play. His ego boundaries include his tools and skills: the work principle teaches him the pleasure of work completion by steady attention and persevering diligence. In all cultures, at this stage, children receive some *systematic instruction,* although it is by no means always in the kind of school which literate people must organize around special teachers who have learned how to teach literacy. In preliterate people and in nonliterate pursuits much is learned from adults who become teachers by dint of gift and inclination rather than by appointment, and perhaps the greatest amount is learned from older children. Thus the fundamentals of technology are developed, as the child becomes ready to handle the utensils, the tools, and the weapons used by the big people. Literate people, with more specialized careers, must prepare the child by teaching him things which first of all make him literate, the widest possible basic education for the greatest number of possible careers. The more confusing specialization becomes, however, the more indistinct are the eventual goals of initiative; and the more complicated social reality, the vaguer are the father's and mother's role in it. School seems to be a culture all by itself, with its own goals and limits, its achievements and disappointment.

The child's danger, at this stage, lies in a sense of inadequacy and inferiority. If he despairs of his tools and skills or of his status among his tool partners, he may be discouraged from identification with them and with a section of the tool world. To lose the hope of such "industrial" association may pull him back to the more isolated, less tool-conscious familial rivalry of the oedipal time. The child despairs of his equipment in the tool world and in anatomy, and considers himself doomed to mediocrity or inadequacy. It is at this point that wider society becomes significant in its ways of admitting the child to an understanding of meaningful roles in its technology and economy. Many a child's development is disrupted when family life has failed to prepare him for school life, or when school life fails to sustain the promises of earlier stages.

Regarding the period of a developing sense of industry, I have referred to *outer and inner hindrances* in the use of new capacities but not to aggravations of new human drives, nor to submerged rages resulting from their frustration. This stage differs from the earlier ones in that it is not a swing from an inner upheaval to a new mastery. Freud calls it the latency stage because violent drives are normally dormant. But it is only a lull before the storm of puberty, when all the earlier drives reemerge in a new combination, to be brought under the dominance of genitality.

On the other hand, this is socially a most decisive stage: since industry involves doing things beside and with others, a first sense of division of labor and of differential opportunity, that is, a sense of the *technological ethos* of a culture, develops at this time. We have pointed in the last section to the danger threatening individual and society where the schoolchild begins to feel that the color of his skin, the background of his parents, or the fashion of his clothes rather than his wish and his will to learn will decide his worth as an apprentice, and thus his sense of *identity*—to which we must now turn. But there is another, more fundamental danger, namely man's restriction of himself and constriction of his horizons to include only his work to which, so the Book says, he has been sentenced after his expulsion from paradise. If he accepts work as his only obligation, and "what works" as his only criterion of worthwhileness, he may become the conformist and thoughtless slave of his technology and of those who are in a position to exploit it.

5. Identity vs. Role Confusion

With the establishment of a good initial relationship to the world of skills and tools, and with the advent of puberty, childhood proper comes to an end. Youth begins. But in puberty and adolescence all samenesses and continuities relied on earlier are more or less questioned again, because of a rapidity of body growth which equals that of early childhood and because of the new addition of genital maturity. The growing and developing youths, faced with this physiological revolution within them, and with tangible adult tasks ahead of them are now primarily concerned with what they appear to be in the eyes of others as compared with what they feel they are, and with the question of how to connect the roles and skills cultivated earlier with the occupational prototypes of the day. In their search for a new sense of continuity and sameness, adolescents have to refight many of the battles of earlier years, even though to do so they must artificially appoint perfectly well-meaning people to play the roles of adversaries; and they are ever ready to install lasting idols and ideals as guardians of a final identity.

The integration now taking place in the form of ego identity is, as pointed out, more than the sum of the childhood identifications. It is the accrued experience of the ego's ability to integrate all identifications with the vicissitudes of the libido, with the aptitudes developed out of endowment, and with the opportunities offered in social roles. The sense of ego identity, then, is the accrued confidence that the inner sameness and continuity prepared in the past are matched by the sameness and continuity of one's meaning for others, as evidenced in the tangible promise of a "career."

The danger of this stage is role confusion. Where this is based on a strong previous doubt as to one's sexual identity, delinquent and outright psychotic episodes are not uncommon. If diagnosed and treated correctly, these incidents do not have the same fatal significance which they have at other ages. In most instances, however, it is the inability to settle on an occupational identity which disturbs individual young people. To keep themselves together they temporarily overidentify, to the point of apparent complete loss of identity, with the heroes of cliques and crowds. This initiates the stage of "falling in love," which is by no means entirely, or even primarily, a sexual matter—except where the mores demand it. To a considerable extent adolescent love is an attempt to arrive at a definition of one's identity by projecting one's diffused ego image on another and by seeing it thus reflected and gradually clarified. This is why so much of young love is conversation.

Young people can also be remarkably clannish, and cruel in their exclusion of all those who are "different," in skin color or cultural background, in tastes and gifts, and often in such petty aspects of dress and gesture as have been temporarily selected as the signs of an in-grouper or out-grouper. It is important to understand (which does not mean condone or participate in) such intolerance as a defense against a sense of identity confusion. For adolescents not only help one another temporarily through much discomfort by forming cliques and by stereotyping themselves, their ideals, and their enemies; they also perversely test each other's capacity to pledge fidelity. The readiness for such testing also explains the appeal which simple and cruel totalitarian doctrines have on the minds of the youth of such countries and classes as have lost or are losing their group identities (feudal, agrarian, tribal, national) and face world-wide industrialization, emancipation, and wider communication.

The adolescent mind is essentially a mind of the *moratorium,* a psychosocial stage between childhood and adulthood, and between the morality learned by the child, and the ethics to be developed by the adult. It is an ideological mind—and, indeed, it is the ideological outlook of a society that speaks most clearly to the adolescent who is eager to be affirmed by his peers, and is ready to be confirmed by rituals, creeds, and programs which at the same time define what is evil, uncanny, and inimical. In searching for the social values which guide identity, one therefore confronts the problems of *ideology* and *aristocracy,* both in their widest possible sense which connotes that within a defined world image and a predestined course of history, the best people will come to rule and rule develops the best in people. In order not to become cynically or apathetically lost, young people must somehow be able to convince themselves that those who succeed in their anticipated adult world thereby shoulder the obligation of being the best. We will discuss later the dangers which emanate from human ideals harnessed to the management of super-machines, be they guided by nationalistic or international, communist or capitalist ideologies. In the last part of this book we shall discuss the way in which the revolutions of our day attempt to solve and also to exploit the deep need of youth to redefine its identity in an industrialized world.

11

Dear Professor Marlowe:

I wanted to tell you about a weird parent conference question I just got the other night. I've got this kid in my class named Tanika and her mother is all concerned about her behavior, which isn't great, but seems pretty normal to me. After I was telling Tanika's mom about what a great job she's doing adjusting to first grade, learning to read, etc., etc., she launches into this strange kind of moralistic rant about how Tanika only seems to obey rules ". . . if she thinks there's something in it for her." Then, for comparison, I guess, she starts telling me about her 14-year-old daughter who makes decisions based on what she really thinks is the right thing to do. Tanika's mom is convinced that her older daughter is her "good kid" and she is worried that her younger daughter is her "bad kid" who will likely grow up to be an adolescent with serious behavior problems.

How can I convince her that Tanika is just your average 6 year old?

Robert Kingsley

❖ HOW WOULD YOU RESPOND?

How do children and adults come to understand the difference between what is right and wrong? How do they make moral judgments? Do these kinds of decisions depend on how old they are? In what ways do Tanika and her sister differ with respect to moral development? How can teachers help students become more morally sophisticated in their thinking? In what ways does the moral development of children influence teaching and learning? If you were Robert Kingsley, what would you say to Tanika's mother?

Do children differ in terms of how they solve moral dilemmas? For example, would children in Nigeria and the United States go about determining whether a hypothetical situation was wrong or right in the same way? Would they use the same criteria to make such a judgment? Keep these questions in mind as you read "Continuities and Discontinuities in Childhood and Adult Moral Development" by L. Kohlberg and R. Kramer. What questions do *you* have about moral development? How can you help extend the discussion of these ideas in class? Finally, how would you respond to Robert Kingsley?

❖ CONTINUITIES AND DISCONTINUITIES IN
    CHILDHOOD AND ADULT MORAL DEVELOPMENT

L. Kohlberg and R. Kramer

It is fairly common to talk loosely of adult development and stages in terms of developmental tasks. Such discussion assumes that there are age-typical changes in personality, linked to focal tasks, and that successful resolution of these tasks leads to characteristic attitudinal outcomes. Even if "stages" in this sense can be clearly documented empirically, they would not deal with the basic issues I have mentioned. Before explaining why "developmental tasks" will not deal with these issues, let me first clarify what child psychology in the Piaget-Werner tradition has meant by "development" and "stage" [Werner, 1948; Piaget, 1964; Kohlberg, 1968]. There are three criteria used by the tradition to distinguish psychological development from behavior change in general.

The first criterion is that development involves change in the general shape, pattern, or organization of response, rather than change in the frequency or intensity of emission of an already patterned response. Under reinforcement, bar-pressing increases in frequency; such increase is not development. Under food deprivation, hunger behaviors increase in frequency and intensity; such behavior is not development. With age, sexual impulses wax or wane in intensity. Such changes are not development.

A second criterion, closely related to the first, is that developmental change involves newness, a qualitative difference in response. Developmental change does not have to be sudden or saltatory but it does entail the emergence of a novel structure of response. Novelty involves the quality-quantity distinction, which in turn involves the distinction between form and content. In a sense, any change in content is new. A really new kind of experience, a really new mode of response, however, is one that is different in its form or organization, not simply in the element or the information it contains.

The third criterion implied by the word development is irreversibility. Once a developmental change has occurred, it cannot be reversed by the conditions and experiences which gave rise to it. Learned bar pressing can be reversed or extinguished by withdrawing the reinforcement which conditioned it. A developmental change cannot. Smedslund [1961] has used this criterion to distinguish cognitive development from associationistic learning. He reports that if a Piaget conservation was taught to a preconserver by instruction and reinforcement, it could be reversed by use of the same mechanisms. Naturally developing conservation could not be reversed by the same procedures. The concept of developmental irreversibility does not rule out the existence of behavior change backward to a previous pattern. As an example, seniles and schizophrenics seem to lose the Piaget conservations. Such backward changes are labeled regression; however, it is important to point out that they are rare and their conditions or causes are markedly different from the conditions or causes of forward development.

The three criteria of development just mentioned, plus three others, are involved in the concept of developmental stage. The stage concept not only postulates irreversible qualitative structural change, but in addition postulates a fourth condition that this change occurs in a pattern of universal stepwise invariant sequences. Fifth, the stage concept postulates that the stages form a hierarchy of functioning within the individual. This implies, sixth, that each stage is a differentiation and integration of a set of functional contents present at the prior stage.

On the face of it, developmental task conceptions meet none of the criteria we have mentioned. Sexual intimacy and marriage, vocational identity and achievement, parenthood, acceptance of life's completion and conclusion are matters of content, not form. According to Erikson, [1950] the *content* of parenthood forms the focus of development of an generalized or *formal* attitude of generativity toward the world and toward the self which is new in development. It is just the question of whether such a novel formal attitude develops in part from parental content which lies at the cart of any investigation of Erikson's adult ego stages.

Related to the ambiguity of the formal aspects of stages defined as resolutions of developmental tasks is the ambiguity of their irreversibility and invariance of sequence. Developmental tasks of content in themselves have no order, i.e., individuals can face vocational commitment or identity before or after sexual intimacy and parenthood. Psychologically it is even possible to develop competent parental attitudes before developing capacity for sexual intimacy. Finally, the irreversibility of development defined in terms of developmental tasks is much in question. There are certainly many older adults, apparently mature and ready to face the tasks of integrity vs. despair, who suddenly seem to prefer regression to the tasks of establishing heterosexual intimacy.

My sketch of the developmental task approach does justice neither to its usefulness for personality study nor to its theoretical richness as elaborated by Erikson [1950]. My caricature does, however, point to the inability of the developmental task approach to speak to the two problems mentioned. A study of adult developmental tasks will tell us little about the general role of experience in childhood structural change. It will also do little to establish communication between the generations. The older may indeed have wisdom in the sense of awareness of the problems that the young have not faced and will inevitably face. That does not, however, prove that it is wise for the young to face their problems in terms of the problems of their elders. The old may have developed a style of coping with the immanence of death which is effective and admirable. This does not mean that the young should cope with the problem or use a similar style. Only if there is a form of thought or a form of coping more mature or integrated in its application to a problem that is also the youth's problem, can the development of the older help the younger.

We have talked of the potential value for adult psychology of the rigorous conception of stage used in Piagetian child psychology. Before considering its application to adulthood, let me first quickly sketch how the criteria implied by this rigorous conception have been met in child psychology. For obvious reasons, our example will come from our work on stages of moral judgment [Kohlberg, 1958, 1963, 1968, 1969]. Table 11.1 presents a summary characterization of six stages of moral judgment.

Table 11.1   Definition of Moral Stages

I.   Preconventional Level

At this level the child is responsive to cultural rules and labels of good and bad, right or wrong, but interprets these labels in terms of either the physical or the hedonistic consequences of action (punishment, reward, exchange of favors) or in terms of the physical power of those who enunciate the rules and labels. The level is divided into the following two stages:

Stage 1: *The punishment and obedience orientation.* The physical consequences of action determine its goodness or badness regardless of the human meaning or value of these consequences. Avoidance of punishment and unquestioning deference to power are valued in their own right, not in terms of respect for an underlying moral order supported by punishment and authority (the latter being Stage 4).

Stage 2: *The instrumental relativist orientation.* Right action consists of that which instrumentally satisfies one's own needs and occasionally the needs of others. Human relations are viewed in terms like those of the market place. Elements of fairness, or reciprocity and equal sharing are present, but they are always interpreted in a physical pragmatic way. Reciprocity is a matter of "you scratch my back and I'll scratch yours," not of loyalty, gratitude or justice.

II.   Conventional Level

At this level, maintaining the expectations of the individual's family, group, or nation is perceived as valuable in its own right, regardless of immediate and obvious consequences. The attitude is not only one of conformity to personal expectations and social order, but of loyalty to it, of actively maintaining, supporting, and justifying the order and of identifying with the persons or group involved in it. At this level, there are the following two stages:

Stage 3: *The interpersonal concordance or "good boy–nice girl" orientation.* Good behavior is that which pleases or helps others and is approved by them. There is much conformity to stereotypical images of what is majority or "natural" behavior. Behavior is frequently judged by intention—"he means well" becomes important for the first time. One earns approval by being "nice."

Stage 4: *The "law and order" orientation.* There is orientation toward authority, fixed rules, and the maintenance of the social order. Right behavior consists of doing one's duty, showing respect for authority and maintaining the given social order for its own sake.

III. Post-Conventional, Autonomous, or Principled Level

At this level, there is a clear effort to define moral values and principles which have validity and application apart from the authority of the groups or persons holding these principles and apart from the individual's own identification with these groups. This level again has two stages:

(Continued)

Table 11.1 (Continued)

Stage 5: *The social-contract legalistic orientation generally with utilitarian overtones.* Right action tends to be defined in terms of general individual rights and in terms of standards which have been critically examined and agreed upon by the whole society. There is a clear awareness of the relativism of personal values and opinions and a corresponding emphasis upon procedural rules for reaching consensus. Aside from what is constitutionally and democratically agreed upon, the fight is a matter of personal "values" and "opinion." The result is an emphasis upon the "legal point of view," but with an emphasis upon the possibility of changing law in terms of rational considerations of social utility, (rather than freezing it m terms of Stage 4 "law and order"). Outside the legal realm, free agreement, and contract is the binding element of obligation. This is the "official" morality of the American government and Constitution.

Stage 6: *The universal ethical principle orientation.* Right is defined by the decision of conscience in accord with self-chosen ethical principles appealing to logical comprehensiveness, universality, and consistency. These principles are abstract and ethical, (the Golden Rule, the categorical imperative) they are not concrete moral rules like the Ten Commandments. At heart, these are universal principles of justice of the reciprocity and equality of the human rights and of respect for the dignity of human beings as individual persons.

The concept of human life is valued at each stage. The way in which this value is conceived differs, however, at each stage. In parentheses we indicate the sense in which each higher stage involves a differentiation in thinking about life's values not made at the immediately preceding stage of thought. The sense in which each stage is a new integration is more difficult to define, but will be intuitively evident to you in reading the examples. The table illustrates this one aspect of moral development with responses from two boys in the 10-year longitudinal study. Tommy was first interviewed at 10, and then again at 13, and 16. At 10 he is Stage 1, at 13 Stage 2, at 16 Stage 3. To represent more mature stages we have used Jim.

Jim, when first interviewed at 13, is primarily Stage 2. At 16 he is Stage 4, at 20 Stage 5, at 24 Stage 6 on this aspect. These two boys, then, suggest a sequential pattern holding for each individual. While Tommy is slower in development than Jim and likely will never get as far, both go through the same steps insofar as they move at all. While various statistical qualifications are required in making the generalization, it is

Table 11.2   Six Stages in Conceptions of Moral Worth of Human Life

Stage 1: No differentiation between moral value of life and its physical or social-status value.

Tommy, age ten (III, Why should the druggist give the drug to the dying woman when her husband couldn't pay for it?): "If someone important is in a plane and is allergic to heights and the stewardess won't give him medicine because she's only got enough for one and she's got a sick one, a friend, in back, they'd probably put the stewardess in a lady's jail because she didn't help the important one."

(Is it better to save the life of one important person or a lot of unimportant people?): "All the people that aren't important because one man just has one house, maybe a lot of furniture, but a whole bunch of people have an awful lot of furniture and some of these poor people might have a lot of money and it doesn't look it."

Stage 2: The value of a human life is seen as instrumental to the satisfaction of the needs of its possessor or of other persons. Decision to save life is relative to, or to be made by, its possessor. (Differentiation of physical and interest value of life, differentiation of its value to self and to other.)

Tommy, age thirteen (IV, Should the doctor "mercy kill" a fatally ill woman requesting death because of her pain?): "Maybe it would be good to put her out of her pain, she'd be better off that way. But the husband wouldn't want it, it's not like an animal. If a pet dies you can get along without it—it isn't something you really need. Well, you can get a new wife, but it's not really the same."

Jim, age thirteen (same question): "If she requests it, it's really up to her. She is in such terrible pain, just the same as people are always putting animals out of their pain."

Stage 3: The value of a human life is based on the empathy and affection of family members and others toward its possessor. (The value of human life, as based on social sharing, community and love, is differentiated from the instrumental and hedonistic value of life applicable also to animals.)

Tommy, age sixteen (same question): "It might be best for her, but her husband-it's a human life—not like an animal. it just doesn't have the same relationship that a human being does to a family. You can become attached to a dog, but nothing like a human you know."

Stage 4: Life is conceived as sacred in terms of its place in a categorical moral or religious order of rights and duties. (The value of human life, as a categorical member of a moral order, is differentiated from its value to specific other people in the family, etc. Value of life is still partly dependent upon serving the group, the state, God, however.)

Jim, age sixteen (same question): "I don't know. In one way, it's murder, it's not a right or privilege of man to decide who shall live and who should die. God

(Continued)

Table 11.2 (Continued)

put life into everybody on earth and you're taking away something from that person that came directly from God, and you're destroying something that is very sacred, it's in a way part of God and it's almost destroying a part of God when you kill a person. There's something of God in everyone."

Stage 5: Life is valued both in terms of its relation to community welfare and in terms of being a universal human right. (Obligation to respect the basic right to life is differentiated from generalized respect for the socio-moral order. The general value of the independent human life is a primary autonomous value not dependent upon other values.)

Jim, age twenty (same question): "Given the ethics of the doctor who has taken on responsibility to save human life—from that point of view he probably shouldn't but there is another side, there are more and more people in the medical profession who are thinking it is a hardship on everyone, the person, the family, when you know they are going to die. When a person is kept alive by an artificial lung or kidney it's more like being a vegetable than being a human who is alive. If it's her own choice I think there are certain rights and privileges that go along with being a human being. I am a human being and have certain desires for life and I think everybody else does too. You have a world of which you are the center and everybody else does too and in that sense we're all equal."

Stage 6: Belief in the sacredness of human life as representing a universal human value of respect for the individual. (The moral value of a human being, as an object of moral principle, is differentiated from a formal recognition of his rights.)

Jim, age twenty-four (III, Should the husband steal the drug to save his wife? How about for someone he just knows?): "Yes. A human life takes precedence over any other moral or legal value, whoever it is. A human life has inherent value."

---

true that the pattern of most of our longitudinal data is a pattern of directed irreversible one-step progressions.

We have said that our sequence is invariant for individuals in the United States. Our evidence also suggests that this sequence is culturally universal.

Moral development involves a continual process of matching a moral view to one's experience of life in a social world. Experiences of conflict in this process generate movement from structural stage to structural stage. Even after attainment of the highest stage an individual will reach, there is continued experience of conflict. The developmental product of such conflict is stabilization, i.e. a greater consistency of structure with itself (greater stage "purity") and a greater consistency between thought structure and action. The evidence that adult stabilization is the integration of conflict rather than "social learning" or socialization, is indicated by our finding one pattern of adult stabilization that involves temporary retrogression. The integration of conflict in adult development may be conceived in terms of functional "stages" of ego development which are quite different from structural stages. While I have discussed only moral change at the "ego stage" of late adolescent identity, the moral changes in late adulthood of the Tolstoys or the Saint Pauls presumably could be discussed in the same general terms.

There is, then, a sense in which there is adult moral development. There is an adult movement toward integration in the use of moral structures, in the integration of moral thought in its application to life. There may even by typical phases in this integrative process. There are, however, no adult stages in the structural sense, and accordingly no clear solution to the two problems of adult development which we initially posed. We cannot integrate childhood and adult moral development into a single theoretical series or sequence of stages. Nor can we claim that adulthood has a moral wisdom denied to the youth.

References

Bayley, N. (1953). *On the growth of intelligence. Amer. J. Psychol. 10*, 805–815.

Erikson, E. (1950). *Childhood and society.* New York: Norton.

Haan, N., Smith, M. B. and Block, J. (1968). *The moral reasoning of young adults: Political-social behavior, family background, and personality correlates.*

Hobhouse, L. T. (1906). *Morals in evolution.* London: Chapman and Hall.

Holstein, C. (1969). *The relation of children's moral judgment to that of their parents and to communications patterns in the family.* Unpublished dissertation, University of California, Berkeley.

Kohlberg, L. (1963). Psychological analysis and literary forms. A study of the doubles in Dostoevsky. *Daedalus 92:* 345–363.

Kohlberg, L. (1968). Stage and sequence: the cognitive-developmental approach to socialization, in Goslin, *Handbook of socialization theory.* Chicago: Rand McNally.

Kohlberg, L. (1969). *Stages in the development of moral thought and action.* New York: Holt, Rinehart, and Winston.

Kramer, R. (March 26, 1969). Progression and regression in adolescent moral development. *Soc. Res. Child Development,* Santa Monica.

Perry, W. *Forms of intellectual and ethical development in the college years.* Mimeo monograph. Bureau at Study Counsel, Harvard University.

Piaget, J. (1960). The general problems of the psychobiological development of the child; in Tanner and Inhelder, *Discussions on child development:*

Proceedings of the World Health Organization study group on the psychobiological development of the child (vol. IV, pp. 3–27). New York: International Univ. Press.

Piaget, J. (1964). Cognitive development in children; in Ripple and Rockcastle, *Piaget rediscovered: A report on cognitive studies in curriculum development.* Ithaca, NY: Cornell Univ. School of Education.

Rest, J. (1968). *Developmental hierarchy in preference and comprehension of moral judgment.* Unpublished doctoral dissertation. Univ. of Chicago.

Rest, J., Turiel, E. and Kohlberg, L. (1969). Relations between level of moral judgment and preference and comprehension of the moral judgment of others. *Journal of Personality.*

Smedslund, J. (1961). The acquisition of conservation of substance and weight in children. *Scandinavian Journal of Psychology 2:* 85–87, 156–160, 203–210.

Turiel, E. (1969). Developmental processes in the child's moral thinking; in Mussen, Langer and Covington, *New directions in developmental psychology.* New York: Rhinehart.

Werner, H. (1948). *The comparative psychology of mental development.* Chicago: Wilcox and Follett.

12

Dear Dr. Canestrari:

My cooperating teacher did an interesting experiment in class the other day that I wanted to get your feedback on. He asked everyone in the 11th-grade social studies section I'm student teaching in to write a brief auto-biographical paragraph. The only other directions he gave them was something like this: "Be sure a stranger reading your paragraph would have a pretty good idea about what kind of person you are from reading it." Well, a fascinating thing happened. Almost all the boys in the class wrote about their hobbies, interests, the sports they liked, and their accomplishments. Some of them also included information about physical features that described how they looked; but mostly the boys' pieces were about what the boys had done, what they were proud of, that sort of thing. The girls, on the other hand, wrote almost exclusively about whom they were connected to and how they were connected. Their paragraphs really focused on relationships, the people in their family, their friends. What do you make of this difference? My cooperating teacher thinks that boys tend to be more self-centered and girls tend to think of others first, sometimes to the exclusion of themselves.

Susan Perry

❖ HOW WOULD YOU RESPOND?

Are boys and girls fundamentally different when it comes to how they define themselves in the world? Do they solve problems differently? Are their values different too? How might these differences show up in school settings? What social forces may help shape these differences? Keep these questions in mind as you read "Images of Relationship" by Carol Gilligan. What questions do you have about gender differences? How might you extend the discussion of these ideas in class? Finally, how would you respond to Susan Perry?

❖ IMAGES OF RELATIONSHIP

Carol Gilligan

Since the imagery of relationships shapes the narrative of human development, the inclusion of women, by changing that imagery, implies a change in the entire account.

The shift in imagery that creates the problem in interpreting women's development is elucidated by the moral judgments of two eleven-year-old children, a boy and a girl, who see, in the same dilemma, two very different moral problems. While current theory brightly illuminates the line and the logic of the boy's thought, it casts scant light on that of the girl. The choice of a girl whose moral judgments elude existing categories of developmental assessment is meant to highlight the issue of interpretation rather than to exemplify sex differences per se. Adding a new line of interpretation, based on the imagery of the girl's thought, makes it possible not only to see development where previously development was not discerned but also to consider differences in the understanding of relationships without scaling these differences from better to worse.

The two children were in the same sixth-grade class at school and were participants in the rights and responsibilities study, designed to explore different conceptions of morality and self. The sample selected for this study was chosen to focus the variables of gender and age while maximizing developmental potential by holding constant, at a high level, the factors of intelligence, education, and social class that have been associated with moral development, at least as measured by existing scales. The two children in question, Amy and Jake, were both bright and articulate and, at least in their eleven-year-old aspirations, resisted easy categories of sex-role stereotyping, since Amy aspired to become a scientist while Jake preferred English to math. Yet their moral judgments seem initially to confirm familiar notions about differences between the sexes, suggesting that the edge girls have on moral development during the early school years gives way at puberty with the ascendance of formal logical thought in boys.

The dilemma that these eleven-year-olds were asked to resolve was one in the series devised by Kohlberg to measure moral development in adolescence by presenting a conflict between moral norms and exploring the logic of its resolution. In this particular dilemma, a man named Heinz considers whether or not to steal a drug which he cannot afford to buy in order to save the life of his wife. In the standard format of Kohlberg's interviewing procedure, the description of the dilemma itself—Heinz's predicament, the wife's disease, the druggist's refusal to lower his price—is followed by the question, "Should Heinz steal the drug?" The reasons for and against stealing are then explored through a series of questions that vary and extend the parameters of the dilemma in a way designed to reveal the underlying structure of moral thought.

Jake, at eleven, is clear from the outset that Heinz should steal the drug. Constructing the dilemma, as Kohlberg did, as a conflict between the values of property and life, he discerns the logical priority of life and uses that logic to justify his choice:

> For one thing, a human life is worth more than money, and if the druggist only makes $1,000, he is still going to live, but if Heinz doesn't steal the drug, his wife is going to die. (*Why is life worth more than money?*) Because the druggist can get a thousand dollars later from rich people with cancer, but Heinz can't get his wife again. (*Why not?*) Because people are all different and so you couldn't get Heinz's wife again.

Asked whether Heinz should steal the drug if he does not love his wife, Jake replies that he should, saying that not only is there "a difference between hating and killing," but also, if Heinz were caught, "the judge would probably think it was the right thing to do." Asked about the fact that, in stealing, Heinz would be breaking the law, he says that "the laws have mistakes, and you can't go writing up a law for everything that you can imagine."

Thus, while taking the law into account and recognizing its function in maintaining social order (the judge, Jake says, "should give Heinz the lightest possible sentence"), he also sees the law as man-made and therefore subject to error and change. Yet his judgment that Heinz should steal the drug, like his view of the law as having mistakes, rests on the assumption of agreement, a societal consensus around moral values that allows one to know and expect others to recognize what is "the right thing to do."

Fascinated by the power of logic, this eleven-year-old boy locates truth in math, which, he says, is "the only thing that is totally logical." Considering the moral dilemma to be "sort of like a math problem with humans," he sets it up as an equation and proceeds to work out the solution. Since his solution is rationally derived, he assumes that anyone following reason would arrive at the same conclusion and thus that a judge would also consider stealing to be the right thing for Heinz to do. Yet he is also aware of the limits of logic. Asked whether there is a right answer to moral problems, Jake replies that "there can only be right and wrong in judgment," since the parameters of action are variable and complex. Illustrating how actions undertaken with the best of intentions can eventuate in the most disastrous of consequences, he says, "like if you give an old lady your seat on the trolley, if you are in a trolley crash and that seat goes through the window, it might be that reason that the old lady dies."

Theories of developmental psychology illuminate well the position of this child, standing at the juncture of childhood and adolescence, at what Piaget describes as the pinnacle of childhood intelligence, and beginning through thought to discover a wider universe of possibility. The moment of preadolescence is caught by the conjunction of formal operational thought with a description of self still anchored in the factual parameters of his childhood world—his age, his town, his father's occupation, the substance of his likes, dislikes, and beliefs. Yet as his self-description radiates the self-confidence of a child who has arrived, in Erikson's terms, at a favorable balance of industry over inferiority—competent, sure of himself, and knowing well the rules of the game—so his emergent capacity for formal thought, his ability to think about thinking and to reason things out in a logical way, frees him from dependence on authority and allows him to find solutions to problems by himself.

This emergent autonomy follows the trajectory that Kohlberg's six stages of moral development trace, a three-level progression from an egocentric understanding of fairness based on individual need (stages one and two), to a conception of fairness anchored in the shared conventions of societal agreement (stages three and four), and finally to a principled understanding of fairness that rests on the free-standing logic of equality and reciprocity (stages five and six). While this boy's judgments at eleven are scored as conventional on Kohlberg's scale, a mixture of stages three and four, his ability to bring deductive logic to bear on the solution of moral dilemmas, to differentiate morality from law, and to see how laws can be considered to have mistakes points toward the principled conception of justice that Kohlberg equates with moral maturity.

In contrast, Amy's response to the dilemma conveys a very different impression, an image of development stunted by a failure of logic, an inability to think for herself. Asked if Heinz should steal the drug, she replies in a way that seems evasive and unsure:

> Well, I don't think so. I think there might be other ways besides stealing it, like if he could borrow the money or make a loan or something, but he really shouldn't steal the drug—but his wife shouldn't die either.

Asked why he should not steal the drug, she considers neither property nor law but rather the effect that theft could have on the relationship between Heinz and his wife:

> If he stole the drug, he might save his wife then, but if he did, he might have to go to jail, and then his wife might get sicker again, and he couldn't get more of the drug, and it might not be good. So, they should really just talk it out and find some other way to make the money.

Seeing in the dilemma not a math problem with humans but a narrative of relationships that extends over time, Amy envisions the wife's continuing need for her husband and the husband's continuing concern for his wife and seeks to respond to the druggist's need in a way that would sustain rather than sever connection. Just as she ties the wife's survival to the preservation of relationships, so she considers the value of the wife's life in a context of relationships, saying that it would be wrong to let her die because "if she died, it hurts a lot of people and it hurts her." Since Amy's moral judgment is grounded in the belief that, "if somebody has something that would keep somebody alive, then it's not right not to give it to them," she considers the problem in the dilemma to arise not from the druggist's assertion of rights but from his failure of response.

As the interviewer proceeds with the series of questions that follow from Kohlberg's construction of the dilemma, Amy's answers remain essentially unchanged, the various probes serving neither to elucidate nor to modify her initial response. Whether or not Heinz loves his wife, he still shouldn't steal or let her die; if it were a stranger dying instead,

Amy says that "if the stranger didn't have anybody near or anyone she knew," then Heinz should try to save her life, but he should not steal the drug. But as the interviewer conveys through the repetition of questions that the answers she gave were not heard or not right, Amy's confidence begins to diminish, and her replies become more constrained and unsure. Asked again why Heinz should not steal the drug, she simply repeats, "Because it's not right." Asked again to explain why, she states again that theft would not be a good solution, adding lamely, "if he took it, he might not know how to give it to his wife, and so his wife might still die." Failing to see the dilemma as a self-contained problem in moral logic, she does not discern the internal structure of its resolution; as she constructs the problem differently herself, Kohlberg's conception completely evades her.

Instead, seeing a world comprised of relationships rather than of people standing alone, a world that coheres through human connection rather than through systems of rules, she finds the puzzle in the dilemma to lie in the failure of the druggist to respond to the wife. Saving that "it is not right for someone to die when their life could be saved," she assumes that if the druggist were to see the consequences of his refusal to lower his price, he would realize that "he should just give it to the wife and then have the husband pay back the money later." Thus she considers the solution to the dilemma to lie in making the wife's condition more salient to the druggist or, that failing, in appealing to others who are in a position to help.

Just as Jake is confident the judge would agree that stealing is the right thing for Heinz to do, so Amy is confident that, "if Heinz and the druggist had talked it out long enough, they could reach something besides stealing." As he considers the law to "have mistakes," so she sees this drama as a mistake, believing that "the world should just share things more and then people wouldn't have to steal." Both children thus recognize the need for agreement but see it as mediated in different ways—he impersonally through systems of logic and law, she personally through communication in relationship. Just as he relies on the conventions of logic to deduce the solution to this dilemma, assuming these conventions to be shared, so she relies on a process of communication, assuming connection and believing that her voice will be heard. Yet while his assumptions about agreement are confirmed by the convergence in logic between his answers and the questions posed, her assumptions are belied by the failure of communication, the interviewer's inability to understand her response.

Although the frustration of the interview with Amy is apparent in the repetition of questions and its ultimate circularity, the problem of interpretation is focused by the assessment of her response. When considered in the light of Kohlberg's definition of the stages and sequence of moral development, her moral judgments appear to be a full stage lower in maturity than those of the boy. Scored as a mixture of stages two and three, her responses seem to reveal a feeling of powerlessness in the world, an inability to think systematically about the concepts of morality or law, a reluctance to challenge authority or to examine the logic of received moral truths, a failure even to conceive of acting directly to save a life or to consider that such action, if taken, could possibly have an effect. As her reliance on relationships seems to reveal a continuing dependence and vulnerability, so her belief in communication as the mode through which to resolve moral dilemmas appears naive and cognitively immature.

Yet Amy's description of herself conveys a markedly different impression. Once again, the hallmarks of the preadolescent child depict a child secure in her sense of herself, confident in the substance of her beliefs, and sure of her ability to do something of value in the world. Describing herself at eleven as "growing and changing," she says that she "sees some things differently now, just because I know myself really well now, and I know a lot more about the world." Yet the world she knows is a different world from that refracted by Kohlberg's construction of Heinz's dilemma. Her world is a world of relationships and psychological truths where an awareness of the connection between people gives rise to a recognition of responsibility for one another, a perception of the need for response. Seen in this light, her understanding of morality as arising from the recognition of relationship, her belief in communication as the mode of conflict resolution, and her conviction that the solution to the dilemma will follow from its compelling representation seem far from naive or cognitively immature. Instead, Amy's judgments contain the insights central to an ethic of care, just as Jake's judgments reflect the logic of the justice approach. Her incipient awareness of the "method of truth," the central tenet of nonviolent conflict resolution, and her belief in the restorative activity of care, lead her to see the actors in the dilemma arrayed not as opponents in a contest of rights but as members of a network of relationships on whose continuation they all depend. Consequently her solution to the dilemma lies in activating the network by communication, securing the inclusion of the wife by strengthening rather than severing connections.

But the different logic of Amy's response calls attention to the interpretation of the interview itself. Conceived as an interrogation, it appears instead as a dialogue, which takes on moral dimensions of its own, pertaining to the interviewer's uses of power and to the manifestations of respect. With this shift in the conception of the interview, it immediately becomes clear that the interviewer's problem in understanding Amy's response stems from the fact that Amy is answering a different question from the one the interviewer thought had been posed. Amy is considering not *whether* Heinz should act in this situation ("*should* Heinz steal the drug?") but rather *how* Heinz should act in response to his awareness of his wife's need ("Should Heinz *steal* the drug?"). The interviewer takes the mode of action for granted, presuming it to be a matter of fact; Amy assumes the necessity for action and considers what form it should take. In the interviewer's failure to imagine a response not dreamt of in Kohlberg's moral philosophy lies the failure to hear Amy's question and to see the logic in her response, to discern that what appears, from one perspective, to be an evasion of the dilemma signifies in other terms a recognition of the problem and a search for a more adequate solution.

Thus in Heinz's dilemma these two children see two very different moral problems—Jake a conflict between life and property that can be resolved by logical deduction, Amy a fracture of human relationship that must be mended with its own thread. Asking different questions that arise from different conceptions of the moral domain, the children arrive at answers that fundamentally diverge, and the arrangement of these answers as successive stages on a scale of increasing moral maturity calibrated by the logic of the boy's response misses the different truth revealed in the judgment of the girl. To the question, "What does he see that she does not?" Kohlberg's theory provides a ready response, manifest in the scoring of Jake's judgments a full stage higher than Amy's in moral maturity; to the question, "What does she see that he does not?" Kohlberg's theory has nothing to say. Since most of her responses fall through the sieve of Kohlberg's scoring system, her responses appear from his perspective to lie outside the moral domain.

Yet just as Jake reveals a sophisticated understanding of the logic of justification, so Amy is equally sophisticated in her understanding of the nature of choice. Recognizing that "if both the roads went in totally separate ways, if you pick one, you'll never know what would happen if you went the other way," she explains that "that's the chance you have to take, and like I said, it's just really a guess." To illustrate her point "in a simple way," she describes her choice to spend the summer at camp:

> I will never know what would have happened if I had stayed here, and if something goes wrong at camp, I'll never know if I stayed here if it would have been better. There's really no way around it because there's no way you can do both at once, so you've got to decide, but you'll never know.

In this way, these two eleven-year-old children, both highly intelligent and perceptive about life, though in different ways, display different modes of moral understanding, different ways of thinking about conflict and choice. In resolving Heinz's dilemma, Jake relies on theft to avoid confrontation and turns to the law to mediate the dispute. Transposing a hierarchy of power into a hierarchy of values, he defuses a potentially explosive conflict between people by casting it as an impersonal conflict of claims. In this way he abstracts the moral problem from the interpersonal situation, finding in the logic of fairness an objective way to decide who will win the dispute. But this hierarchical ordering, with its imagery of winning and losing and the potential for violence which it contains gives way in Amy's construction of the dilemma to a network of connection, a web of relationships that is sustained by a process of communication. With this shift, the moral problem changes from one of unfair domination, the imposition of property over life, to one of unnecessary exclusion, the failure of the druggist to respond to the wife.

This shift in the formulation of the moral problem and the concomitant change in the imagery of relationships appear in the responses of two eight-year-old children, Jeffrey and Karen, asked to describe a situation in which they were not sure what was the right thing to do:

Jeffrey	Karen
When I really want to go to my friends and my mother is cleaning the cellar, I think about my friends, and then I think about my mother, and then I think about the right thing to do. (*But how do you know it's the right thing to do?*) Because some things go before other things.	I have a lot of friends, and I can't always play with all of them, so everybody's going to have to take a turn, because they're all my friends. But like if someone's all alone, I play with them. (*What kinds of things do you think about when you are trying to make that decision?*) Um, someone all alone, loneliness.

While Jeffrey sets up a hierarchical ordering to resolve a conflict between desire and duty, Karen describes a network of relationships that includes all of her friends. Both children deal with the issues of exclusion and priority created by choice, but while Jeffrey thinks about what goes first, Karen focuses on who is left out.

The contrasting images of hierarchy and network in children's thinking about moral conflict and choice illuminate two views of morality which are complementary rather than sequential or opposed. But this construction of differences goes against the bias of developmental theory toward ordering differences in a hierarchical mode. The correspondence between the order of developmental theory and the structure of the boys' thought contrasts with the disparity between existing theory and the structure manifest in the thought of the girls. Yet in neither comparison does one child's judgment appear as a precursor of the other's position. Thus, questions arise concerning the relation between these perspectives: what is the significance of this difference, and how do these two modes of thinking connect? These questions are elucidated by considering the relationship between the eleven-year-old children's understanding of morality and their descriptions of themselves:

Jake	Amy
(How would you describe yourself to yourself?)	
Perfect. That's my conceited side. What do you want—any way that I choose to describe myself?	You mean my character? (*What do you think?*) Well. I don't know. I'd describe myself as, well, what do you mean?
(If you had to describe the person you are in a way that you yourself would know it was you, what would you say?)	
I'd start off with eleven years old, Jake [last name]. I'd have to add that I live in [town], because that is a big part of me, and also that my father is a doctor, because I think that does change me a little bit, and that I don't believe in crime, except for when your name is Heinz; that I think school is boring, because I think that kind of changes your character a	Well, I'd say that I was someone who likes school and studying, and that's what I want to do with my life. I want to be some kind of a scientist or something, and I want to do things, and I want to help people. And I think that's what kind of person I am, or what kind of person I try to be. And that's probably how I'd describe

Jake	Amy
little bit. I don't sort of know how to describe myself, because I don't know how to read my personality. (*If you had to describe the way you actually would describe yourself, what would you say?*) I like corny jokes. I don't really like to get down to work, but I can do all the stuff in school. Every single problem that I have seen in school I have been able to do, except for ones that take knowledge, and after I do the reading, I have been able to do them, but sometimes I don't want to waste my time on easy homework. And also I'm crazy about sports. I think, unlike a lot of people, that the world still has hope . . . Most people that I know I like, and I have the good life, pretty much as good as any I have seen, and I am tall for my age.	myself. And I want to do something to help other people. (*Why is that?*) Well, because I think that this world has a lot of problems, and I think that everybody should try to help somebody else in some way, and the way I'm choosing is through science.

In the voice of the eleven-year-old boy, a familiar form of self-definition appears, resonating to the inscription of the young Stephen Daedalus in his geography book: "himself, his name and where he was," and echoing the descriptions that appear in *Our Town,* laying out across the coordinates of time and space a hierarchical order in which to define one's place. Describing himself as distinct by locating his particular position in the world, Jake sets himself apart from that world by his abilities, his beliefs, and his height. Although Amy also enumerates her likes, her wants, and her beliefs, she locates herself in relation to the world, describing herself through actions that bring her into connection with others, elaborating ties through her ability to provide help. To Jake's ideal of perfection, against which he measures the worth of himself, Amy counterposes an ideal of care, against which she measures the worth of her activity. While she places herself in relation to the world and chooses to help others through science, he places the world in relation to himself as it defines his character, his position, and the quality of his life.

The contrast between a self defined through separation and a self delineated through connection, between a self measured against an abstract ideal of perfection and a self assessed through particular activities of care, becomes clearer and the implications of this contrast extend by considering the different ways these children resolve a conflict between responsibility to others and responsibility to self. The question about responsibility followed a dilemma posed by a woman's conflict between her commitments to work and to family relationships. While the details of this conflict color the text of Amy's response, Jake abstracts the problem of responsibility from the context in which it appears, replacing the themes of intimate relationship with his own imagery of explosive connection:

Jake	Amy
(When responsibility to oneself and responsibility to others conflict, how should one choose?)	
You go about one-fourth to the others and three-fourths to yourself.	Well, it really depends on the situation. If you have a responsibility with somebody else, then you should keep it to a certain extent, but to the extent that it is really going to hurt you or stop you from doing something that you really, really want, then I think maybe you should put yourself first. But if it is your responsibility to somebody really close to you, you've just got to decide in that situation which is more important, yourself or that person, and like I said, it really depends on what kind of person you are and how you feel about the other person or persons involved.
(Why?)	
Because the most important thing in your decision should be yourself, don't let yourself be guided totally by other people, but you have to take them into consideration. So, if what you want to do is blow yourself up with an atom bomb, you should maybe blow yourself up with a	Well, like some people put themselves and things for themselves before they put other people, and some people really care about other people. Like, I don't think your job is as important as somebody that you really love, like your husband or your parents or a very close friend. Somebody that you really care for—or if it's just your

Jake	Amy
hand grenade because you are thinking about your neighbors who would die also.	responsibility to your job or somebody that you barely know, then maybe you go first—but if it's somebody that you really love and love as much or even more than you love yourself, you've got to decide what you really love more, that person, or that thing, or yourself. (*And how do you do that?*) Well, you've got to think about it, and you've got to think about both sides, and you've got to think which would be better for everybody or better for yourself, which is more important, and which will make everybody happier. Like if the other people can get somebody else to do it, whatever it is, or don't really need you specifically, maybe it's better to do what you want, because the other people will be just fine with somebody else so they'll still be happy, and then you'll be happy too because you'll do what you want.

(What does responsibility mean?)

It means pretty much thinking of others when I do something and like if I want to throw a rock, not throwing it at a window, because I thought of the people who would have to pay for that window, not doing it just for yourself, because you have to live with other people and live with your community, and if you do something that hurts them all, a lot of people will end up suffering, and that is sort of the wrong thing to do.	That other people are counting on you to do something. And you can't just decide, "Well, I'd rather do this or that." (*Are there other kinds of responsibility?*) Well, to yourself. If something looks really fun but you might hurt yourself doing it because you don't really know how to do it and your friends say, "Well, come on, you can do it, don't worry," if you're really scared to do it, it's your responsibility to yourself that you think you might hurt your self, you shouldn't do it, because you have to take care of yourself and that's your responsibility to yourself.

Again Jake constructs the dilemma as a mathematical equation, deriving a formula that guides the solution: one-fourth to others, three-fourths to yourself. Beginning with his responsibility to himself, a responsibility that he takes for granted, he then considers the extent to which he is responsible to others as well. Proceeding from a premise of separation but recognizing that "you have to live with other people," he seeks rules to limit interference and thus to minimize hurt. Responsibility in his construction pertains to a limitation of action, a restraint of aggression, guided by the recognition that his actions can have effects on others, just as theirs can interfere with him. Thus rules, by limiting interference, make life in community safe, protecting autonomy through reciprocity, extending the same consideration to others and self.

To the question about conflicting responsibilities, Amy again responds contextually rather than categorically, saying "it depends" and indicating how choice would be affected by variations in character and circumstance. Proceeding from a premise of connection, that "if you have a responsibility with somebody else, you should keep it," she then considers the extent to which she has a responsibility to herself. Exploring the parameters of separation, she imagines situations where, by doing what you want, you would avoid hurting yourself or where, in doing so, you would not thereby diminish the happiness of others. To her, responsibility signifies response, an extension rather than a limitation of action. Thus it connotes an act of care rather than the restraint of aggression. Again seeking the solution that would be most inclusive of everyone's needs, she strives to resolve the dilemma in a way that "will make everybody happier." Since Jake is concerned with limiting interference, while Amy focuses on the need for response, for him the limiting condition is, "Don't let yourself be guided totally by others," but for her it arises when "other people are counting on you," in which case "you can't just decide, 'Well, I'd rather do this or that.'" The interplay between these responses is clear in that she, assuming connection, begins to explore the parameters of separation, while he, assuming separation, begins to explore the parameters of connection. But the primacy of separation or connection leads to different images of self and of relationships.

Most striking among these differences is the imagery of violence in the boy's response, depicting a world of dangerous confrontation and explosive connection, where she sees a world of care and protection, a life lived with others whom "you may love as much or even more than you love yourself." Since the conception of morality reflects the understanding of social relationships, this difference in the imagery of relationships gives rise to a change in the moral injunction itself. To Jake, responsibility means not doing what he wants because he is thinking of others; to Amy, it means doing what others are counting on her to do regardless of what she herself wants. Both children are concerned with avoiding hurt but construe the problem in different ways—he seeing hurt to arise from the expression of aggression, she from a failure of response.

Questions for Reflection

Look back at the letters and readings in **Part III, What Role Does Maturation Play in Learning?** Consider the following questions as you begin formulating your own ideas about how to apply theories of learning and development into planned instructional practice.

1. What do you think about the idea that development occurs in continuous stages? Is it possible that development occurs in some way other than in stages? Are recent pressures to introduce complex ideas and skills to increasingly younger and younger children consistent with what you have read regarding student readiness? For what kinds of students might content standards or grade level expectations be inappropriate?

2. What connections do you see between Kohlberg's theory of moral development and Piaget's theory of cognitive development? Does one need to be in Piaget's formal operations stage to solve a moral dilemma? How do Erikson's ideas about psychosocial development relate to Gilligan's ideas about moral development? How would you respond to a teacher in your building who says, "Teaching is about learning skills and acquiring content knowledge. Paying attention to what you *think* is going on with them emotionally is a waste of time"?

3. Gilligan suggests that boys use a justice orientation, whereas girls use an ethic of care orientation when solving moral problems. If psychosocial development were to differ by gender, how might girls differ from boys in their social-emotional development?

4. Cite examples of instructional activities that support each of the developmental theories you read about in this chapter.

❖ YOUR OWN IDEAS

What ideas seem most important to you as you reflect about teaching and learning in real classrooms? What do you think is most important for new teachers to consider? What further questions did the authors raise for you in Part III that have not been adequately answered?

_____

_____

_____

_____

_____

_____

_____

_____

_____

_____

_____

_____

_____

_____

Suggested Readings

American Association of University Women. (1991). *Shortchanging girls, shortchanging America.* Washington, DC: Author.

Arnold, M. L. (2000). Stage, sequence, and sequels: Changing conceptions of morality, post-Kohlberg. *Educational Psychology Review, 12,* 365–383.

DeVries, R., & Zan, B. (1994). *Moral classrooms, moral children: Creating a constructivist atmosphere in early education.* New York: Teachers College Press.

Erikson, E. (1968). *Identity, youth, and crisis.* New York: Norton.

Gilligan, C., & Attanucci, J. (1988). Two moral orientations: Gender differences and similarities. *Merrill-Palmer Quarterly, 34,* 223–237.

Kohlberg, L. (1975). The cognitive-developmental approach to moral education. *Phi Delta Kappan, 56,* 670–677.

Kohlberg, L. (1984). *Essays on moral development.* San Francisco: Harper & Row.

Likona, T. (1991). *Educating for character: How our schools can teach respect and responsibility.* New York: Bantam.

Piaget, J. (1954). *The construction of reality in the child.* New York: Basic Books.

PART IV

How Should
Student Diversity
Affect Teaching Practice?

13

Dear Dr. Marlowe:

As a young child I grew up in one of Rhode Island's five core cities, Providence. I guess it's not a surprise that after I got my degree in education that I ended up back there in the city that raised me. It's my way of giving back to my hometown. Right now, I'm teaching a first-grade classroom in one of the schools in Providence's old southside. I grew up on the southside of Providence and I feel that I can connect with the students here because of this. Growing up, I came from the same socio-economic status that most of them come from. I know what it is like as a child to come from a one-parent family and be on public assistance. My primary goal in the Providence public school system is to act as an example to my students. I want to show them that you can make something out of nothing. You can obtain success even if you do not come from a successful background. Your background does not decide who you will become, you do. My mission is to not only educate them about academics, it is also to educate them about life.

I've been struggling with a question about how to help them succeed in school and life though. So many kids here speak English as a second language and a lot of the kids don't speak proper English, even though it is their first language. Should I try to change how they speak in my class?

Candice McLean

❖ HOW WOULD YOU RESPOND?

How should teachers respond to students who do not speak Standard English? And what about English-language learners? Should teachers meet students where they are? What is the proper role of a teacher when he or she hears non-Standard or rudimentary English skills in the classroom? How does constant correction affect students who have not mastered Standard English? Should all students in American schools learn Standard English? When is Ebonics okay? What do you think of the decision made in many states, including Massachusetts and California, to outlaw bilingual education?

Think about the letter from Candice McLean. What teacher behaviors likely contributed to her success? What does she hold dear that will likely help her future students? Why is it that students of color, and those in poverty, are more likely to face teachers with authoritarian approaches to instruction? What do you think? Why is it that school districts with higher rates of poverty invariably identify more students as eligible for special education? Should English-language learners be identified as students in need of special education?

❖ ENGLISH ONLY: THE TONGUE-TYING OF AMERICA

Donaldo Macedo

During the past decade conservative educators such as ex-secretary of education William Bennett and Diane Ravitch have mounted an unrelenting attack on bilingual and multicultural education. These conservative educators tend to recycle old assumptions about the "melting pot theory" and our "common culture," assumptions designed primarily to maintain the status quo. Maintained is a status quo that functions as a cultural reproduction mechanism which systematically does not allow other cultural subjects, who are considered outside of the mainstream, to be present in history. These cultural subjects who are profiled as the "other" are but palely represented in history within our purportedly democratic society in the form of Black History Month, Puerto Rican Day, and so forth. This historical constriction was elegantly captured by an 11th-grade Vietnamese student in California:

> I was so excited when my history teacher talked about the Vietnam War. Now at last, I thought, now we will study about my country. We didn't really study it. Just for one day, though, my country was real again. (Olsen, 1988, p. 68)

The incessant attack on bilingual education which claims that it serves to tongue-tie students in their native language not only negates the multilingual and multicultural nature of U.S. society, but blindly ignores the empirical evidence that has been amply documented in support of bilingual education . . . [T]he present overdose of monolingualism and Anglocentrism that dominates the current educational debate not only contributes to a type of mind-tied America, but also is incapable of producing educators and leaders who can rethink what it means to prepare students to enter the ever-changing, multilingual, and multicultural world of the 21st century.

It is both academically dishonest and misleading to simply point to some failures of bilingual education without examining the lack of success of linguistic minority students within a larger context of a general failure of public education in major urban centers. Furthermore, the English Only position points to a pedagogy of exclusion that views the learning of English as education itself. English Only advocates fail to question under what conditions English will be taught and by whom. For example, immersing non-English-speaking students in English as a Second Language [ESL] programs taught by untrained music, art and social science teachers (as is the case in Massachusetts with the grandfather clause in ESL certification) will hardly accomplish the avowed goals of the English Only Movement. The proponents of English Only also fail to raise two other fundamental question. First, if English is the most effective educational language, how can we explain that over 60 million Americans are illiterate or functionally illiterate (Kozol, 1982, p. 4)? Second, if education solely in English can guarantee linguistic minorities a better future, as educators like William Bennett promise, why do the majority of Black Americans, whose ancestors have been speaking English for over 200 years, find themselves still relegated to ghettos?

I want to argue in this paper that the answer lies not in technical questions of whether English is a more viable language of instruction or the repetitive promise that it offers non-English-speaking students "full participation first in their school and later in American society" (Silber, 1991, p. 7). This position assumes that English is in fact a superior language and that we live in a classless, race-blind society. I want to propose that decisions about how to educate non-English-speaking students cannot be in a full understanding of the ideological elements that generate and sustain linguistic, racial, and sex discrimination. That is, educators need to develop, as Henry Giroux has suggested, "a politics and pedagogy around a new language capable of acknowledging the multiple, contradictory, and complex subject positions people occupy within different social, cultural, and economic locations" (1992, p. 27). By shifting the linguistic issue to an ideological terrain we will challenge conservative educators to confront the Berlin Wall of racism, classism, and economic deprivation which characterizes the lives experiences of minorities in U.S. public schools. For example, J. Anthony Lukas succinctly captures the ideological elements that promote racism and segregation in schools in his analysis of desegregation in the Boston Public Schools. Lukas cites a trip to Charlestown High School, where a group of Black parents experienced firsthand the stark reality their children were destined to endure. Although the headmaster assured them that "violence, intimidation, or racial slurs would not be tolerated," they could not avoid the racial epithets on the walls: "Welcome Niggers," "Niggers Suck," "White Power," "KKK," "Bus is for Zulu," and "Be illiterate, fight busing." As those parents were boarding the bus, "they were met with jeers and catcalls 'go home niggers. Keep going all the way to Africa!'" This racial intolerance led one parent to reflect, "My god, what kind of hell am I sending my children into?" (Lukas, 1985, p. 282). What could her children learn at a school like that except to hate? Even though forced integration of schools in Boston exacerbated the racial tension in the Boston Public Schools, one should not overlook the deep-seeded racism that permeates all levels of the school structure. . . .

Against this landscape of violent racism perpetrated again racial minorities, and also against linguistic minorities, one can understand the reasons for the high dropout rate in the Boston public schools (approximately 50%). Perhaps racism and other ideological elements are part of a school reality which forces a high percentage of students to leave school, only later to be profiled by the very system as dropouts or "poor and unmotivated students." One could argue that the above incidents occurred during a tumultuous time of racial division in Boston's history, but I do not believe that we have learned a great deal from historically dangerous memories to the degree that our leaders continue to invite racial tensions as evidenced in the Willie Horton presidential campaign issue and the present quota for jobs as an invitation once again to racial divisiveness.

It is very curious that this new-found concern of English Only advocates for limited English proficiency students does not interrogate those very ideological elements that psychologically and emotionally harm these students far more than the mere fact that English may present itself as a temporary barrier to an effective education. It would be more socially constructive and beneficial if the zeal that propels the English Only movement were diverted toward social struggles designed to end violent racism and structures of poverty, homelessness, and family breakdown, among other social ills that characterize the lived experiences of minorities in the United States. If these social issues are not dealt with appropriately, it is naïve to think that the acquisition of the English language alone will, somehow, magically eclipse the raw and cruel injustices and oppression perpetrated against the dispossessed class of minorities in the United States. According to Peter McLaren, these dispossessed minority students who

> populate urban settings in places such as Howard Beach, Ozone Park, El Barrio, are more likely to be forced to learn about Eastern Europe in ways set forth by neo-conservative multiculturalists than they are to learn about the Harlem Renaissance, Mexico, Africa, the Caribbean, or Aztec or Zulu culture. (McLaren, 1991, p. 7)

While arguing for the use of the students' native language in their educational development, I would like to make it very clear that the bilingual education goal should never be to restrict students to their own vernacular. This linguistic constriction inevitably leads to a linguistic ghetto. Educators must understand fully the broader meaning of the use of students' language as a requisite for their empowerment. That is, empowerment should never be limited to what Stanley Aronowitz describes as "the process of appreciating and loving oneself" (1985). In addition to this process, empowerment should also be a means that enables students "to interrogate and selectively appropriate those aspects of the dominant culture that will provide them with the basis for defining and transforming, rather than merely serving, the wider social order" (Giroux & McLaren, 1986, p. 17). This means that educators should understand the value of mastering the standard English language that linguistic minority students find themselves linguistically empowered to engage in dialogue with various sectors of the wider society. What I must reiterate is that educators should never allow the limited proficient students' native language to be silenced by a distorted legitimation of the standard English language. Linguistic minority students' language should never be sacrificed, since it is the only means through which they make sense of their own experience in the world.

Given the importance of the standard English language in the education of linguistic minority students, I must agree with the members of the Institute for Research in English Acquisition and Development when they quote Antonio Gramsci in their brochure:

> Without the mastery of the common standard version of the national language, one is inevitably destined to function only at

the periphery of national life and, especially, outside the national and political mainstream. (READ, 1990)

But these English Only advocates fail to tell the other side of Antonio Gramsci's argument, which warns us:

> Each time that in one way or another, the question of language comes to the fore, that signifies that a series of other problems is about to emerge, the formation and enlarging of the ruling class, the necessity to establish more "intimate" and sure relations between the ruling groups and the popular masses, that is, the reorganization of cultural hegemony. (Gramsci, 1971, p. 16)

This selective selection of Gramsci's position on language points to the hidden curriculum with which the English Only movement seeks to promote a monolithic ideology. It is also part and parcel of an ongoing attempt at "reorganization of cultural hegemony" as evidenced by the unrelenting attack by conservative educators on multicultural education and curriculum diversity. . . .

In contrast to the zeal for a common culture and English only, these conservative educators have remained ominously silent about forms of racism, inequality, subjugation, and exploitation that daily serve to wage symbolic and real violence against those children who by virtue of their language, race, ethnicity, class, or gender are not treated in schools with the dignity and respect all children warrant in a democracy. Instead of reconstituting education around an urban and cultural studies approach which takes the social, cultural, political and economic divisions of education and everyday life as the primary categories for understanding contemporary schooling, conservative educators have recoiled in an attempt to salvage the status quo. That is, they try to keep the present unchanged even through, as Renato Constantino points out:

> Within the living present there are imperceptible changes which make the status quo a moving reality . . . Thus a new policy based on the present as past and not on the present as future is backward for it is premised not on evolving conditions that are already dying away. (1978, p. 201)

One such not so imperceptible change is the rapid growth of minority representation in the labor force. As such, the conservative leaders and educators are digging this county's economic grave by their continued failure to educate minorities. As Lew Ferleger and Jay Mandle convincingly argue, "Unless the educational attainment of minority populations in the United States improves, the country's hopes for resuming high rates of growth and an increasing standard of living look increasingly dubious" (1991, p. 12).

In addition to the real threat to the economic fabric of the United States, the persistent call for English language only in education smacks of backwardness in the present conjuncture of our ever-changing multicultural and multilingual society. Furthermore, these conservative educators base their language policy argument on the premise that English education in this country is highly effective. On the contrary, as Patrick Courts clearly argues in his book *Literacy for Empowerment* (1991), English education is failing even middle-class and upper-class students. He argues that English reading and writing classes are mostly based on workbooks and grammar lessons, lessons which force students to "bark at print" or fill in the blanks. Students engage in grudgingly banal exercises such as practicing correct punctuation and writing sample business letters. Books used in their classes are, Courts points out, too often in the service of commercially prepared ditto sheets and workbooks. Court's account suggests that most school programs do not take advantage of the language experiences that the majority of students have had before they reach school. These teachers become the victims of their own professional ideology when they delegitimize the language experiences that students bring with them into the classroom

Courts's study is basically concerned with middle-class and upper-middle-class students unburdened by racial discrimination and poverty, students who have done well in elementary and high school settings and are now populating the university lecture halls and seminar rooms. If schools are failing these students, the situation does not bode well for those students less economically, socially, and politically advantaged. It is toward the linguistic minority students that I would like to turn my discussion now.

The Role of Language in the
Education of Linguistic Minority Students

Within the last two decades, the issue of bilingual education has taken on a heated importance among educators. Unfortunately, the debate that has emerged tends to recycle old assumptions and values regarding the meaning and usefulness of the students' native language in education. The notion that education of linguistic minority students is a matter of learning the standard English language still informs the vast majority of bilingual programs and manifests its logic in the renewed emphasis on technical reading and writing skills.

I want to reiterate in this paper that the education of linguistic minority students cannot be viewed as simply the development of skills aimed at acquiring the standard English language. English Only proponents seldom discuss the pedagogical structures that will enable these students to access other bodies of knowledge. Nor do they interrogate the quality of ESL instruction provided to the linguistic minority students and the adverse material conditions under which these students learn English. The view that teaching English constitutes education sustains a notion of ideology that systematically negates rather than makes meaningful the cultural experiences of the subordinate linguistic groups who are, by and large, the objects of its policies. For the education of linguistic minority students to become meaningful it has to be situated within a theory of cultural production and viewed as an integral part of the way in which people produce, transform, and reproduce meaning. Bilingual education, in this sense, must be seen as a medium that constitutes and affirms the historical and existential moments of lived culture. Hence, it is an eminently political phenomenon, and it must be analyzed within the context of a theory of power relations and an understanding of social and cultural reproduction and production. By "cultural reproduction" I refer to collective experiences that function in the interest of the dominant groups rather than in the interest of the oppressed groups that are objects of its policies. Bilingual education programs in the United States have been developed and implemented under the cultural reproduction model leading to a de facto neocolonial educational model. I use "cultural production" to refer to specific groups of people producing, mediating, and confirming the mutual ideological elements that merge from and reaffirm their daily lived experiences. In this case, such experiences are rooted in the interest of individual and collective self-determination. It is only through a cultural production model that we can achieve a truly democratic and liberatory educational experience. I will return to this issue later.

While the various debates in the past two decades may differ in their basic assumptions about the education of linguistic minority students, they all share one common feature: they all ignore the role of language as a major force in the construction of human subjectivities. That is, they ignore the way language may either confirm or deny the life histories and experiences of the people who use it.

The pedagogical and political implications in education programs for linguistic minority students are far-reaching and yet largely ignored. These programs, for example, often contradict a fundamental principle of reading, namely that students learn to read faster and with better comprehension when taught in their native tongue. The immediate recognition of familiar words and experiences enhances the development of a positive self-concept in children who are somewhat insecure about the status of their language and culture. For this reason, and to be consistent with the plan to construct a democratic society free from vestiges of oppression, a minority literacy program must be rooted in the cultural capital of subordinate groups and have as its point of departure their own language.

Educators must develop radical pedagogical structures which provide students with the opportunity to use their own reality as a basis of literacy. This includes, obviously, the language they bring to the classroom. To do otherwise is to deny minority students the rights that lie at the core of a democratic education. The failure to base a literacy program on the minority students' language means that oppositional forces can neutralize the efforts of educators and political leaders to achieve decolonization of schooling. It is of tantamount importance that the incorporation of the minority language as the primary language of instruction in education of linguistic minority students be given top priority. It is through their own language that linguistic minority students will be able to reconstruct their history and their culture.

I want to argue that the minority language has to be understood within the theoretical framework that generates it. Put another way, the ultimate meaning and value of the minority language is not to be found by determining how systematic and rule-governed it is. We know that already. Its real meaning has to be understood through the assumptions that govern it, and it has to be understood via the social, political, and ideological relations to which it points. Generally speaking, this issue of effectiveness and validity often hides the true role of language in the maintenance of the values and interests of the dominant class. In other words, the issue of effectiveness and validity becomes a mask that obfuscates questions about the social, political, and ideological order within which the minority language exists.

If an emancipatory and critical education program is to be developed in the United States for linguistic minority students in which they become "subjects" rather than "objects," educators must understand the productive quality of language. James Donald puts it this way:

I take language to be productive rather than reflective of social reality. This means calling into question the assumption that we, as speaking subjects, simply use language to organize and express our ideas and experiences. On the contrary, language is one of the most important social practices through which we come to experience ourselves as subjects . . . My point here is that once we get beyond the idea of language as not more than a medium of communication, as a tool equally and neutrally available to all parties in cultural exchanges, then we can begin to examine language both as a practice of signification and also as a site for culture struggle and as a mechanism which produces antagonistic relations between different social groups. (Donald, 1982, p. 44)

It is to the antagonistic relationship between the minority and dominant speakers that I want to turn now. The antagonistic nature of the minority language has never been fully explored. In order to more clearly discuss the issue of antagonism, I will use Donald's distinction between oppressed language and repressed language. Using Donald's categories, the "negative" way of posting the minority language question is to view it in terms of oppression—that is, seeing the minority language as "lacking" the dominant standard features which usually serve as a point of reference for the minority language. By far the most common questions concerning the minority language in the United States are posed from the oppression perspective. The alternative view of the minority language is that it is repressed in the standard dominant language. In this view, minority language as a repressed language could, if spoken, challenge the privileged standard linguistic dominance. Educators have failed to recognize the "positive" promise and antagonistic nature of the minority language. It is precisely on these dimensions that educators must demystify the standard dominant language and the old assumptions about its inherent superiority. Educators must develop liberatory and critical bilingual programs informed by a radical pedagogy so that the minority language will cease to provide the speakers the experience of subordination and, moreover, may be brandished as a weapon of resistance to the dominance of the dominant standard language of the curriculum.

In this sense, the students' language is the only means by which they can develop their own voice, a prerequisite to the development of a positive sense of self-worth. As Giroux elegantly states, the students' voice "is the discursive means to makes themselves 'heard' and to define themselves as active authors of their worlds" (Giroux & McLaren, 1986,

p. 235). The authorship of one's own world also implies the use of one's own language, and relates to what Mikhail Bakhtin describes as "retelling a story in one's own words" (Giroux & McLaren, 1986, p. 235).

A Democratic and Liberatory
Education for Linguistic Minority Students

In maintaining a certain coherence with the educational plan to reconstruct new and more democratic educational programs for linguistic minority students, educators and political leaders need to create a new school grounded in a new educational praxis, expressing different concepts of education consonant with the principles of a democratic, multicultural, and multilingual society. In order for this to happen, the first step is to identify the objectives of the inherent colonial education that informs the majority of bilingual programs in the United States. Next, it is necessary to analyze how colonialist methods used by the dominant schools function, legitimize the Anglocentric values and meaning, and at the same time negate the history, culture, and language practices of the majority of linguistic minority students. The new school, so it is argued, must also be informed by a radical bilingual pedagogy, which would make concrete such values as solidarity, social responsibility, and creativity. In the democratic development of bilingual programs rooted in a liberatory ideology, linguistic minority students become "subjects" rather than mere "objects" to be assimilated blindly into an often hostile dominant "common" culture. A democratic and liberatory education needs to move away from traditional approaches, which emphasize the acquisition of mechanical basic skills while divorcing education from its ideological and historical contexts. In attempting to meet this goal, it purposely must reject the conservative principles embedded in the English Only movement I have discussed earlier. Unfortunately, many bilingual programs sometimes unknowingly reproduce one common feature of the traditional approaches to education by ignoring the important relationship between language and the cultural capital of the students at whom bilingual education is aimed. The result is the development of bilingual programs whose basic assumptions are at odds with the democratic spirit that launched them.

Bilingual program development must be largely based on the notion of a democratic and liberatory education, in which education is viewed "as one of the major vehicles by which 'oppressed' people are able to participate in the sociohistorical transformation of their society" (Walmsley, 1981, p. 74). Bilingual education, in this sense, is grounded in a critical reflection of the cultural capital of the oppressed. It becomes a vehicle by which linguistic minority students are equipped with the necessary tools to reappropriate their history, culture, and language practices. It is, thus, a way to enable the linguistic minority students to reclaim "those historical and existential experiences that are devalued in everyday life by the dominant culture in order to be both validated and critically understood" (Giroux, 1983, p. 226). To do otherwise is to deny these students their very democratic rights. In fact, the criticism that bilingual and multicultural education unwisely question the traditions and values of our so-called "common culture" as suggested by Kenneth T. Jackson (1991) is both antidemocratic and academically dishonest. Multicultural education and curriculum diversity did not create the S & L scandal, the Iran-Contra debacle, or the extortion of minority properties by banks, the stewards of the "common culture," who charged minorities exorbitant loan-sharking interest rates. Multicultural education and curriculum diversity did not force Joachim Maitre, dean of the College of Communication at Boston University, to choose the hypocritical moral high ground to excoriate the popular culture's "bleak moral content," all the while plagiarizing 15 paragraphs of a conservative comrade's text.

The learning of English language skills alone will not enable linguistic minority students to acquire the critical tools "to awaken and liberate them from their mystified and distorted views of themselves and their world" (Giroux, 1983, p. 226). For example, speaking English has not enabled African-Americans to change this society's practice of jailing more Blacks than even South Africa, and this society spending over 7 billion dollars to keep African-American men in jail while spending only 1 billion dollars educating Black males (Black, 1991).

Educators must understand the all-encompassing role the dominant ideology has played in this mystification and distortion of our so-called "common culture" and our "common language." They must also recognize the antagonistic relationship between the "common culture" and those who, by virtue of their race, language, ethnicity, and gender, have been relegated to the margins. Finally, educators must develop bilingual programs based on the theory of cultural production. In other words, linguistic minority students must be provided the opportunity to become actors in the reconstruction of a more democratic and just society. In short, education conducted in English only is alienating to linguistic minority students, since it denies them the fundamental tools for reflection, critical thinking, and social interaction. Without the cultivation of their native language, and robbed of the opportunity for reflection and critical thinking, linguistic minority students find themselves unable to re-create their culture and history. Without the reappropriation of their culture, the valorization of their lived experiences, English Only supporters' vacuous promise that the English language will guarantee students "full participation first in their school and later in American society" (Silber, 1991, p. 7) can hardly be a reality.

References

Aronowitz, S. (1985, May). "Why should Johnny read." *Village Voice Literary Supplement,* p. 13.

Black, C. (1991, January 13). Paying the high price for being the world's no. 1 jailor. *Boston Sunday Globe,* p. 67.

Constantino, R. (1928). *Neocolonial identity and counter consciousness.* London: Merlin Press.

Courts, P. (1991). *Literacy for empowerment.* South Hadley, MA: Bergin & Garvey.

Donald, J. (1982). Language, literacy, and schooling. In *The state and popular culture.* Milton Keynes: Open University Culture Unit.

Ferlerger, L., & Mandle, J. (1991). *African-Americans and the future of the U.S. economy.* Unpublished manuscript.

Giroux, H. A. (1983). *Theory and resistance: A pedagogy for the opposition.* South Hadley, MA: Bergin & Garvey.

Giroux, H. (1991). *Border crossings: Cultural workers and the politics of education.* New York: Routledge.

Giroux, H. A., & McLaren, P. (1986). Teacher education and the politics of engagement: The case for democratic schooling. *Harvard Educational Review, 56*(3), 213–238.

Gramsci, A. (1971). *Selections from Prison Notebooks,* (Ed. and Trans. Quinten Hoare & Geoffrey Smith). New York: International Publishers.

Jackson, D. (1991, December 8). The end of the second Reconstruction. *Boston Globe,* p. 27.

Jackson, K. T. (1991, July 7). Cited in a *Boston Sunday Globe* editorial.

Kozol, J. (1985). *Illiterate America.* New York: Doubleday Anchor.

Lukas, J. A. (1985). *Common ground.* New York: Alfred A. Knopf.

McLaren, P. (1991). Critical pedagogy: Constructing an arch of social dreaming and a doorway to hope. *Journal of Education, 173*(1), 9–34.

Olsen, L. (1988). *Crossing the schoolhouse border: Immigrant students and the California public schools.* San Francisco: California Tomorrow.

Silber, J. (1991, May). *Boston University Commencement Catalogue.*

Walmsley, S. (1991). On the purpose and content of secondary reading programs: Educational and ideological perspectives. *Curriculum Inquiry, 11,* 73–79.

14

Dear Professor Canestrari:

Just wanted to drop you a line. As you know, I have relocated to Arizona. I was interviewed for a sixth-grade position over the telephone 8 weeks ago. It went so well that they flew me out for a face-to-face interview with the board. Well, I just completed my first week.

Now to the fun stuff. I teach one math, one language arts, and three science classes. I had all of one day of training and transitioning and the following day was orientation. What was I thinking?

I wasn't given a classroom until 2 pm on Tuesday, the parent and student orientation was scheduled for 5 to 7 pm. I had to go to a teaching store (an hour away), buy stuff to decorate, and have my room looking like a classroom in 3 hours. By the way, I didn't have desks or chairs yet. Somehow I did it. I'm an East Coast guy (that's how the principal refers to me).

I received my roster at 4:45 (so I had an excellent chance to prep). Parents started to arrive at 5. What a nightmare. First, half of the parents spoke zero English. Students with severe disabilities were not assigned yet, so the parents were told they would be in regular ed classrooms. They didn't respond well to this (the parents that is). I had the mother of a severely autistic girl tell me that her daughter has always been in Special Ed or with an aide and that she was unable to perform in a regular ed classroom. She was yelling at me as if I had placed her in my classroom. Her child was petrified of me and hid under a desk. I think I was more scared than anyone. I calmed the parent and told her that everything would be in order by start of school the following day. What a liar. What was I to do? I didn't want to get yelled at anymore and I didn't want anyone to know I had absolutely no idea what was going on here. So I kept smiling and reassuring . . . reassuring everyone but myself.

When the orientation was over, I realized I had one autistic child, two mildly mentally retarded children, and one blind child . . . oh yeah, and no Special Ed department and no classroom aide to my knowledge. Things were looking promising. Also, I was told that the classroom size would be approximately 27 students. Try 33 and growing.

Michael Parrillo

❖ HOW WOULD YOU RESPOND?

School districts all over the nation are moving toward full-inclusion classrooms. Change to a full-inclusion model can be problematic. Are all districts ready for the transition? What is the rationale for full inclusion? Has the school district developed a culture of inclusion prior to its implementation? How will the district provide for transition to a full-inclusion model? As you read "Can Inclusion Work? A Conversation With Jim Kauffman and Mara Sapon-Shevin," think about how you might respond to Michael Parrillo.

❖ CAN INCLUSION WORK? A CONVERSATION WITH JIM KAUFFMAN AND MARA SAPON-SHEVIN

John O'Neil

To what extent should schools provide services to students with disabilities in regular classrooms? Jim Kauffman and Mara Sapon-Shevin debate the potential and pitfalls of trying to make schools more inclusive.

Mara, you're a supporter of more inclusive schools. How do you define inclusion, and what's your rationale for wanting schools to be more inclusive?

Sapon-Shevin: The vision of inclusion is that all children would be served in their neighborhood schools, in the "regular classroom" with children their own age. The idea is that these schools would be restructured so that they are supportive, nurturing communities that really meet the needs of all the children within them: rich in resources and support for both students and teachers.

As far as a rationale, we should not have to defend inclusion—we should make others defend exclusion. There's very little evidence that some children need segregated settings in which to be educated. At another level, we know that the world is an inclusive community. There are lots of people in it who vary, not only in terms of disabilities, but in race, class, gender, and religious background. It's very important for children to have the opportunity to learn and grow within communities that represent the kind of world they'll live in when they finish school. So we should begin with the assumptions that all children are included and that we must meet their needs within an inclusive setting.

Jim, some critics say that special education has emerged as the place to put kids who "don't fit" in traditional classrooms. Would you agree that many schools are too quick to remove children from regular classrooms? And if so, then why not seek ways to meet their special needs in regular classrooms?

Kauffman: A lot of schools do move too quickly to remove kids from a regular classroom. But many others are too reluctant to consider alternatives to the regular class. I'm convinced that we must maintain the alternative of moving kids to other places when that appears necessary in the judgment of teachers and parents.

Educators have to defend every placement decision, inclusive or otherwise. Sure, we ought to meet special needs in a regular class when that's possible. But there isn't anything wrong with meeting special needs outside the regular class if that is required. In fact, the law and best practice say we must consider both possibilities.

Mara, Jim supports the idea of maintaining a continuum of possible placements, ranging from a regular classroom to a special separate school. Do you agree?

Sapon-Shevin: Clearly, what we need is a continuum of services, but that's not the same as a continuum of placements. To deny children with special needs some type of service, whether it's speech therapy, physical therapy, occupational therapy, or something else, is not what inclusion's about. Inclusion is saying: How can we meet children's individual educational needs within the regular classroom context— the community of students—without segregating them?

The problem with maintaining this "continuum of placements" is that it keeps districts from making the far-reaching changes they need to make. They continue to try to fix special education or make this dual system of regular and special education work better.

In many places, special education has become a kind of safety valve that allows schools to keep doing business as usual—labeling, sorting, and segregating students. You can see that when you look at different schools. While one school is able to teach large numbers of students with disabilities in regular classrooms, others refer every other child to special education.

How do you respond to that, Jim? It does appear that some schools manage to serve all kids in regular classrooms, while others almost reflexively place students elsewhere.

Kauffman: I agree that there are differences in the capacity of schools and teachers to deal with differences. But we don't have research showing that all students can be taught well in regular classrooms and regular schools. Reflexive placement decisions are bad practice and illegal, whether the reflex is to place children in regular classrooms or elsewhere.

Trying to force everybody into the inclusion mold promises to be just as coercive as trying to force everybody into the mold of special class or institution. There are wide differences in children's needs and the kinds of environments that can address those differences. Inclusion is going to be great for some kids, and some parents will love it. The opposite is also true. I believe in giving options to parents and kids. A continuum of placement options is sensible; it's also the law.

Much of the support for special education in the first place came from parents and advocates for disabled students. Are they sold on inclusion?

Kauffman: Some are, but certainly not all. If you talk to parents of kids with disabilities, there are wide differences in the kind of school or the kind of place that they want their child to attend. Quite a number of parents want their child in a special class or in a special school. Many parents fought for that option, and many parents will fight for it again.

Mara, what would you say to parents who argued strongly for their child to be in a special class or a special school? Should their choice take precedence?

Sapon-Shevin: I would want to sit down with those parents to find out, very carefully, about their hopes for that child. But I have never, ever met a parent of a child with disabilities who did not hope that that child would someday have friends and connections with the broader community—not just with the community of other children with autism, for example, or the community of other people who are blind.

Some parents and advocates for children with disabilities have strenuously objected to the move toward inclusion because they see it as a way for districts to cut costs and to reduce services to their children. Don't they have good reason to worry that inclusion is not being done to help their kids, but is being done in the name of convenience or cutting costs?

Sapon-Shevin: Do they have reason to worry? Absolutely. Inclusion without resources, without support, without teacher preparation time, without commitment, without a vision statement, without restructuring, without staff development, won't work. This leads some people to say we shouldn't do it. My conclusion is that, knowing all that we know about what it takes to make it happen right, we'd better do it right.

There are children who are dumped into classrooms in the name of inclusion, when in fact, nothing is in place to make that an inclusive classroom except that they've put a child with significant disabilities into it. That's not a problem about inclusion; it's irresponsible planning, irresponsible fiscal management, irresponsible teaching. But to call that inclusion is a real mistake.

Inclusion is much bigger than special education, much bigger than individual classrooms; it's even much bigger than the school. Inclusion really calls for a fundamental restructuring of the school districts and the schools. It means changes in the curriculum, changes of pedagogy, in staff allocation, teacher education, and so on.

But, if I were a parent, telling me that schools need to be restructured for inclusion to work would worry me. All that restructuring will take a long time, but my child's in school this year. Isn't that a valid concern?

Sapon-Shevin: I've been an expert witness in quite a few lawsuits in which parents were suing districts because they wanted their child more fully included, and the districts were reluctant to do so. I think these parents were very realistic about what kinds of major restructuring may need to happen eventually and what kinds of changes need to happen right away.

In any case, the kinds of changes that parents who advocate inclusion want are changes that end up being beneficial for all children. I do not see situations in which an effort to do inclusion has in any way minimized or damaged efforts to make school programs more responsive. I see lots of examples of inclusion efforts improving education for all kids. A lot of the "best" practices that are now being advocated—authentic assessment, portfolios, an emphasis on critical thinking, collaborative planning, teamwork—they're all absolutely complementary and part and parcel of an inclusion program.

Jim, much of the support for inclusion seems to be coming from people who are dissatisfied with the outcomes of special education. Some people think that students with disabilities will benefit socially from being in regular classrooms, and they certainly wouldn't do any worse on educational outcomes. How do you respond to that?

Kauffman: Well, there are two points to consider. One is that some studies do show that students have performed better in pull-out programs than in the regular class. The other point is that it's far more important to improve instruction for kids in alternative settings than to try to get all kids into regular classes.

The fact is, we need different instruction for different kids, and you can't have all types of instruction happening in the same place at the same time. Some kids learn very well through an exploratory approach, for example, but others don't learn well this way. Direct instruction is going to produce much better outcomes for them. I think the literature is very clear on that. Some, like deaf kids, need special instruction that can't be provided in a regular class. Many kids with severe emotional or behavioral disorders need a more supportive environment than any regular classroom can possibly provide. Besides, research on inclusion shows that the results for many kids are disappointing. It is possible for kids to do worse, both academically and socially, in inclusive settings than in alternative placements.

Sapon-Shevin: When Jim says that there's research that shows that children in segregated classrooms do better than children in inclusive classrooms, you have to ask: Better at what? Better at spelling? Or better at making friends? Better at being part of the community? Better at being connected with other people? I'm not saying that one sacrifices academic knowledge by moving toward inclusion, but if you look at the differences in terms of children's social connections, children's friends, children's being part of a community, there is absolutely no way that a child in a segregated classroom can learn to be part of the broader community.

Kauffman: Well, let's talk some about the word segregation. Certainly racial segregation is a great evil, and segregation that is forced and universal and unrelated to legitimate educational purposes certainly is wrong. But when separate programs are freely chosen and placement decisions are made on a case-by-case basis—not forced, not universal— I think it's inappropriate to call that segregation.

If you ask kids, you'll find many who say that they want to be in a special school, or that they like their special class. I think we should listen to them. And, yes, some have better social experiences in special schools or classes.

Mara said earlier that the world is an inclusive place. That's not really true in many ways. We're not all included in the same place doing the same or parallel activities; we go to many different places for different purposes. We may go to different places of worship and different places of work, for example, but that doesn't exclude us from being part of other communities outside those places, and it doesn't demean us. We ought to celebrate a diversity of places where we learn and work and play and have friends.

Sapon-Shevin: I think it's a complete rewriting of history to say that special education placements have been freely chosen. If you look at the over-representation of children of color in special education classrooms, if you look at the vast numbers of children who are never given a choice of the inclusive placement, it's a real mistake to say that these parents or children are freely choosing to be segregated.

When children report that they would rather be in a segregated classroom, very often what they're telling you is that there is something about that regular classroom that isn't hospitable and accepting. Of course they want to exit that setting. But removing kids doesn't do anything to change the nature of that regular classroom setting to make it a more warm and welcoming community.

Mara, if a school or district were to move toward inclusion, what specifically would it need to do to make it work?

Sapon-Shevin: Again, we shouldn't think of choosing between special education services and regular classrooms as they currently look, but to rethink, restructure, and recreate a different kind of regular education classroom. These would be classrooms in which, for example, curriculum is flexible and appropriate for different levels and modalities. There would probably be things like thematic instruction, cooperative learning, authentic assessment—practices that are really encouraging, and foster individualized and cooperative learning activities.

But surely there are students with very profound disabilities who have different needs than just thematic learning, for example.

Sapon-Shevin: That's true, but there are ways of addressing those needs. For example, aides are often assigned to help children who need additional kinds of supports. Some people are finding that it's much more helpful to think of that aide as someone who also supports the entire classroom. We need to move away from the kind of isolation where we have one teacher who is in charge of 30 kids. Instead, we need to say: How do we arrange classrooms where there may be two or three adults who share responsibility and expertise and collaborate to meet the needs of a wide range of learners? I think there are some fundamental ways of restructuring that really make it much more possible to meet a diverse range of needs.

Jim, do you think Mara has identified the kinds of supports that would be needed, or do you think she's underestimating it?

Kauffman: I think she's underestimating, especially for kids with learning disabilities and emotional or behavioral disorders. Although it sounds very engaging and intriguing, I doubt that it's possible to provide all needed services in one place at the same time for all the types of children one might have. People are eager to say that they don't exclude anybody from a particular classroom, but there is no credible research showing that the regular classroom can actually provide superior services for all kids with disabilities.

But do you think that techniques like thematic instruction, using adults in the classroom more flexibly, and so on, will help make inclusion work?

Kauffman: They're insufficient. I think all of them have some merit and can be of some help to some kids. But there just isn't sound research to support the idea that the practices Mara is mentioning are effective for instructing all kids with learning and behavior problems or other disabilities.

I agree with Mara that inclusion should be the "default" setting for schools, and it is so by law. But there are children for whom the default setting is inappropriate, and there are many parents and teachers who feel that these practices that Mara refers to are not going to be adequate to meet the needs of their kids. And many of those parents and teachers are correct.

Obviously, there are strong arguments on both sides of the inclusion debate. What do you foresee happening with inclusion in schools?

Kauffman: The movement has been going strong for a decade, and I think it's already had a major impact. It's seen as the thing to do, and it's taken on a bandwagon effect that is gaining momentum. I have really mixed feelings about that because I'm a supporter of inclusion for kids for whom it's appropriate. I think we have an obligation to try to make accommodations for kids in a regular classroom.

On the other hand, I see a lot of dumping of kids and a lot of pretense about what's happening with inclusion. My fear is that inclusion will be very poorly implemented and pushed to destructive extremes. As a result, we may have a counter movement that will result in more—not less—needless separation of kids.

What I hope happens is that people come back to the principles articulated in the Individuals with Disabilities Education Act. We should ask first "What does this child need?" and then ask "What's the least restrictive environment in which we can provide these services?"

For many kids, but not all, the least restrictive place is the regular classroom. But if we lose placement options, we're going to fail a large number of kids. Eventually, and I hope very soon, people will recognize this and reject the radical rhetoric that calls for the full inclusion of all kids with disabilities in regular classrooms.

Mara, where do you see the inclusion movement going?

Sapon-Shevin: Certainly, the goal is not going to go away: the idea that we want to create a world in which all children are welcome, in which all children grow up comfortable with, knowledgeable about, and supportive of, all kinds of other children. Inclusion is consistent with multicultural education, with wanting to create a world in which many more people have opportunities to know, play, and work with one another. So I can't foresee the many people who have fought so hard for their children's right to be full members of the community changing their minds.

Of course, I also worry a lot that school districts will do inclusion badly, that they'll leap into it with no planning or preparation.

But in general, I see educators recognizing that we need to create schools and classrooms that meet the needs of all children. And I really believe that we'll see many more innovative, creative ways of providing services. We might find that multi-age grouping is most conducive to working with diversity. Maybe we'll have teachers taking more initiative in designing curriculum, and we'll find ways to prepare them and to help them collaborate with aides and support staff in new ways.

Inclusion will succeed to the extent that it links itself with other ongoing restructuring efforts: with the detracking movement, authentic assessment, site-based management, and so on. Restructuring means looking at not just what kind of classrooms we want, but what kind of a world we want, and how we prepare children to be members of that broader community.

15

Dear Dr. Marlowe:

Student teaching is great, but teaching high school is challenging. I swear some of these kids are smarter than me. But, then there's Ben. My cooperating teacher has made him my "project" and I have to tell you it's been pretty challenging. Looking through all the paperwork that's accumulated over the years on this guy is daunting. In different years, he's been labeled as learning disabled, mentally retarded, language impaired, and probably other stuff I haven't even gotten to yet.

When I work with him individually, it's clear that he does have difficulty expressing himself and his writing is atrocious. Besides the handwriting, which is basically illegible, he can't even write in complete sentences. I don't know how he ever got to 10th grade. His reading is pretty sketchy too. But, the thing is, he's got some talent. For example, if you ask him about clocks or watches or car engines or virtually anything mechanical he can tell you everything about it and he can draw all the inner workings of these things. It's uncanny. Sort of like those David Macaulay drawings. Really detailed, precise. His eyes light up when he does that sort of stuff and my cooperating teacher told me that Ben can also repair just about anything, including transmissions. I'm not really sure what to do with this guy because I'm a mechanical klutz to begin with and anyway shouldn't a kid like this be in voc-tech? He doesn't really seem to be smart enough for the regular high school curriculum. Am I just off base here?

Sarah Johnson

❖   HOW WOULD YOU RESPOND?

What does it mean to be smart? Is it possible for one to be "book smart" and lack common sense? How is intelligence measured? Is there a common understanding of what intelligence is, or might people in Polynesia, Brazil, and China each have a different understanding about what it means to be intelligent? Students can learn to be better readers; can they learn to become more intelligent or is this something fixed, like eye color? What teacher behaviors might foster intellectual growth? Keep these questions in mind as you read Kathy Checkley's interview with Howard Gardner. What questions do you have about intelligence? How can you help extend the discussion of these ideas in class? Finally, how would you respond to Sarah Johnson?

❖   THE FIRST SEVEN . . . AND THE EIGHTH:
     A CONVERSATION WITH HOWARD GARDNER

Kathy Checkley

Howard Gardner's theory of multiple intelligences, described in *Frames of Mind* (1985), sparked a revolution of sorts in classrooms around the world, a mutiny against the notion that human beings have a single, fixed intelligence. The fervor with which educators embraced his premise that we have multiple intelligences surprised Gardner himself. "It obviously spoke to some sense that people had that kids weren't all the same and that the tests we had only skimmed the surface about the differences among kids," Gardner said.

Here Gardner brings us up-to-date on his current thinking on intelligence, how children learn, and how they should be taught.

How do you define intelligence?

Intelligence refers to the human ability to solve problems or to make something that is valued in one or more cultures. As long as we can find a culture that values an ability to solve a problem or create a product in a particular way, then I would strongly consider whether that ability should be considered an intelligence.

First, though, that ability must meet other criteria: Is there a particular representation in the brain for the ability? Are there populations that are especially good or especially impaired in an intelligence? And, can an evolutionary history of the intelligence be seen in animals other than human beings?

I defined seven intelligences (see box) in the early 1980s because those intelligences all fit the criteria. A decade later when I revisited the task, I found at least one more ability that clearly deserved to be called an intelligence.

The Intelligences, in Gardner's Words

- Linguistic intelligence is the capacity to use language, your native language, and perhaps other languages, to express what's on your mind and to understand other people. Poets really specialize in linguistic intelligence, but any kind of writer, orator, speaker, lawyer, or a person for whom language is an important stock in trade highlights linguistic intelligence.

- People with a highly developed logical-mathematical intelligence understand the underlying principles of some kind of a causal system, the way a scientist or a logician does; or can manipulate numbers, quantities, and operations, the way a mathematician does.

- Spatial intelligence refers to the ability to represent the spatial world internally in your mind—the way a sailor or airplane pilot navigates the large spatial world, or the way a chess player or sculptor represents a more circumscribed spatial world. Spatial intelligence can be used in the arts or in the sciences. If you are spatially intelligent and oriented toward the arts, you are more likely to become a painter or a sculptor or an architect than, say, a musician or a writer. Similarly, certain sciences like anatomy or topology emphasize spatial intelligence.

- Bodily kinesthetic intelligence is the capacity to use your whole body or parts of your body—your hand, your fingers, your arms—to solve a problem, make something, or put on some kind of a production. The most evident examples are people in athletics or the performing arts, particularly dance or acting.

- Musical intelligence is the capacity to think in music, to be able to hear patterns, recognize them, remember them, and perhaps manipulate them. People who have a strong musical intelligence don't just remember music easily—they can't get it out of their minds, it's so omnipresent. Now, some people will say, "Yes, music is important, but it's a talent, not an intelligence." And I say, "Fine, let's call it a talent." But, then we have to leave the word *intelligent* out of *all* discussions of human abilities. You know, Mozart was damned smart!

- Interpersonal intelligence is understanding other people. It's an ability we all need, but is at a premium if you are a teacher, clinician, salesperson, or politician. Anybody who deals with other people has to be skilled in the interpersonal sphere.

- Intrapersonal intelligence refers to having an understanding of yourself, of knowing who you are, what you can do, what you want to do, how you react to things, which things to avoid, and which things to gravitate toward. We are drawn to people who have a good understanding of themselves because those people tend not to screw up. They tend to know what they can do. They tend to know what they can't do. And they tend to know where to go if they need help.

- Naturalist intelligence designates the human ability to discriminate among living things (plants, animals) as well as sensitivity to other features of the natural world (clouds, rock configurations). This ability was clearly of value in our evolutionary past as hunters, gatherers, and farmers; it continues to be central in such roles as botanist or chef. I also speculate that much of our consumer society exploits the naturalist intelligences, which can be mobilized in the discrimination among cars, sneakers, kinds of makeup, and the like. The kind of pattern recognition valued in certain of the sciences may also draw upon naturalist intelligence.

That would be the naturalist intelligence. What led you to consider adding this to our collection of intelligences?

Somebody asked me to explain the achievements of the great biologists, the ones who had a real mastery of taxonomy, who understood about different species, who could recognize patterns in nature and classify objects. I realized that to explain that kind of ability, I would have to manipulate the other intelligences in ways that weren't appropriate.

So I began to think about whether the capacity to classify nature might be a separate intelligence. The naturalist ability passed with flying colors. Here are a couple of reasons: First, it's an ability we need to survive as human beings. We need, for example, to know which animals to hunt and which to run away from. Second, this ability isn't restricted to human beings. Other animals need to have a naturalist intelligence to survive. Finally, the big selling point is that brain evidence supports the existence of the naturalist intelligence. There are certain parts of the brain particularly dedicated to the recognition and the naming of what are called "natural" things.

How do you describe the naturalist intelligence to those of us who aren't psychologists?

The naturalist intelligence refers to the ability to recognize and classify plants, minerals, and animals, including rocks and grass and all variety of flora and fauna. The ability to recognize cultural artifacts like cars or sneakers may also depend on the naturalist intelligence.

Now, everybody can do this to a certain extent—we can all recognize dogs, cats, trees. But, some people from an early age are extremely good at recognizing and classifying artifacts. For example, we all know kids who, at age 3 or 4, are better at recognizing dinosaurs than most adults.

Darwin is probably the most famous example of a naturalist because he saw so deeply into the nature of living things.

Are there any other abilities you're considering calling intelligences?

Well, there may be an existential intelligence that refers to the human inclination to ask very basic questions about existence. Who are we? Where do we come from? What's it all about? Why do we die? We might say that existential intelligence allows us to know the invisible, outside world. The only reason I haven't given a seal of approval to the existential intelligence is that I don't think we have good brain evidence yet on its existence in the nervous system—one of the criteria for an intelligence.

You have said that the theory of multiple intelligences may be best understood when we know what it critiques. What do you mean?

The standard view of intelligence is that intelligence is something you are born with; you have only a certain amount of it; you cannot do much about how much of that intelligence you have; and tests exist that can tell you how smart you are. The theory of multiple intelligences challenges that view. It asks, instead, "Given what we know about the brain, evolution, and the differences in cultures, what are the sets of human abilities we all share?"

My analysis suggested that rather than one or two intelligences, all human beings have several (eight) intelligences. What makes life interesting, however, is that we don't have the same strength in each intelligence area, and we don't have the same amalgam of intelligences. Just as we look different from one another and have different kinds of personalities, we also have different kinds of minds.

This premise has very serious educational implications. If we treat everybody as if they are the same, we're catering to one profile of intelligence, the language-logic profile. It's great if you have that profile, but it's not great for the vast majority of human beings who do not have that particular profile of intelligence.

Can you explain more fully how the theory of multiple intelligences challenges what has become known as IQ?

The theory challenges the entire notion of IQ. The IQ test was developed about a century ago as a way to determine who would have trouble in school. The test measures linguistic ability, logical-mathematical ability, and, occasionally, spatial ability.

What the intelligence test does not do is inform us about our other intelligences; it also doesn't look at other virtues like creativity or civic mindedness, or whether a person is moral or ethical.

We don't do much IQ testing anymore, but the shadow of IQ tests is still with us because the SAT—arguably the most potent examination in the world—is basically the same kind of disembodied language-logic instrument.

The truth is, I don't believe there is such a general thing as scholastic aptitude. Even so, I don't think that the SAT will fade until colleges indicate that they'd rather have students who know how to use their minds well—students who may or may not be good test takers, but who are serious, inquisitive, and know how to probe and problem-solve. That is really what college professors want, I believe.

Can we strengthen our intelligences? If so, how?

We can all get better at each of the intelligences, although some people will improve in an intelligence area more readily than others, either because biology gave them a better brain for that intelligence or because their culture gave them a better teacher.

Teachers have to help students use their combination of intelligences to be successful in school, to help them learn whatever it is they want to learn, as well as what the teachers and society believe they have to learn.

Now, I'm not arguing that kids shouldn't learn the literacies. Of course they should learn the literacies. Nor am I arguing that kids shouldn't learn the disciplines. I'm a tremendous champion of the disciplines. What I argue against is the notion that there's only one way to learn how to read, only one way to learn how to compute, only one way to learn about biology. I think that such contentions are nonsense.

It's equally nonsensical to say that everything should be taught seven or eight ways. That's not the point of the MI theory. The point is to realize that any topic of importance, from any discipline, can be taught in more than one way. There are things people need to know, and educators have to be extraordinarily imaginative and persistent in helping students understand things better.

A popular activity among those who are first exploring multiple intelligences is to construct their own intellectual profile. It's thought that when teachers go through the process of creating such a profile, they're more likely to recognize and appreciate the intellectual strengths of their students. What is your view on this kind of activity?

My own studies have shown that people love to do this. Kids like to do it, adults like to do it. And, as an activity, I think it's perfectly harmless.

I get concerned, though, when people think that determining your intellectual profile—or that of someone else—is an end in itself.

You have to use the profile to understand the ways in which you seem to learn easily. And, from there, determine how to use those strengths to help you become more successful in other endeavors. Then, the profile becomes a way for you to understand yourself better, and you can use that understanding to catapult yourself to a better level of understanding or to a higher level of skill.

How has your understanding of the multiple intelligences influenced how you teach?

My own teaching has changed slowly as a result of multiple intelligences because I'm teaching graduate students psychological theory and there are only so many ways I can do that. I am more open to group work and to student projects of various sorts, but even if I wanted to be an "MI professor" of graduate students, I still have a certain moral obligation to prepare them for a world in which they will have to write scholarly articles and prepare theses.

Where I've changed much more, I believe, is at the workplace. I direct research projects and work with all kinds of people. Probably 10 to 15 years ago, I would have tried to find people who were just like me to work with me on these projects.

I've really changed my attitude a lot on that score. Now I think much more in terms of what people are good at and in putting together teams of people whose varying strengths complement one another.

How should thoughtful educators implement the theory of multiple intelligences?

Although there is no single MI route, it's very important that a teacher take individual differences among kids very seriously. You cannot be a good MI teacher if you don't want to know each child and try to gear how you teach and how you evaluate to that particular child. The bottom line is a deep interest in children and how their minds are different from one another, and in helping them use their minds well.

Now, kids can be great informants for teachers. For example, a teacher might say, "Look, Benjamin, this obviously isn't working. Should we try using a picture?" If Benjamin gets excited about that approach, that's a pretty good clue to the teacher about what could work.

The theory of multiple intelligences, in and of itself, is not going to solve anything in our society, but linking the multiple intelligences with a curriculum focused on understanding is an extremely powerful intellectual undertaking.

When I talk about understanding, I mean that students can take ideas they learn in school, or anywhere for that matter, and apply those appropriately in new situations. We know people truly understand something when they can represent the knowledge in more than one way. We have to put understanding up front in school. Once we have that goal, multiple intelligences can be a terrific handmaiden because understandings involve a mix of mental representations, entailing different intelligences.

People often say that what they remember most about school are those learning experiences that were linked to real life. How does the theory of multiple intelligences help connect learning to the world outside the classroom?

The theory of multiple intelligences wasn't based on school work or on tests. Instead, what I did was look at the world and ask, What are the things that people do in the world? What does it mean to be a surgeon? What does it mean to be a politician? What does it mean to be an artist or a sculptor? What abilities do you need to do those things? My theory, then, came from the things that are valued in the world.

So when a school values multiple intelligences, the relationship to what's valued in the world is patent. If you cannot easily relate this activity to something that's valued in the world, the school has probably lost the core idea of multiple intelligences, which is that these intelligences evolved to help people do things that matter in the real world.

School matters, but only insofar as it yields something that can be used once students leave school.

How can teachers be guided by multiple intelligences when creating assessment tools?

We need to develop assessments that are much more representative of what human beings are going to have to do to survive in this society. For example, I value literacy, but my measure of literacy should not be whether you can answer a multiple-choice question that asks you to select the best meaning of a paragraph. Instead, I'd rather have you read the paragraph and list four questions you have about the paragraph and figure out how you would answer those questions. Or, if I want to know how you can write, let me give you a stem and see whether you can write about that topic, or let me ask you to write an editorial in response to something you read in the newspaper or observed on the street.

The current emphasis on performance assessment is well supported by the theory of multiple intelligences. Indeed, you could not really be an advocate of multiple intelligences if you didn't have some dissatisfaction with the current testing because it's so focused on short-answer, linguistic, or logical kinds of items.

MI theory is very congenial to an approach that says: one, let's not look at things through the filter of a short-answer test. Let's look directly at the performance that we value, whether it's a linguistic, logical, aesthetic, or social performance; and, two, let's never pin our assessment of understanding on just one particular measure, but let's always allow students to show their understanding in a variety of ways.

You have identified several myths about the theory of multiple intelligences. Can you describe some of those myths?

One myth that I personally find irritating is that an intelligence is the same as a learning style. Learning styles are claims about ways in which individuals purportedly approach everything they do. If you are planful, you are supposed to be planful about everything. If you are logical-sequential, you are supposed to be logical-sequential about everything. My own research and observations suggest that that's a dubious assumption. But whether or not that's true, learning styles are very different from multiple intelligences.

Multiple intelligences claims that we respond, individually, in different ways to different kinds of content, such as language or music or other people. This is very different from the notion of learning style.

You can say that a child is a visual learner, but that's not a multiple intelligences way of talking about things. What I would say is, "Here is a child who very easily represents things spatially, and we can draw upon that strength if need be when we want to teach the child something new."

Another widely believed myth is that, because we have seven or eight intelligences, we should create seven or eight tests to measure students' strengths in each of those areas. That is a perversion of the theory. It's re-creating the sin of the single intelligence quotient and just multiplying it by a larger number. I'm personally against assessment of intelligences unless such a measurement is used for a very specific learning purpose—we want to help a child understand her history or his mathematics better and, therefore, want to see what might be good entry points for that particular child.

What experiences led you to the study of human intelligence?

It's hard for me to pick out a single moment, but I can see a couple of snapshots. When I was in high school, my uncle gave me a textbook in psychology. I'd never actually heard of psychology before. This textbook helped me understand color blindness. I'm color blind, and I became fascinated by the existence of plates that illustrated what color blindness was. I could actually explain why I couldn't see colors.

Another time when I was studying the Reformation, I read a book by Erik Erikson called *Young Man Luther* (1958). I was fascinated by the psychological motivation of Luther to attack the Catholic Church. That fascination influenced my decision to go into psychology.

The most important influence was actually learning about brain damage and what could happen to people when they had strokes. When a person has a stroke, a certain part of the brain gets injured, and that injury can tell you what that part of the brain does. Individuals who lose their musical abilities can still talk. People who lose their linguistic ability still might be able to sing. That understanding not only brought me into the whole world of brain study, but it was really the seed that led ultimately to the theory of multiple intelligences. As long as you can lose one ability while others are spared, you cannot just have a single intelligence. You have to have several intelligences.

16

Dear Professor Canestrari:

I don't know if you remember me but I had you in a foundations of ed class. Since graduation, I've been teaching fourth grade for the last four years and, well, actually, I'm thinking about quitting and it reminded me of a conversation we had in your class about teachers needing to take a stand. So, I guess I'm trying to decide about taking a stand or simply doing something less stressful.

The thing that's been really bothering me is that it seems as if kids, in my building anyway, are getting asked to answer questions in the same way. It's like the district makes a big fuss about how we should come up with all these interesting activities and questions to do with kids in our classes but at the same time they want the kids to all have the same answer in the same format. Is this a good idea? Shouldn't we be encouraging all sorts of answers and approaches to solving problems? Even my principal, who I like, wants us to make sure the kids all do their math problems in a certain way and all do their writing a certain way. Even the art teacher is being asked to evaluate her kids' painting based on a rubric where each kid is compared to the same criteria. Doesn't this squash individuality? What if a kid comes up with a painting style that doesn't fit? Do we really want to say the painting's no good or inadequate? What if it's really just so original? I don't know anymore but when I started it seemed like there was a lot more room for kids to explore and be creative and now it all seems so narrow. Do you think I'm being silly? Is this something you think is worth taking a stand about?

Alice Chen

❖ HOW WOULD YOU RESPOND?

What teacher behaviors or school district policies inhibit/enhance creativity? Can creativity be taught? How would you define creativity? What does creativity look like in the classroom? How might the recent emphasis on student, teacher, and school district accountability jeopardize the creativity of students? Of teachers? Keep these questions in mind as you read "Insights About Creativity: Questioned, Rejected, Ridiculed, Ignored" by Edward P. Torrance. What questions do you have about creativity? How might you extend the discussion of these ideas in class? Finally, how would you respond to Alice Chen?

❖ INSIGHTS ABOUT CREATIVITY:
    QUESTIONED, REJECTED, RIDICULED, IGNORED

Edward P. Torrance

Introduction

During my 46 years of experience in creativity research and study I have developed numerous insights about creative behavior that are counter to accepted and established ideas. These insights have been questioned, rejected, ridiculed, or ignored. This should not have surprised me because I know that a person who has an original idea is always in a minority of one, at least at first. Fortunately some of these insights have been accepted by a few people and this has diminished my discomfort enough to enable me to continue. In other cases, someone of a later generation comes along and develops the same insight and it is readily accepted. Then, there was readiness for them.

The latter route to the partial acceptance of the insight is especially important. Let me offer a couple of examples. Very early in my attempts to understand what made for creative achievement, I developed the insight that being in love with what you are doing was very important in creative achievement. I began collecting data that would enable me to find out. For example, I tried to find out what elementary school children were in love with year after year in my longitudinal studies launched in 1958. Later (1980, 1981a, 1983, 1987), I published evidence in support of this insight. This finding was ignored. None paid attention to this finding. If they did, they were opposed to it and disbelieved it. It was unthinkable for children this young to know what they were in love with. The fact is that many of them did know, recorded this fact in their own handwriting, and as adults they were doing what they loved, and they were doing it creatively.

Then Teresa M. Amabile independently came out with the same insight (1986, 1989) and wrote, "Extraordinary talent, personality, and cognitive ability do not seem to be enough—it's the 'labor of love' aspect that determines creativity" (Amabile, 1986, p. 12).

Early in my research, I developed the idea that information processed (read) with a creative mind set was more likely to be used creatively. My associates and I conducted several experiments and found consistent support for this insight (Torrance and Harmon, 1961, 1962; Torrance, 1969). Again, Ellen Langer, a generation later and using different terminology, came up with the same indight (Langer *et al.*, 1989; Langer, 1989, 1990). She used the terms "mindfulness" and "mindlessness" for the sets that she gave, but she was dealing with the same phenomena. No one listened to me, and no one I know applied the results. Langer's results made headlines and *Reader's Digest* (March, 1990).

A whole generation separates my work from the works of Amabile and Langer. Neither Amabile nor Langer appear to be familiar with this work, yet their findings were almost immediately accepted. Perhaps I unknowingly have done the same thing, although I deliberately searched the old literature and used it.

Changing the Golden Rule

Some ideas are so widely accepted that no one thinks of questioning them, preventing the emergence of new insights. For example, the Golden Rule, "do under others as you would have them do unto you," is one such established rule. For a long time, I have had the information that could have led to the insight that we should also "treat people like they want to be treated." I have seen and accepted the value of the "role reversal" technique (Moreno, 1946) in psychodrama, sociodrama, and role playing. I have heard and accepted the American Indian prayer, "Great Spirit, let me not judge a man (woman) until I have walked a mile in his (her) moccasins." I have embraced Harry Stack Sullivan's theory (1953) that human relations and lives go wrong when people behave toward others as through they have attitudes, motivations, skills and other qualities different from what they actually have.

I had taught it and written about it. Let us examine a couple of examples of what happens.

I know a tremendously gifted, creative 17-year-old boy who had been "in love with science" practically all of his life. In elementary school, he had achieved quite well and he had been looking forward to high school when he could take science courses. He had already done a lot of reading in science and had conducted some science experiments. When he entered high school, his counselor refused to permit him to register for the General Science course, telling him that it was too difficult for him. His older brother tried to intervene for him with the counselor. However, the counselor told the brother that it would be unfair to place his younger brother in a science course and have him fail. The mother also tried to intervene, but the counselor lectured her about trying to push her son too hard.

The boy, however, was able to find a science teacher at a nearby college to work with him. This professor said that the boy's understanding of chemistry was superior to his college students. Through the influence of this professor, some of the high school teachers permitted him to take other science courses and he excelled in them. In his senior year, he won a scholarship in the Westinghouse National Science Talent Search and achieved top scores in the College Board Examinations. The local newspaper wanted to interview the boy, the school principal, and some of the teachers.

The principal and teachers called in for the interview would not believe he had won this honor and wondered if he had cheated. Fortunately, he was defended by one of the science teachers. Using his cumulative folder, it was discovered that his home room number and IQ had been transposed in his permanent record when he entered high school.

I have since learned that this kind of situation is not uncommon. In Japan, a professor and principal of a university high school told me of a similar case with which he was dealing at the time. This laboratory school included a group of "feeble minded" students of high school age. There was one boy among this certified "feeble minded" group who was excited about science and asked to take physics at his new school. The principal allowed him to enroll in the regular high school physics course. At the time I taked to this principal, this "feeble minded" boy was leading the class in physics, and he had been retested and attained an IQ of 115. The principal had treated him as he wanted to be treated.

Being a speech writer is a profession which demands a high degree of the kind of creativity involved in treating a person as s/he wants to be treated. Peggy Noonan (*American Legion*, April 1991) worked as a speech writer for Presidents Reagan and Bush. She says that being a presidential writer, the challenge was not so much determining what they wanted to say, but how they wanted to say it. Reagan liked to be sharply declarative, to be very clear and very blunt; whereas Bush saw the benefits in a certain amount of vagueness, so he often confused his enemies. Noonan found the creativity required in speech writing for these presidents exciting and fun.

There are other examples just as dramatic as the ones I have described. Behaving toward others as they want to be treated certainly challenges one's creativity more than does the Golden Rule and appears to facilitate creativity and result in more satisfying outcomes.

Firmly Established Ideas

When I went to the University of Minnesota as Director of the Bureau of Educational Research, the Dean of the College of Education said to all of the faculty at the annual banquet and faculty meeting, "Over half of what you teach is false. It's time you got busy and found which are true and which are false." Every Fall until his untimely death, he gave us the same challenge. I was deeply impressed by this challenge. I soon found out that it was difficult to question something that you have been teaching and that is widely accepted. Then if you stumble upon an original insight, you are afraid to make it known. Being a minority of one is very uncomfortable.

A few of my original insights have been rather widely accepted, but the ones I would like to share with you have not been accepted. Some of them have been rejected, ignored, or ridiculed. Some of them have angered some educators. Let's examine one of them.

Is Past Performance the Best Predicator of Future Performance?

Do you accept the idea that the best predictor of future behavior (performance, achievement) is past behavior (performance, achievement)? Almost all educational institutions live by this "law." Business lives by it. The Army lives by it. I shall never forget the stories, told to me in World War II, by men who had been court martialed and were being dishonorably discharged. It was a story repeated over and over. They would reach their units before their records did and they performed exceedingly well until their records arrived. From then on, their attempts to perform well seemed impossible.

The same phenomenon occurred in some of the school drop-out students (Lichter, Rapien, Siebert, and Sklansky, 1962). One school had a very successful program for potential drop-outs. The students were achieving well, attending class regularly, and behaved well. When they returned to their regular classrooms, their teachers responded to them not as they now were, bust as they were before the counseling and intensive academic program. As would be expected, the students failed. Their teachers apparently would not let them succeed.

When I came to the University of Georgia, I was delighted, in most respects, with the policy of admitting students to the Graduate School. Under this policy the Graduate School could admit students who met certain requirements involving their past performance (GRE score and undergraduate grade point average). They had a section of the application blank which called for the applicant's future career image, although some candidates left this blank and it was never used in admitting students. Each department could admit students who did not quite meet the requirements as "unclassified post graduates." If their performance was satisfactory, they could be admitted to a degree program. The Department of Educational Psychology had a policy which provided an opportunity to admit students as "unclassified post graduates." Generally we looked at their future career image as expressed on the application blank, their strong motivation, and their clear indication of commitment to a career in Educational Psychology.

After about 10 years, the Dean of the Graduate School decided that we were admitting too many students under this policy. He then decreed that the Graduate School would not admit any more Educational Psychology students under this provision. One of the things I did at this time was to take a look at the records and positions held by these students after graduation. To my surprise, the students who entered degree programs upon admittance to the University of Georgia had statistically significant lower GPAs than the ones who had come into the graduate school as "unclassified post graduates." I also found that they held professional positions as good as those who had been admitted outright. With this kind of evidence, the Graduate Dean relented and admitted students in Educational Psychology under the "unclassified post graduate" category.

Now that 20 more years have elapsed, we find from the list of ten students who were not admitted on the standard criteria that there have been: three past presidents of the National Association for Gifted Children, the founder and first president of the American Creativity Association, the authors of hundreds of professional articles in Educational Psychology, dozens of Educational Psychology texts and other books, one Educational Psychology Department head, the founders of several innovative programs, a Distinguished Scholar Award winner, and other distinctions, far exceeding the accomplishments of those who were admitted outright without question.

There have been many studies conducted by professionals from educational psychology and personnel that appear to support the contention that as performance is indeed the best predictor of future performance. None of these studies, however, have used a measure or indicator of future image. Of course, there is no standardized measure of future self-image. I have been wrestling with this problem for at least 35 years. I have experimented with the following types of measures or indicators:

1. Both fantasy and realistic expressions of future self images (two longitudinal studies) (Torrance, 1972, 1981).

2. Future orientation based upon scoring of the verbal TTCT (Torrance, 1972, 1981).

3. Persistence in realization of career choice made in elementary school over a three-year period (longitudinal 22-year study) (Torrance, 1987).

4. Scenarios scored for Achievement Motivation (learning disabled students).

5. Biographical inventories scored for future achievement motivation and clearness of future images.

Thus far, the results have been positive and statistically significant, but much more work needs to be done. The implications are far reaching.

Examples of Insight About Creativity That Have Been Questioned, Rejected, Ridiculed, or Ignored

The following are examples of some of the insights which have been developed over the years. These examples are intended to give readers something to think about:

1. *Insight.* Creativity tests, such as the TTCT, are lacking in economic and racial bias, especially if the tests are given early (Torrance, 1977).

   Accepted Belief and Practice. All standardized tests, including creativity tests, are culturally biased (Torrance, 1977).

2. *Insight.* In administering creativity tests, subjects must be motivated to give the kinds of responses you are looking for (Torrance, 1974).

   Accepted Belief and Practice. Students should not be motivated toward test items or be told what is expected of them as that will bias the results of the test.

3. *Insight.* In giving creativity tests, subjects should be "aroused" rather than being relaxed or stressed (Treffinger, Torrance, and Ball, 1987).

   Accepted Belief and Practice. Students should have a relaxed or playful atmosphere to perform on creativity tests or should take tests in strict, standardized conditions.

4. *Insight.* The way to evaluate an educational program to develop creativity is not to give a pretest in October and a post test in May or June or to give a pretest early in June and a post test in July or August. Such procedures give spurious results. The pretests are given when students are at their peak and the post tests are given when they are past their peak.

   Accepted Belief and Practice. Students are given pre and post tests under whatever conditions exist at the time to evaluate whether they have learned anything from their creativity training.

5. *Insight.* Disadvantaged children may perform better than affluent or gifted students in brainstorming (Torrance, 1977).

   Accepted Belief and Practice. Disadvantaged students do not have sufficient experience with creativity materials to compete with affluent or gifted students in brainstorming exercises.

6. *Insight.* Disadvantaged children perform as well or better than affluent children on tests of ability to improvise with commonplace materials (Torrance, 1977).

   Accepted Belief and Practice. Affluent children perform better than disadvantaged children on all tests of creativity.

7. *Insight.* In longitudinal studies using creativity tests scores as predictors of adult creative achievement, give enough time for

creative achievement to "pay off." I found only a moderate correlation after 6 years, a higher one after 12 years, and a lower one after 30 years when other indicators like love of one's work, risk taking, persistence, courage, and the like are more important.

Accepted Belief and Practice. For creativity tests to accurately predict future creative achievements, you must measure the subjects' creativity in regular, short-term intervals.

8. *Insight.* Apparent procrastination may result in greater incubation and creative achievement (Torrance and Safter, 1991).

    Accepted Belief and Practice. Procrastination is a negative trait and should be dealt with as an impediment to creative production.

9. *Insight.* High creatives, not so high IQ, have higher creative achievement than high IQs, not so high creatives, and equal those high in both (Torrange and Wu, 1981).

    Accepted Belief and Practice. High IQ is necessary for real creative achievement of any kind.

10. *Insight.* Fourth graders are less creative than third graders (Torrance, 1968).

    Accepted Belief and Practice. Creativity is developmental and consistently increases with age and education.

11. *Insight.* It is not necessary in scoring for originality to adjust to group, culture, gender, and so forth (Rungsinan, 1976).

    Accepted Belief and Practice. Scoring of all creativity factors must be adjusted to account for cultural or gender variables.

12. *Insight.* Generally, disadvantaged children do not have mentors, yet they need them more than more affluent children (Torrance, 1991).

    Accepted Belief and Practice. Disadvantaged children have as much access to significant role models as advantaged children but because they do not think that they need them, they ignore these opportunities.

13. *Insight.* The willingness to disagree in a group facilitates creativity and the making of better decisions (Torrance, 1957).

    Accepted Belief and Practice. Group cohesion and cooperation is the best facilitator of creativity and decision making and disagreement is disruptive to this process.

14. *Insight.* Young children can begin learning negotiation skills (Murdock and Torrance, 1988).

> *Accepted Belief and Practice.* Young children do not have the ability to learn negotiation skills, nor should they take time away from their basic skills instruction.

15. *Insight.* Creatively gifted children with learning disabilities may attain a high degree of success in a field that he/she loves in his/her strengths are regarded positively (Torrance, 1992).

> *Accepted Belief and Practice.* There is no such thing as a gifted child with learning disabilities. If a child is learning disable he/she will always be so handicapped, he/she cannot achieve success.

References

Amabile, T. (1986). The personality of creativity. *Creat. Learn.* 15(3): 12–16.

Amabile, T. (1989). *Growing up Creative,* Crown Publishers. New York.

Haley, G. A. (1979). Training Advantaged and Disadvantaged Black Kindergarteners in Sociodrama: Effects on Creativity and Free Recall Variables of Oral Language. Doctoral dissertation, University of Georgia, Dissertation Abstracts International, 39.4139A, University Microfilms Order No. 79091, 642.

Langer, E. (1989). *Mindfulness,* Addison-Wesley, Reading, MA.

Langer, E. (March 1990). The power of an open mind. *Reader's Dig.* 15–16.

Langer, E., Hatem, M., Joss, J., and Howell, M. (1989). Conditional teaching and mindful learning. *Creativ. Res. J.,* 2: 150–161.

Lichter, S. O., Rapien, E. B., Seibert, S. M., and Sklansky, N. O. (1962). *The Dropouts,* Free Press, New York.

Moreno, J. L. (1946). *Psychodrama* (Vol. 1), Beacon House, Beacon, NY.

Murdock, M. C., and Torrence, E. P. (1988). Using the Torrance sociodramatic model as a vehicle for negotiation. *Creat. Child Adult Quart.* 13(3): 108–114.

Noonan, P. (1991). White House wordsmith. *Am. Legion Mag.* 130(4): 28–29, 65.

Rungsinan, W. (1976). Scoring of Originality of Creative Thinking Across Cultures. Doctoral Dissertation. University of Georgia, *Dissertation Abstracts International,* 37, 5003-A, No. 77–47, 58.

Singer, B. (1974). The future-focused role-image. In Toffler, A. (ed.), *Learning for Tomorrow: The Role of the Future in Education,* Vintage Books, New York.

Sullivan, H. S. (1953). *The Interpersonal Theory of Psychiatry,* W. W. Norton and Company, New York.

Toffler, A. (ed.). (1974). *Learning for Tomorrow,* Random House, New York.

Torrance, E. P. (1957). Group decision making and disagreement. *Soc. Forces,* 35: 314–318.

Torrance, E. P. (1965a). *Constructive Behavior: Stress, Personality, and Mental Health,* Wadsworth, Belmont, CA.

Torrance, E. P. (1965b). *Rewarding Creative Behavior,* Prentice-Hall, Englewood Cliffs, NJ.

Torrance, E. P. (1968). A longitudinal examination of the fourth grade slump in creativity. *Creat. Child Adult Quart.,* 12: 195–199.

Torrance, E. P. (1969). Influence on a student's learning of the type of test to be administered. In Ingenkamp, K. (ed.), *Developments in Educational Testing,* University of London Press, London.

Torrance, E. P. (1970). Achieving socialization without sacrificing creativity. *J. Creat. Behav.* 4: 183–189.

Torrance, E. P. (1972). Predictive validity of the Torrance tests of creative thinking. *J. Creat Behav.* 6: 236–252.

Torrance, E. P. (1974). *The Torrance Tests of Creative Thinking: Norms-Technical Manual,* Personal Press, Lexington, MA.

Torrance, E. P. (1977). *Discovery and Nurturance of Giftedness in the Culturally Different,* Council for Exceptional Children, Reston, VA.

Torrance, E. P. (November 1980). Predicting the Young Adult Creative Achievements of Elementary School Children. Paper presented before the National Association for Gifted Children, Minneapolis, MN.

Torrance, E. P. (1981a). Predicting the creativity of elementary school children (1958–1980)—and the teacher who made a difference. *Gifted Child Quart.,* 25: 55–62.

Torrance, E. P. (1981b). *Thinking Creatively in Action and Movement,* Scholastic Testing Service, Bensenville, IL.

Torrance, E. P. (1983). The importance of falling in love with "something." *Creat. Child Adult Quart.,* 8(2), 72–78.

Torrance, E. P. (1987). Future career image as a predictor of creative achievement in the 22-year longitudinal study. *Psychol. Rep.* 60: 574.

Torrance, E. P., and Harmon, J. A. (1961). Effects of memory, evaluation and creative sets on test performances. *J. Educ. Psychol.* 52: 204–214.

Torrance, E. P., and Harmon, J. A. (1962). *A Study of Instructional Set for Four Types of Test Items.* Unpublished manuscript, Department of Educational Psychology, University of Minnesota.

Torrance, E. P., and Safter, T. (1991). *The Incubation Model of Teaching,* Bearly Limited, Buffalo, NY.

Torrance, E. P., and Wu, T. H. (1981). A comparative longitudinal study of adult creative achievements of elementary school children identified as high intelligent and highly creative. *Creat. Child Adult Quart.,* 6: 71–76.

Treffinger, D. J., Torrance, E. P., and Ball, O. E. (1987). *Guidelines for Administration and Scoring Comments on Using the Torrance Tests of Creative Thinking,* Scholastic Testing Service, Bensenville, IL.

Questions for Reflection

Let's look back at the letters and readings in **Part IV: How Should Student Diversity Affect Teaching Practice?** Consider the following questions as you begin formulating your own ideas about how to apply theories of development into planned instructional practice.

1. Define diversity. How does student diversity affect learning? How might instruction be differentiated to meet the needs of increasingly diverse classroom populations?

2. What are the advantages and disadvantages of teaching students in their primary language? Should English language learning instruction serve to replace native language?

3. Why do substantial IQ test score differences persist between different racial and ethnic groups? What might Torrance and Howard Gardner suggest that teachers and school districts do to eliminate these differences?

4. Think about Aronson's idea about the jigsaw classroom. How would he suggest that teachers should think about grouping students in classrooms as diverse as those Macedo describes?

❖ YOUR OWN IDEAS

What ideas seem most important to you as you reflect about teaching and learning in real classrooms? What do you think is most important for new teachers to consider? What further questions did the authors raise for you in Part IV that have not been adequately answered?

Suggested Readings

Amabile, T. M. (1996). *Creativity in context.* Boulder, CO: Westview.

Banks, J. A. (2002). *An introduction to multicultural education* (3rd ed.). Boston: Allyn & Bacon.

Cummins, J. (1984). *Bilingualism and special education.* San Diego, CA: College Hill Press.

Delpit, L. (1995). *Other people's children: Cultural conflict in the classroom.* New York: New Press.

Gardner, H. (1983). *Frames of mind: The theory of multiple intelligences.* New York: Basic Books.

Kozol, J. (1995). *Amazing grace: The lives of children and the conscience of a nation.* New York: Perennial.

Oakes, J. (1990). *Multiplying inequities: The effects of race, social class, and tracking on opportunities to learn mathematics and science.* Santa Monica, CA: Rand.

Ogbu, J. U. (1999). Beyond language: Ebonics, proper English and identity in a Black-American speech community. *American Educational Research Journal, 36,* 147–184.

Sternberg, R. J. (1985). *Beyond IQ: A triarchic theory of human intelligence.* New York: Cambridge University Press.

Tomlinson, C. A. (2001). *How to differentiate instruction in mixed ability classrooms* (2nd ed.). Alexandria, VA: Association for Supervision and Curriculum Development.

Torrance, E. P., & Hall, L. K. (1980). Assessing the future reaches of creative potential. *Journal of Creative Behavior, 14,* 1–19.

PART V

What Factors Influence Student Motivation?

17

Dear Professor Marlowe:

OK, you asked me to write you a letter about how I motivate kids in my classroom. Here goes. First of all, some kids just don't have any motivation for anything. I know you probably disagree but you don't work with sixth graders every day and I do. And now that I have my own classroom for a couple of years, I can tell you that I think you're just wrong about what you told us in that psychology of learning class. Here's the thing: Some kids won't do anything unless you give them something. It's just that simple. And, I don't blame them. Learning isn't always fun. Some things, like math or learning grammar is simply boring, but you still have to learn it and to make sure my kids do learn it I have to give them something. Sometimes I have to threaten them, sometimes it seems like I have to bribe them, and sometimes I just have to praise them over and over again when they're learning something really awful like the rules for punctuating complex sentences.

I don't know if this is what you had in mind, but I guess if I had to sum it up I'd simply say some kids are motivated and most are not. Usually, you just have to offer something or threaten kids and you can get them to do their work. Frankly, I don't feel bad about it either because they do have to learn dates, and how to add and subtract fractions. It's just not fun. But, I get them to do it.

Aaron Cooke

❖ HOW WOULD YOU RESPOND?

What is the best way to motivate students to engage in activities they are convinced are boring, useless, and/or irrelevant to their lives? What teacher behaviors enhance student motivation? How might providing rewards, incentives, or other forms of positive reinforcement undermine student motivation? Keep these questions in mind as you read Alfie Kohn. What questions do you have about student motivation? How will you extend these ideas in class? Finally, how will you respond to Aaron Cooke?

❖ FIVE REASONS TO STOP SAYING "GOOD JOB!"

Alfie Kohn

Plenty of books and articles advise us against relying on punishment, from spanking to forcible isolation ("time out"). Occasionally someone will even ask us to rethink the practice of bribing children with stickers or food. But you'll have to look awfully hard to find a discouraging word about what is euphemistically called positive reinforcement.

Lest there be any misunderstanding, the point here is not to call into question the importance of supporting and encouraging children, the need to love them and hug them and help them feel good about themselves. Praise, however, is a different story entirely. Here's why.

1. *Manipulating children.* Suppose you offer a verbal reward to reinforce the behavior of a two-year-old who eats without spilling, or a five-year-old who cleans up her art supplies. Who benefits from this? Is it possible that telling kids they've done a good job may have less to do with their emotional needs than with our convenience?

Rheta DeVries, a professor of education at the University of Northern Iowa, refers to this as "sugar-coated control." Very much like tangible rewards—or, for that matter, punishments—it's a way of doing something to children to get them to comply with our wishes. It may be effective at producing this result (at least for a while), but it's very different from working *with* kids—for example, by engaging them in conversation about what makes a classroom (or family) function smoothly, or how other people are affected by what we have done—or failed to do. The latter approach is not only more respectful but more likely to help kids become thoughtful people.

The reason praise can work in the short run is that young children are hungry for our approval. But we have a responsibility not to exploit that dependence for our own convenience. A "Good job!" to reinforce something that makes our lives a little easier can be an example of taking advantage of children's dependence. Kids may also come to feel manipulated by this, even if they can't quite explain why.

2. *Creating praise junkies.* To be sure, not every use of praise is a calculated tactic to control children's behavior. Sometimes we compliment kids just because we're genuinely pleased by what they've done. Even then, however, it's worth looking more closely. Rather than bolstering a child's self-esteem, praise may increase kids' dependence on us. The more we say, "I like the way you. . . ." or "Good going," the more kids come to rely on *our* evaluations, *our* decisions about what's good and bad, rather than learning to form their own judgments. It leads them to measure their worth in terms of what will lead us to smile and dole out some more approval.

Mary Budd Rowe, a researcher at the University of Florida, discovered that students who were praised lavishly by their teachers were more tentative in their responses, more apt to answer in a questioning tone of voice ("Um, seven?"). They tended to back off from an idea they had proposed as soon as an adult disagreed with them. And they were less likely to persist with difficult tasks or share their ideas with other students.

In short, "Good job!" doesn't reassure children; ultimately, it makes them feel less secure. It may even create a vicious circle such that the more we slather on the praise, the more kids seem to need it, so we praise them some more. Sadly, some of these kids will grow into adults who continue to need someone else to pat them on the head and tell them whether what they did was OK. Surely this is not what we want for our daughters and sons.

3. *Stealing a child's pleasure.* Apart from the issue of dependence, a child deserves to take delight in her accomplishments, to feel pride in what she's learned how to do. She also deserves to decide when to feel that way. Every time we say, "Good job!," though, we're telling a child how to feel.

To be sure, there are times when our evaluations are appropriate and our guidance is necessary—especially with toddlers and preschoolers.

But a constant stream of value judgments is neither necessary nor useful for children's development. Unfortunately, we may not have realized that "Good job!" is just as much an evaluation as "Bad job!" The most notable feature of a positive judgment isn't that it's positive, but that it's a judgment. And people, including kids, don't like being judged.

I cherish the occasions when my daughter manages to do something for the first time, or does something better than she's ever done it before. But I try to resist the knee-jerk tendency to say, "Good job!" because I don't want to dilute her joy. I want her to share her pleasure with me, not look to me for a verdict. I want her to exclaim, "I did it!" (which she often does) instead of asking me uncertainly, "Was that good?"

4. *Losing interest.* "Good painting!" may get children to keep painting for as long as we keep watching and praising. But, warns Lilian Katz, one of the country's leading authorities on early childhood education, "once attention is withdrawn, many kids won't touch the activity again." Indeed, an impressive body of scientific research has shown that the more we reward people for doing something, the more they tend to lose interest in whatever they had to do to get the reward. Now the point isn't to draw, to read, to think, to create—the point is to get the goody, whether it's an ice cream, a sticker, or a "Good job!"

In a troubling study conducted by Joan Grusec at the University of Toronto, young children who were frequently praised for displays of generosity tended to be slightly less generous on an everyday basis than other children were. Every time they had heard "Good sharing!" or "I'm so proud of you for helping," they became a little less interested in sharing or helping. Those actions came to be seen not as something valuable in their own right but as something they had to do to get that reaction again from an adult. Generosity became a means to an end.

Does praise motivate kids? Sure. It motivates kids to get praise. Alas, that's often at the expense of commitment to whatever they were doing that prompted the praise.

5. *Reducing achievement.* As if it weren't bad enough that "Good job!" can undermine independence, pleasure, and interest, it can also interfere with how good a job children actually do. Researchers keep finding that kids who are praised for doing well at a creative task tend to stumble at the next task—and they don't do as well as children who weren't praised to begin with.

Why does this happen? Partly because the praise creates pressure to "keep up the good work" that gets in the way of doing so. Partly because their *interest* in what they're doing may have declined. Partly because they become less likely to take risks—a prerequisite for creativity—once they start thinking about how to keep those positive comments coming.

More generally, "Good job!" is a remnant of an approach to psychology that reduces all of human life to behaviors that can be seen and measured. Unfortunately, this ignores the thoughts, feelings, and values that lie behind behaviors. For example, a child may share a snack with a friend as a way of attracting praise, or as a way of making sure the other child has enough to eat. Praise for sharing ignores these different motives. Worse, it actually promotes the less desirable motive by making children more likely to fish for praise in the future.

Once you start to see praise for what it is—and what it does—these constant little evaluative eruptions from adults start to produce the same effect as fingernails being dragged down a blackboard. You begin to root for a child to give his teachers or parents a taste of their own treacle by turning around to them and saying (in the same saccharine tone of voice), "Good praising!"

Still, it's not an easy habit to break. It can seem strange, at least at first, to stop praising; it can feel as though you're being chilly or withholding something. But that, it soon becomes clear, suggests that *we praise more because we need to say it than because children need to hear it.* Whenever that's true, it's time to rethink what we're doing.

What kids do need is unconditional support, love with no strings attached. That's not just different from praise—it's the *opposite* of praise. "Good job!" is conditional. It means we're offering attention and acknowledgement and approval for jumping through our hoops, for doing things that please us.

This point, you'll notice, is very different from a criticism that some people offer to the effect that we give kids too much approval, or give it too easily. They recommend that we become more miserly with our praise and demand that kids "earn" it. But the real problem isn't that children expect to be praised for everything they do these days. It's that we're tempted to take shortcuts, to manipulate kids with rewards instead of explaining and helping them to develop needed skills and good values.

So what's the alternative? That depends on the situation, but whatever we decide to say instead has to be offered in the context of genuine affection and love for who kids are rather than for what they've done. When unconditional support is present, "Good job!" isn't necessary; when it's absent, "Good job!" won't help.

If we're praising positive actions as a way of discouraging misbehavior, this is unlikely to be effective for long. Even when it works, we can't really say the child is now "behaving himself"; it would be more accurate to say the praise is behaving him. The alternative is to work *with* the child, to figure out the reasons he's acting that way. We may have to reconsider our own requests rather than just looking for a way to get kids to obey. (Instead of using "Good job!" to get a four-year-old to sit quietly through a long class meeting or family dinner, perhaps we should ask whether it's reasonable to expect a child to do so.)

We also need to bring kids in on the process of making decisions. If a child is doing something that disturbs others, then sitting down with her later and asking, "What do you think we can do to solve this problem?" will likely be more effective than bribes or threats. It also helps a child learn how to solve problems and teaches that her ideas and feelings are important. Of course, this process takes time and talent, care and courage. Tossing off a "Good job!" when the child acts in the way we deem appropriate takes none of those things, which helps to explain why "doing to" strategies are a lot more popular than "working with" strategies.

And what can we say when kids just do something impressive? Consider three possible responses:

• *Say nothing.* Some people insist a helpful act must be "reinforced" because, secretly or unconsciously, they believe it was a fluke. If children are basically evil, then they have to be given an artificial reason for being nice (namely, to get a verbal reward). But if that cynicism is unfounded—and a lot of research suggests that it is—then praise may not be necessary.

• *Say what you saw.* A simple, evaluation-free statement ("You put your shoes on by yourself" or even just "You did it") tells your child that you noticed. It also lets her take pride in what she did. In other cases, a more elaborate description may make sense. If your child draws a picture, you might provide feedback—not judgment—about what you noticed: "This mountain is huge!" "Boy, you sure used a lot of purple today!"

If a child does something caring or generous, you might gently draw his attention to the effect of his action *on the other person*: "Look at Abigail's face! She seems pretty happy now that you gave her some of your snack." This is completely different from praise, where the emphasis is on how *you* feel about her sharing.

• *Talk less, ask more.* Even better than descriptions are questions. Why tell him what part of his drawing impressed *you* when you can ask him what he likes best about it? Asking "What was the hardest part to draw?" or "How did you figure out how to make the feet the right size?" is likely to nourish his interest in drawing. Saying "Good job!," as we've seen, may have exactly the opposite effect.

This doesn't mean that all compliments, all thank-you's, all expressions of delight are harmful. We need to consider our *motives* for what we say (a genuine expression of enthusiasm is better than a desire to manipulate the child's future behavior) as well as the actual *effects* of doing so. Are our reactions helping the child to feel a sense of control over her life—or to constantly look to us for approval? Are they helping her to become more excited about what she's doing in its own right—or turning it into something she just wants to get through in order to receive a pat on the head?

It's not a matter of memorizing a new script, but of keeping in mind our long-term goals for our children and watching for the effects of what we say. The bad news is that the use of positive reinforcement really isn't so positive. The good news is that you don't have to evaluate in order to encourage.

18

Professor Marlowe:

I miss being on campus this semester but student teaching in Mrs. Silvia's first-grade class at the Juanita Chavez School has been great. The kids are a lot of fun and the teachers here really believe that all kids can learn. It can be challenging though. I have a concern, a story to share with you if you don't mind. The story starts with a simple math problem. "If Peter has 24 stamps and each letter needs 2 stamps to be mailed, how many letters can Peter mail?" I was watching a handful of kids at the math table using the problem solving strategies they learned. It was fascinating watching the kids draw sets of 2 squares to represent the stamps needed for each letter and then counting the 12 sets. The kids worked quickly and confidently. When each of the children finished, I went over to each of them and asked them about how they thought about solving the problem and then gave them each a little tougher problem. "If Peter had 19 stamps and each letter needs 2 stamps to be mailed, how many letters can Peter mail?" I noticed that Sam got pretty quiet, sitting for a long time before writing then erasing, writing and erasing, over and over again. I was surprised when I saw him get flushed and on the verge of tears. I went over to give Sam some help and encouragement. Later, Mrs. Silvia told me that she had Sam's older brother in class 3 years ago, that he was very smart as well and reacted similarly when given challenging tasks. What do you think? What should I say to Sam? How should I approach Sam and other students who get flustered with challenging tasks and not just in math but reading as well?

Maria Dias

❖ HOW WOULD YOU RESPOND?

In the Kohn piece (Chapter 17) you just read, Alfie Kohn suggests that teachers and parents should eliminate praise altogether. Isn't it important to provide students with feedback about their performance? Don't students need to hear about how they are doing? For what kinds of tasks or behaviors should teachers consider using praise? Keep these questions in mind as you read the following piece on the dangers of using certain kinds of praise by Carol S. Dweck. What questions do you have about encouragement, feedback, and praise? How might you extend the discussion of these ideas in class? Finally, how would you respond to Maria Dias?

❖ CAUTION—PRAISE CAN BE DANGEROUS

Carol S. Dweck

The self-esteem movement, which was flourishing just a few years ago, is in a state of decline. Although many educators believed that boosting students' self-esteem would boost their academic achievement, this did not happen. But the failure of the self-esteem movement does not mean that we should stop being concerned with what students think of themselves and just concentrate on improving their achievement. Every time teachers give feedback to students, they convey messages that affect students' opinion of themselves, their motivation, and their achievement. And I believe that teachers can and should help students become high achievers who also feel good about themselves. But how, exactly, should teachers go about doing this?

In fact, the self-esteem people were on to something extremely important. Praise, the chief weapon in their armory, is a powerful tool. Used correctly it can help students become adults who delight in intellectual challenge, understand the value of effort, and are able to deal with setbacks. Praise can help students make the most of the gifts they have. But if praise is not handled properly, it can become a negative force, a kind of drug that, rather than strengthening students, makes them passive and dependent on the opinion of others. What teachers—and parents—need is a framework that enables them to use praise wisely and well.

Where Did Things Go Wrong?

I believe the self-esteem movement faltered because of the way in which educators tried to instill self-esteem. Many people held an intuitively appealing theory of self-esteem, which went something like this: Giving students many opportunities to experience success and then praising them for their successes will indicate to them that they are intelligent. If they feel good about their intelligence, they will achieve. They will love learning and be confident and successful learners.

Much research now shows that this idea is wrong. Giving students easy tasks and praising their success tells students that you think they're dumb. It's not hard to see why. Imagine being lavishly praised for something you think is pretty Mickey Mouse. Wouldn't you feel that the person thought you weren't capable of more and was trying to make you feel good about your limited ability?

But what about praising students' ability when they perform well on challenging tasks? In such cases, there would be no question of students' thinking you were just trying to make them feel good. Melissa Kamins, Claudia Mueller, and I decided to put this idea to the test.

Mueller and I had already found, in a study of the relationship between parents' beliefs and their children's expectations, that 85 percent of parents thought they needed to praise their children's intelligence in order to assure them that they were smart. We also knew that many educators and psychologists thought that praising children for being intelligent was of great benefit. Yet in almost 30 years of research, I had seen over and over that children who had maladaptive achievement patterns were already obsessed with their intelligence—and with proving it to others. The children worried about how smart they looked and feared that failing at some task—even a relatively unimportant one—meant they were dumb. They also worried that having to work hard in order to succeed at a task showed they were dumb. Intelligence seemed to be a label to these kids, a feather in their caps, rather than a tool that, with effort, they could become more skillful in using.

In contrast, the more adaptive students focused on the process of learning and achieving. They weren't worried about their intelligence and didn't consider every task a measure of it. Instead, these students were more likely to concern themselves with the effort and strategies they needed in order to master the task. We wondered if praising children for being intelligent, though it seemed like a positive thing to do, could hook them into becoming dependent on praise.

Praise for Intelligence

Claudia Mueller and I conducted six studies, with more than 400 fifth-grade students, to examine the effects of praising children for being intelligent. The students were from different parts of the country (a Midwestern town and a large Eastern city) and came from varied ethnic, racial, and socioeconomic backgrounds. Each of the studies involved several tasks, and all began with the students working, one at a time, on a puzzle task that was challenging but easy enough for all of them to do quite well. After this first set, we praised one-third of the children for their *intelligence*. They were told: "Wow, you got *x* number correct. That's a really good score. You must be smart at this." One-third of the children were also told that they got a very good score, but they were praised for their *effort*: "You must have worked really hard." The final third were simply praised for their *performance*, with no comment on why they were successful. Then, we looked to see the effects of these different types of praise across all six studies.

We found that after the first trial (in which all of the students were successful) the three groups responded similarly to questions we asked them. They enjoyed the task equally, were equally eager to take the problems home to practice, and were equally confident about their future performance.

In several of the studies, as a followup to the first trial, we gave students a choice of different tasks to work on next. We asked whether they wanted to try a challenging task from which they could learn a lot (but at which they might not succeed) or an easier task (on which they were sure to do well and look smart).

The majority of the students who had received praise for being intelligent the first time around went for the task that would allow them to keep on looking smart. Most of the students who had received praise for their effort (in some studies, as many as 90 percent) wanted the challenging learning task. (The third group, the students who had not been praised for intelligence or effort, were right in the middle and I will not focus on them.)

These findings suggest that when we praise children for their intelligence, we are telling them that this is the name of the game: Look smart; don't risk making mistakes. On the other hand, when we praise children for the effort and hard work that leads to achievement, they want to keep engaging in that process. They are not diverted from the task of learning by a concern with how smart they might—or might not—look.

The Impact of Difficulty

Next, we gave students a set of problems that were harder and on which they didn't do as well. Afterwards, we repeated the questions we had asked after the first task: How much had they enjoyed the task? Did they want to take the problems home to practice? And how smart did they feel? We found that the students who had been praised for being intelligent did not like this second task and were no longer interested in taking the problems home to practice. What's more, their difficulties led them to question their intelligence. In other words, the same students who had been told they were smart when they succeeded now felt dumb because they had encountered a setback. They had learned to measure themselves from what people said about their performance, and they were dependent on continuing praise in order to maintain their confidence.

In contrast, the students who had received praise for their effort on the easier task liked the more difficult task just as much even though they missed some of the problems. In fact, many of them said they liked the harder problems even more than the easier ones, and they were even more eager to take them home to practice. It was wonderful to see.

Moreover, these youngsters did not think that the difficulty of the task (and their relative lack of success) reflected on their intelligence. They thought, simply, that they had to make a greater effort in order to succeed. Their interest in taking problems home with them to practice on presumably reflected one way they planned to do this.

Thus, the students praised for effort were able to keep their intellectual self-esteem in the face of setbacks. They still thought they were smart; they still enjoyed the challenge; and they planned to work toward future success. The students who had been praised for their intelligence received an initial boost to their egos, but their view of themselves was quickly shaken when the going got rough.

As a final test, we gave students a third set of problems that were equal in difficulty to the first set—the one on which all the students had been successful. The results were striking. Although all three groups had performed equally well on the first trial, the students who had received praise for their intelligence (and who had been discouraged by their poor showing on the second trial) now registered the worst performance of the three groups. Indeed, they did significantly worse than they had on the first trial. In contrast, students who were praised for working hard performed the best of the three groups and significantly better than they had originally. So the different kinds of praise apparently affected not just what students thought and felt, but also how well they were able to perform.

Given what we had already seen, we reasoned that when students see their performance as a measure of their intelligence, they are likely to feel stigmatized when they perform poorly and may even try to hide the fact. If, however, students consider a poor performance a temporary setback, which merely reflects how much effort they have put in or their current level of skill, then it will not be a stigma. To test this idea, we gave students the opportunity to tell a student at another school about the task they had just completed by writing a brief description on a prepared form. The form also asked them to report their score on the second, more difficult trial.

More than 40 percent of the students who had been praised for their intelligence lied about their score (to improve it, of course). They did this even though they were reporting their performance to an anonymous peer whom they would never meet. Very few of the students in the other groups exaggerated their performance. This suggests that when we praise students for their intelligence, failure becomes more personal and therefore more of a disgrace. As a result, students become less able to face and therefore deal with their setbacks.

The Messages We Send

Finally, we found that following their experiences with the different kinds of praise, the students believed different things about their intelligence. Students who had received praise for being intelligent told us they thought of intelligence as something innate—a capacity that you just had or didn't have. Students who had been praised for effort told us they thought of intelligence more in terms of their skills, knowledge, and motivation—things over which they had some control and might be able to enhance.

And these negative effects of praising for intelligence were just as strong (and sometimes stronger) for the high-achieving students as for their less successful peers. Perhaps it is even easier to get these youngsters invested in looking smart to others. Maybe they are even more attuned to messages from us that tell them we value them for their intellects.

How can one sentence of praise have such powerful and pervasive effects? In my research, I have been amazed over and over again at how quickly students of all ages pick up on messages about themselves—at how sensitive they are to suggestions about their personal qualities or about the meaning of their actions and experiences. The kinds of praise (and criticism) students receive from their teachers and parents tell them how to think about what they do—and what they are.

This is why we cannot simply forget about students' feelings, their ideas about themselves and their motivation, and just teach them the "facts." No matter how objective we try to be, our feedback conveys messages about what we think is important, what we think of them, and how they should think of themselves. These messages, as we have seen, can have powerful effects on many things including performance. And it should surprise no one that this susceptibility starts very early.

Melissa Kamins and I found it in kindergarten children. Praise or criticism that focused on children's personal traits (like being smart or good) created a real vulnerability when children hit setbacks. They saw setbacks as showing that they were bad or incompetent and they were unable to respond constructively. In contrast, praise or criticism that focused on children's strategies or the efforts they made to succeed left them hardy, confident, and in control when they confronted setbacks. A setback did not mean anything bad about them or their personal qualities. It simply meant that something needed to be done, and they set about doing it. Again, a focus on process allowed these young children to maintain their self-esteem and to respond constructively when things went wrong.

Ways of Praising

There are many groups whose achievement is of particular interest to us: minorities, females, the gifted, the underachieving, to name a few. The findings of these studies will tell you why I am so concerned that we not try to encourage the achievement of our students by prais-ing their intelligence. When we worry about low-achieving or vulner-able students, we may want to reassure them they're smart. When we want to motivate high-achieving students, we may want to spur them on by telling them they're gifted. Our research says: Don't do that. Don't get students so invested in these labels that they care more about keeping the label than about learning. Instead of empowering students, praise is likely to render students passive and dependent on something they believe they can't control. And it can hook them into a system in which setbacks signify incompetence and effort is recognized as a sign of weakness rather than a key to success.

This is not to say that we shouldn't praise students. We can praise as much as we please when they learn or do well, but we should wax enthusiastic about their strategies, not about how their performance reveals an attribute they are likely to view as innate and beyond their control. We can rave about their effort, their concentration, the effectiveness of their study strategies, the interesting ideas they came up with, the way they followed through. We can ask them questions that show an intelligent appreciation of their work and what they put into it. We can enthusiastically discuss with them what they learned. This, of course, requires more from us than simply telling them that they are smart, but it is much more appreciative of their work, much more constructive, and it does not carry with it the dangers I've been describing.

What about the times a student really impresses us by doing something quickly, easily—and perfectly? Isn't it appropriate to show our admiration for the child's ability? My honest opinion is that we should not. We should not be giving students the impression that we place a high value on their doing perfect work on tasks that are easy for them. A better approach would be to apologize for wasting their time with something that was too easy, and move them to something that is more challenging. When students make progress in or master that more challenging work, that's when our admiration—for their efforts—should come through.

A Challenging Academic Transition

The studies I have been talking about were carried out in a research setting. Two other studies tracked students with these different viewpoints in a real-life situation, as they were making the transition to junior high school and during their first two years of junior high. This is a point at which academic work generally becomes more demanding than it was in elementary school, and many students stumble. The studies compared the attitudes and achievement of students who believed that intelligence is a fixed quantity with students who believed that they could develop their intellectual potential. We were especially interested in any changes in the degree of success students experienced in junior high school and how they dealt with these changes. For the sake of simplicity, I will combine the results from the two studies, for they showed basically the same thing.

First, the students who believed that intelligence is fixed did indeed feel that poor performance meant they were dumb. Furthermore, they reported, in significantly greater numbers than their peers, that if they did badly on a test, they would seriously consider cheating the next time. This was true even for students who were highly skilled and who had a past record of high achievement.

Perhaps even worse, these students believed that having to make an effort meant they were dumb—hardly an attitude to foster good work habits. In fact, these students reported that even though school achievement was very important to them, one of their prime goals in school was to exert as little effort as possible.

In contrast to the hopelessly counterproductive attitude of the first group, the second group of students, those who believed that intellectual potential can be developed, felt that poor performance was often due to a lack of effort, and it called for more studying. They saw effort as worthwhile and important—something necessary even for geniuses if they are to realize their potential.

So once again, for those who are focused on their fixed intelligence and its adequacy, setbacks and even effort bring a loss of face and self-esteem. But challenges, setbacks, and effort are not threatening to the self-esteem of those who are concerned with developing their potential; they represent opportunities to learn. In fact, many of these students told us that they felt smartest when things were difficult; they gained self-esteem when they applied themselves to meeting challenges.

What about the academic achievement of the two groups making the transition to junior high school? In both studies, we saw that students who believed that intelligence was fixed and was manifest in their performance did more poorly than they had in elementary school. Even many who had been high achievers did much less well. Included among them were many students who entered junior high with high intellectual self-esteem. On the other hand, the students who believed that intellectual potential could be developed showed, as a group, clear gains in their class standing, and many blossomed intellectually. The demands of their new environment, instead of causing them to wilt because they doubted themselves, encouraged them to roll up their sleeves and get to work.

These patterns seem to continue with students entering college. Research with students at highly selective universities found that, although they may enter a situation with equal self-esteem, optimism, and past achievement, students respond to the challenge of college differently: Students in one group by measuring themselves and losing confidence; the others by figuring out what it takes and doing it.

Believing and Achieving

Some of the research my colleagues and I have carried out suggests that it is relatively easy to modify the views of young children in regard to intelligence and effort in a research setting. But is it possible to influence student attitudes in a real-life setting? And do students become set in their beliefs as they grow older? Some exciting new research shows that even college students' views about intelligence and effort can be modified—and that these changes will affect their level of academic achievement. In their study, Aronson and Fried taught minority students at a prestigious university to view their intelligence as a potentiality that could be developed through hard work. For example, they created and showed a film that explained the neural changes that took place in the brain every time students confronted difficulty by exerting effort. The students who were instructed about the relationship between intelligence and effort went on to earn significantly higher grades than their peers who were not. This study, like our intelligence praise studies, shows that (1) students" ideas about their intelligence can be influenced by the messages they receive, and (2) when these ideas change, changes in performance can follow.

But simply getting back to basics and enforcing rigorous standards—which some students will meet and some will not—won't eliminate the pitfalls I have been describing. This approach may convey, even more forcefully, the idea that intelligence is a gift only certain students possess. And it will not, in itself, teach students to value learning and focus on the *process* of achievement or how to deal with obstacles. These students may, more than ever, fear failure because it takes the measure of their intelligence.

A Different Framework

Our research suggests another approach. Instead of trying to convince our students that they are smart or simply enforcing rigorous standards in the hopes that doing so will create high motivation and achievement, teachers should take the following steps: first, get students to focus on their potential to learn; second, teach them to value challenge and learning over looking smart; and third, teach them to concentrate on effort and learning processes in the face of obstacles.

This can be done while holding students to rigorous standards. Within the framework I have outlined, tasks are challenging and effort is highly valued, required, and rewarded. Moreover, we can (and must) give students frank evaluations of their work and their level of skill, but we must make clear that these are evaluations of their current level of performance and skill, not an assessment of their intelligence or their innate ability. In this framework, we do not arrange easy work or constant successes, thinking that we are doing students a favor. We do not lie to students who are doing poorly so they will feel smart: That would rob them of the information they need to work harder and improve. Nor do we just give students hard work that many can't do, thus making them into casualties of the system.

I am not encouraging high-effort situations in which students stay up studying until all hours every night, fearing they will displease their parents or disgrace themselves if they don't get the top test scores. Pushing students to do that is not about valuing learning or about orienting students toward developing their potential. It is about pressuring students to prove their worth through their test scores.

It is also not sufficient to give students piles of homework and say we are teaching them about the importance of effort. We are not talking about quantity here but about teaching students to seek challenging tasks and to engage in an active learning process.

However, we as educators must then be prepared to do our share. We must help students acquire the skills they need for learning, and we must be available as constant resources for learning. It is not enough to keep harping on and praising effort, for this may soon wear thin. And it will not be effective if students don't know *how* to apply their effort appropriately. It is necessary that we as educators understand and teach students how to engage in processes that foster learning, things like task analysis and study skills.

When we focus students on their potential to learn and give them the message that effort is the key to learning, we give them responsibility for and control over their achievement—and over their self-esteem. We acknowledge that learning is not something that someone gives students; nor can they expect to feel good about themselves because teachers tell them they are smart. Both learning and self-esteem are things that students achieve as they tackle challenges and work to master new material.

Students who value learning and effort know how to make and sustain a commitment to valued goals. Unlike some of their peers, they are not afraid to work hard; they know that meaningful tasks involve setbacks; and they know how to bounce back from failure. These are lessons that cannot help but serve them well in life as well as in school.

These are lessons I have learned from my research on students' motivation and achievement, and they are things I wish I had known as a student. There is no reason that every student can't know them now.

References

Aronson, J., & Fried, C. (1998). Reducing stereotype threat and boosting academic achievement of African Americans: The role of conceptions of intelligence. Unpublished manuscript, University of Texas.

Brown, A. L. (1997). Transforming schools into communities of thinking and learning about serious matters. *American Psychologist, 52*, 399–413.

Dweck, C. S., & Sorich, L. (1999). Mastery-oriented thinking. In C. R. Snyder (Ed.), *Coping*. New York: Oxford University Press.

Henderson, V., & Dweck, C. S. (1990). Achievement and motivation in adolescence: A new model and data. In S. Feldman and G. Elliott (Eds.), *At the threshold: The developing adolescent*. Cambridge, MA: Harvard University Press.

Kamins, M. & Dweck, C. S. (1999). Person vs. process praise and criticism: Implications for contingent self-worth and coping. *Developmental Psychology*.

Meyer, W. U. (1982). Indirect communications about perceived ability estimates. *Journal of Educational Psychology, 74*, 888–897.

Mueller, C. M., & Dweck, C. S. (1996). Implicit theories of intelligence: Relation of parental beliefs to children's expectations. Paper presented at the Third National Research Convention of Head Start, Washington, D.C.

Mueller, C. M., & Dweck, C. S. (1998). Intelligence praise can undermine motivation and performance. *Journal of Personality and Social Psychology, 75*, 33–52.

Robins, R. W., & Pals, J. (1998). Implicit self-theories of ability in the academic domain: A test of Dweck's model. Unpublished manuscript, University of California at Davis.

Zhao, W., Dweck, C. S., & Mueller, C. (1998). Implicit theories and depression-like responses to failure. Unpublished manuscript, Columbia University.

19

Dear Dr. Canestrari:

I got a job!! Actually, even though I love it, it's pretty depressing. I'm working in the north-central part of Vermont right near the Canadian border. Most people think about maple syrup and skiing and beautiful snow-covered pine trees. I used to, too. There is so much poverty here. Worse than I could have imagined. A lot of my kids live in cramped trailers without heat. Their clothes are threadbare and I'm pretty sure a lot of them don't eat dinner and I know they come to school without breakfast.

You know, I'm a pretty good teacher but this is challenging. It's like these kids haven't had some of their most basic needs met and I'm asking them to care about their schoolwork. How they even pay attention at all is astounding to me when I really think about it.

One of my colleagues brings in food everyday. And, not as a reward either. She just knows that some kids need to eat more and she's got crackers and pretzels all over the room. Yesterday, I was working with this little guy in my room out in the hall and as the fourth graders lined up for lunch he got all teary-eyed. It dawned on me that he was probably crying thinking about the fact that he didn't have any money with him and his parents didn't pack him anything. I told him I wasn't that hungry and asked him if he could help me out by sharing my lunch with me. He was so happy and not at all self-conscious about it. I don't know how some of these kids make it, I really don't.

Yousef Ibrahim

❖ HOW WOULD YOU RESPOND?

Why do students who have had their basic needs (food, clothing, shelter) met behave better in school? What student needs should teachers and schools meet? Why might students who struggle with the basic needs that Maslow describes have difficulty behaving appropriately in class? What is the relationship between unmet needs and student motivation? Keep these questions in mind as you read the selection from "A Theory of Human Motivation" by Abraham H. Maslow. What questions do you have about the relationship between needs, motivation, and classroom management. How might you extend the discussion of these ideas in class? Finally, how would you respond to Yousef Ibrahim?

❖ A THEORY OF HUMAN MOTIVATION

Abraham H. Maslow

The Basic Needs

The Physiological Needs

Undoubtedly these physiological needs are the most prepotent of all needs. What this means specifically is that in the human being who is missing everything in life in an extreme fashion, it is most likely that the major motivation would be the physiological needs rather than any others. A person who is lacking food, safety, love, and esteem would most probably hunger for food more strongly than for anything else.

If all the needs are unsatisfied, and the organism is then dominated by the physiological needs, all other needs may become simply nonexistent or be pushed into the background. It is then fair to characterize the whole organism by saying simply that it is hungry, for consciousness is almost completely preempted by hunger. All capacities are put into the service of hunger-satisfaction, and the organization of these capacities is almost entirely determined by the one purpose of satisfying hunger. The receptors and effectors, the intelligence, memory, habits, all may now be defined simply as hunger-gratifying tools.

Capacities that are not useful for this purpose lie dormant, or are pushed into the background. The urge to write poetry, the desire to acquire an automobile, the interest in American history, the desire for a new pair of shoes are, in the extreme case, forgotten or become of secondary importance. For the man who is extremely and danger-ously hungry, no other interests exist but food. He dreams food, he remembers food, he thinks about food, he emotes only about food, he perceives only food, and he wants only food. The more subtle determinants that ordinarily fuse with the physiological drives in orga-nizing even feeding, drinking, or sexual behavior, may now be so com-pletely overwhelmed as to allow us to speak at this time (but *only* at this time) of pure hunger drive and behavior, with the one unqualified aim of relief.

Another peculiar characteristic of the human organism when it is dominated by a certain need is that the whole philosophy of the future tends also to change. For our chronically and extremely hungry man, Utopia can be defined simply as a place where there is plenty of food. He tends to think that, if only he is guaranteed food for the rest of his life, he will be perfectly happy and will never want anything more. Life itself tends to be defined in terms of eating. Anything else will be defined as unimportant. Freedom, love, community feeling, respect, philosophy, may all be waved aside as fripperies that are useless, since they fail to fill the stomach. Such a man may fairly be said to live by bread alone.

It cannot possibly be denied that such things are true, but their *gen-erality* can be denied. Emergency conditions are, almost by definition, rare in the normally functioning peaceful society. That this truism can be forgotten is attributable mainly to two reasons. First, rats have few motivations other than physiological ones, and since so much of the research upon motivation has been made with these animals, it is easy to carry the rat picture over to the human being. Second, it is too often not realized that culture itself is an adaptive tool, one of whose main functions is to make the physiological emergencies come less and less often. In most of the known societies, chronic extreme hunger of the emergency type is rare, rather than common. In any case, this is still true in the United States. The average American citizen is experiencing appetite rather than hunger when he says, "I am hungry." He is apt to experience sheer life-and-death hunger only by accident and then only a few times through his entire life.

Obviously a good way to obscure the higher motivations, and to get a lopsided view of human capacities and human nature, is to make the organism extremely and chronically hungry or thirsty. Anyone who attempts to make an emergency picture into a typical one, and who will measure all of man's goals and desires by his behavior during extreme physiological deprivation is certainly being blind to many things. It is quite true that man lives by bread alone—when there is no bread. But what happens to man's desires when there is plenty of bread and when his belly is chronically filled?

At once other (and higher) needs emerge and these, rather than physiological hungers, dominate the organism. And when these in turn are satisfied, again new (and still higher) needs emerge, and so on. This is what we mean by saying that the basic human needs are organized into a hierarchy of relative prepotency.

One main implication of this phrasing is that gratification becomes as important a concept as deprivation in motivation theory, for it releases the organism from the domination of a relatively more physiological need, permitting thereby the emergence of other more social goals. The physiological needs, along with their partial goals, when chronically gratified cease to exist as active determinants or organizers of behavior. They now exist only in a potential fashion in the sense that they may emerge again to dominate the organism if they are thwarted. But a want that is satisfied is no longer a want. The organism is dominated and its behavior organized only by unsatisfied needs. If hunger is satisfied, it becomes unimportant in the current dynamics of the individual.

This statement is somewhat qualified by a hypothesis to be discussed more fully later, namely, that it is precisely those individuals in whom a certain need has always been satisfied who are best equipped to tolerate deprivation of that need in the future, and that furthermore, those who have been deprived in the past will react differently to current satisfactions than the one who has never been deprived.

The Safety Needs

If the physiological needs are relatively well gratified, there then emerges a new set of needs, which we may categorize roughly as the safety needs (security; stability; dependency; protection; freedom from fear, from anxiety and chaos; need for structure, order, law, limits; strength in the protector; and so on). All that has been said to the physiological needs is equally true, although in less degree, of these desires. The organism may equally well be wholly dominated by them. They may serve as the almost exclusive organizers of behavior, recruiting all the capacities of the organism in their service, and we may then fairly describe the whole organism as a safety-seeking mechanism. Again we may say of the receptors, the effectors, of the intellect, and of the other capacities that they are primarily safety-seeking tools. Again, as in the hungry man, we find that the dominating goal is a strong determinant not only of his current world outlook and philosophy but also of his philosophy of the future and of values. Practically everything looks less important than safety and protection (even sometimes the physiological needs, which, being satisfied, are now underestimated). A man in this state, if it is extreme enough and chronic enough, may be characterized as living almost for safety alone.

Although in this chapter we are interested primarily in the needs of the adult, we can approach an understanding of his safety needs perhaps more efficiently by observation of infants and children, in whom these needs are much more simple and obvious. One reason for the clearer appearance of the threat or danger reaction in infants is that they do not inhibit this reaction at all, whereas adults in our society have been taught to inhibit it at all costs. Thus even when adults do feel their safety to be threatened, we may not be able to see this on the surface. Infants will react in a total fashion and as if they were endangered, if they are disturbed or dropped suddenly, startled by loud noises, flashing light, or other unusual sensory stimulation, by rough handling, by general loss of support in the mother's arms, or by inadequate support.[1]

In infants we can also see a much more direct reaction to bodily illnesses of various kinds. Sometimes these illnesses seem to be immediately and *per se* threatening, and seem to make the child feel unsafe. For instance, vomiting, colic, or other sharp pains seem to make the child look at the whole world in a different way. At such a moment of pain, it may be postulated that, for the child, the whole world suddenly changes from sunniness to darkness, so to speak, and become a place in which anything at all might happen, in which previously stable things have suddenly become unstable. Thus a child who because of some bad food is taken ill may for a day or two develop fear, nightmares, and a need for protection and reassurance never seen in him before his illness. The recent work on the psychological effects of surgery on children demonstrates this richly.

Another indication of the child's need for safety is his preference for some kind of undisrupted routine or rhythm. He seems to want a predictable, lawful, orderly world. For instance, injustice, unfairness, or inconsistency in the parents seems to make a child feel anxious and unsafe. This attitude may be not so much because of the injustice *per se* or any particular pains involved, but rather because this treatment threatens to make the world look unreliable, or unsafe, or unpredictable. Young children seem to thrive better under a system that has at least a skeletal outline of rigidity, in which there is a schedule of a kind, some sort of routine, something that can be counted upon, not only for the present but also far into the future. Child psychologists, teachers, and psychotherapists have found that permissiveness within limits, rather than unrestricted permissiveness is preferred as well as *needed* by children. Perhaps, one could express this more accurately by saying that the child needs an organized and structured world rather than an unorganized or unstructured one.

The central role of the parents and the normal family setup are indisputable. Quarreling, physical assault, separation, divorce, or death within the family may be particularly terrifying. Also parental outbursts of rage or threats of punishment directed to the child, calling him names, speaking to him harshly, handling him roughly, or actual physical punishment sometimes elicit such total panic and terror that we must assume more is involved than the physical pain alone. While it is true that in some children this terror may represent also a fear of loss of parental love, it can also occur in completely rejected children, who seem to cling to the hating parents more for sheer safety and protection than because of hope of love.

Confronting the average child with new, unfamiliar, strange, unmanageable stimuli or situations will too frequently elicit the danger or terror reaction, as for example, getting lost or even being separated from the parents for a short time, being confronted with new faces, new situations, or new tasks, the sight of strange, unfamiliar, or uncontrollable objects, illness, or death. Particularly at such times, the child's frantic clinging to his parents is eloquent testimony to their role as protectors (quite apart from their roles as food givers and lover givers).[2]

From these and similar observations, we may generalize and say that the average child and, less obviously, the average adult in our society generally prefers a safe, orderly, predictable, lawful, organized world, which he can count on and in which unexpected, unmanageable, chaotic, or other dangerous things do not happen, and in which, in any case, he has powerful parents or protectors who shield him from harm.

That these reactions may so easily be observed in children is in a way proof that children in our society feel too unsafe (or, in a world, are badly brought up). Children who are reared in an unthreatening, loving family do not ordinarily react as we have described. In such children the danger reactions are apt to come mostly to objects or situations that adults too would consider dangerous.

The healthy and fortunate adult in our culture is largely satisfied in his safety needs. The peaceful, smoothly running, stable, good society ordinarily makes its members feel safe enough from wild animals, extremes of temperature, criminal assault, murder, chaos, tyranny, and so on. Therefore, in a very real sense, he no longer has any safety needs as active motivators. Just as a sated man no longer feels hungry, a safe man no longer feels endangered. If we wish to see these needs directly and clearly we must turn to neurotic or near-neurotic individuals, and to the economic and social underdogs, or else to social chaos, revolution, or breakdown of authority. In between these extremes, we can perceive the expressions of safety needs only in such phenomena as, for instance, the common preference for a job with tenure and protection, the desire for a saving account, and for insurance of various kinds (medical, dental, unemployment, disability, old age).

The safety needs can become very urgent on the social scene whenever there are real threats to law, to order, to the authority of society. The threat of chaos or of nihilism can be expected in most human beings to produce a regression from any higher needs to the more prepotent safety needs. A common, almost an expectable reaction, is the easier acceptance of dictatorship or of military rule. This tends to be true for all human beings, including healthy ones, since they too will tend to respond to danger with realistic regression to the safety need level, and will prepare to defend themselves. But it seems to be most true of people who are living near the safety line. They are particularly disturbed by threats to authority, to legality, and to the representatives of the law.

The Belongingness and Love Needs

If both the physiological and the safety needs are fairly well gratified, there will emerge the love and affection and belongingness needs, and the whole cycle already described will repeat itself with this new center. Now the person will feel keenly, as never before, the absence of friends, or a sweetheart, or a wife, or children. He will hunger for affectionate relations with people in general, namely, for a place in his group or family, and he will strive with great intensity to achieve this goal. He will want to attain such a place more than anything else in the world and may even forget that once, when he was hungry, he sneered at love as unreal or unnecessary or unimportant. Now he will feel sharply the pangs of loneliness, of ostracism, of rejection, of friend-lessness, of rootlessness.

We have very little scientific information about the belongingness need, although this is a common theme in novels, autobiographies, poems, and plays and also in the newer sociological literature. From these we know in a general way the destructive effects on children of moving too often; of disorientation; of the general overmobility that is forced by industrialization; of being without roots, or of despising one's roots, one's origins, one's group; of being torn from one's home and family, and friends and neighbors; of being a transient or a new-comer rather than a native. We still underplay the deep importance of the neighborhood, of one's territory, of one's clan, of one's own "kind," one's class, one's gang, one's familiar working colleagues. I will con-tent myself with recommending a single book that says all this with great poignancy and conviction and that helps us understand our deeply animal tendency to herd, to flock, to join, to belong. Perhaps also, Ardrey's *Territorial Imperative* will help to make all of this conscious. Its very rashness was good for me because it stressed as crucial what I had been only casual about and forced me to think seriously about the matter. Perhaps it will do the same for the reader.

My strong impression is also that *some* proportion of youth rebel-lion groups—I don't know how many or how much—is motivated by the profound hunger for groupiness, for contact, for real togetherness in the face of a common enemy, *any* enemy that can serve to form an amity group simply by posing an external threat. The same kind of thing was observed in groups of soldiers who were pushed into an unwonted brotherliness and intimacy by their common external dan-ger, and who may stick together throughout a lifetime as a conse-quence. Any good society must satisfy this need, one way or another, if it is to survive and be healthy.

The Esteem Needs

All people in our society (with a few pathological exceptions) have a need or desire for a stable, firmly based, usually high evaluation of themselves, for self-respect, or self-esteem, and for the esteem of others. These needs may therefore be classified into two subsidiary sets. These are, first, the desire for strength, for achievement, for adequacy, for mas-tery and competence, for confidence in the face of the world, and for independence and freedom.[3] Second, we have what we may call the desire for reputation or prestige (defining it as respect or esteem from other people), status, fame and glory, dominance, recognition, attention, importance, dignity, or appreciation. These needs have been relatively stressed by Alfred Adler and his followers, and have been relatively neglected by Freud. More and more today, however, there is appearing widespread appreciation of their central importance, among psychoanalysts as well as among clinical psychologists.

Satisfaction of the self-esteem need leads to feelings of self-confidence, worth, strength, capability, and adequacy, of being useful and necessary in the world. But thwarting of these needs produces feelings of inferiority, of weakness, and of helplessness. These feelings in turn give rise to either basic discouragement or else compensatory or neurotic trends. An appreciation of the necessity of basic self-confidence and an understanding of how helpless people are without it can be easily gained from a study of severe traumatic neurosis.

The most stable and therefore most healthy self-esteem is based on deserved respect from others rather than on external fame or celebrity and unwarranted adulation.

The Need for Self-Actualization

Even if all these needs are satisfied, we may still often (if not always) expect that a new discontent and restlessness will soon develop, unless the individual is doing what *he*, individually, is fitted for. A musician must make music, an artist must paint, a poet must write, if he is to be ultimately at peace with himself. What a man can be, he must be. He must be true to his own nature. This need we may call self-actualization.

This term, first coined by Kurt Goldstein is being used in this book in a much more specific and limited fashion. It refers to man's desire for self-fulfillment, namely, to the tendency for him to become actualized in what he is potentially. This tendency might be phrased as the desire to become more and more what one idiosyncratically is, to become everything that one is capable of becoming.

The specific form that these needs will take will of course vary greatly from person to person. In one individual it may take the form of the desire to be an ideal mother, in another it may be expressed athletically, and in still another it may be expressed in painting pictures or in inventions. At this level, individual differences are greatest.

The clear emergence of these needs usually rests upon some prior satisfaction of the physiological, safety, love, and esteem needs.

Notes

1. As the child grows up, sheer knowledge and familiarity as well as better motor development make these dangers less and less dangerous and more and more manageable. Throughout life it may be said that one of the main cognitive functions of education is this neutralizing of apparent dangers through knowledge, e.g., I am not afraid of thunder because I know something about it.

2. A test battery for safety might be confronting the child with a small exploding firecracker, a bewhiskered face, or a hypodermic injection, having the mother leave the room, putting him upon a high ladder, having a mouse crawl up to him, and so on. Of course I cannot seriously recommend the deliberate use of such tests, for they might very well harm the child being tested. But these and similar situations come up by the score in the child's ordinary day-to-day living and may be observed.

3. Whether or not this particular desire is universal we do not know. The crucial question, especially important today, is, will men who are enslaved and dominated inevitably feel dissatisfied and rebellious? We may assume on the basis of commonly known clinical data that a man who has known true freedom (not paid for by giving up safety and security but rather built on the basis of adequate safety and security) will not willingly or easily allow his freedom to be taken away from him. But we do not know for sure that this is true for the person born into slavery.

20

Dear Professor Canestrari:

Why is it that some kids need so much more motivation than others? Why is it that when a teacher says to kids, "If you don't start doing your work, I am going to call your parents," that some will comply and others like Sally will simply return with, "Go ahead, they don't care." Do her parents really not care or is this her way of reaching out? Does she react this way because of the lack of attention and care from her family? Should I appeal first to her obvious lack of attention and care before I try to motivate her to complete her work or should I integrate both at the same time?

Sally is one of 16 in a fourth-grade class. She is extremely bright and grasps concepts very easily. So, when Sally began reacting and responding in this manner, I was truly concerned. At the onset of this behavior, my first response was, "Come on Sally, you are so smart. This is easy for you." She would try a few more problems and then she would give up again. Obviously, this tactic was not going to work with her. She was receiving the attention she desperately wanted, but she was going about it all the wrong way. Next, I tried to have her help other students in the room who were experiencing difficulty hoping that this would demonstrate to her the confidence I had in her and that I believed in her. This worked for a small amount of time, but she returned to the unmotivated child I had encountered earlier. Finally, I asked Sally to come in during recess so that we could talk. I had to try something else before I lost this wonderful child. She deserved to know that someone truly did care about her. I explained to Sally that I understood that it is important to know that someone cares about you. At that point, I just wanted to take her home and give her all the attention and care that she so desperately needed. I told her that she was important to me and I cared about her. I felt she needed to hear that from me. Sally, then said, "Mrs. Henault, I'm glad you had me stay in." We spent the next 15 minutes before the other children came in simply talking about things that were important to her. Sally did not have to say anything else for me to realize that I had filled an empty spot for her. That afternoon, Sally really tried.

When I notice Sally is having a bad day and has retreated back to that unmotivated child, I offer her the opportunity to eat lunch with me, allow her to invite a friend or two to join us, or simply read together during recess time. This might seem insignificant for some, but for Sally it was a lifesaver.

Lori Henault

❖ HOW WOULD YOU RESPOND?

What factors contribute to students giving up on learning? Why do some students drop out of school before graduation? What teacher behaviors might contribute to feelings of student helplessness? What teacher behaviors might help turn around kids who have given up hope? How can we motivate unmotivated students? Can lack of motivation be attributed to some genetic flaw in a child or is a child socialized in a manner that causes an inability to cope or adapt to new situations? Has Sally experienced some trauma? Keep these questions in mind as you read the following piece on learned helplessness by Martin E. P. Seligman and his colleagues. What questions do you have about students who simply give up? How might you extend the discussion of these ideas in class? Finally, how would you respond to Lori Henault?

❖ ALLEVIATION OF LEARNED HELPLESSNESS IN THE DOG[1]

Martin E. P. Seligman, Stephen F. Maier, and James H. Geer

Dogs given inescapable shock in a Pavlovian harness later seem to "give up" and passively accept traumatic shock in shuttlebox escape/avoidance training. A theoretical analysis of this phenomenon was presented. As predicted by this analysis, the failure to escape was alleviated by repeatedly compelling the dog to make the response which terminated shock. This maladaptive passive behavior in the face of trauma may be related to maladaptive passive behavior in humans. The importance of instrumental control over aversive events in the cause, prevention, and treatment of such behaviors was discussed.

This paper discusses a procedure that produces a striking behavior abnormality in dogs, outlines an analysis which predicts a method for eliminating the abnormality, and presents data which support the prediction. When a normal, naïve dog receives escape/avoidance training in a shuttlebox, the following behavior typically occurs: At the onset of electric shock, the dog runs frantically about, defecating, urinating, and howling, until it scrambles over the barrier and so escapes from shock. On the next trial, the dog, running and howling, crosses the barrier more quickly, and so on until efficient avoidance emerges. See Solomon and Wynne (1953) for a detailed description.

Overmier and Seligman (1967) have reported the behavior of dogs which had received *inescapable* shock while strapped in a Pavlovian harness 24 hr. before shuttlebox training. Typically, such a dog reacts *initially* to shock in the shuttlebox in the same manner as the naïve dog. However, in dramatic contrast to the naïve dog, it soon stops running and remains silent until shock terminates. The dog does not cross the barrier and escape from shock. Rather, it seems to "give up" and passively "accept" the shock. On succeeding trials, the dog continues to fail to make escape movements and thus takes 50 sec. of severe, pulsating shock on each trial. If the dog makes an escape or avoidance response, this does not reliably predict occurrence of future responses, as it does for the normal dog. Pretreated dogs occasionally escape or avoid by jumping the barrier and then revert to taking the shock. The behavior abnormality produced by prior inescapable shock is highly maladaptive: a naïve dog receives little shock in shuttlebox training because it escapes quickly and eventually avoids shock altogether. A dog previously exposed to inescapable shock, in contrast, may take unlimited shock without escaping or avoiding at all.

Method

Subjects

The Ss were four mongrel dogs. They weighed 25–29 lb., were 15–19 in. high at the shoulder, and were housed in individual cages with food and water freely available. Each dog chronically failed to escape shock (see Procedure) as a result of receiving inescapable shock in Experiment I of Seligman and Maier (1967).

Apparatus

The apparatus is described fully by Overmier and Seligman (1967). In brief, it consisted of two separate units: a Pavlovian harness, in which initial exposure to inescapable shock occurred, and a dog shuttlebox, in which escape/avoidance training and modification of the failure to escape were carried out.

The unit in which each S was exposed to inescapable shock was a rubberized cloth hammock located inside a shielded white sound-reducing cubicle. The hammock was constructed so that S's legs hung down below his body through four holes. The S's legs were secured in this position, and S was strapped into the hammock. The S's head was held in position by panels placed on either side and a yoke between them across S's neck. Shock was applied from a 500-VAC transformer through a fixed resistor of 20,000 ohms. The shock was applied to S through brass-plate electrodes coated with electrode paste and taped to the footpath of S's hind feet. The shock intensity was 6.0 ma.

The unit in which S received escape/avoidance trials was a two-way shuttlebox with two black compartments separated by an adjustable barrier. Running along the upper part of the front of the shuttlebox were two one-way mirror windows, through which E could observe and which E could open. The barrier was set at S's shoulder height. Each compartment was illuminated by two 50-w. and one 73½-w. lamps. The CS consisted of turning off the four 50-w. lamps which resulted in a sharp decrease in illumination. The UCS was 4.5-ma. electric shock applied through the grid floors from a 500-VAC source. The polarity pattern of the grid bars was scrambled four times a second. Whenever S crossed from one side of the shuttlebox to the other, photocell beams were interrupted, and the trial was terminated. Latency of crossing was measured from CS onset to the nearest .01 sec. by an electric clock. Seventy decibels (SPL) white noise was present in both units.

Procedure

Inescapable shock exposure. Each S was strapped into the harness and given 64 trials of inescapable shock. The shocks were presented in a sequence of trials of diminishing duration. The mean intershock interval was 90 sec. with a 60–120-sec. range. Each S received a total of 226 sec. of shock.

Instrumental escape/avoidance training. Twenty-four hours after inescapable shock exposure, Ss received 10 trials of instrumental escape/avoidance training in the shuttlebox. The onset of the CS (dimmed illumination) initiated each trial, and the CS remained on until trial termination. The CS-UCS onset interval was 10 sec. If S crossed to the other compartment during this interval, the CS terminated, and no shock was presented. If S did not cross during the CS-UCS interval, shock came on and remained on until S crossed. If no response occurred within 60 sec. of CS onset, the trial was automatically terminated, and a 60-sec. latency was recorded. The average intertrial interval was 90 sec. with a 60–120-sec. range.

All four Ss failed to escape shock on each of the 10 trials. Thus each S took 500 sec. of shock during the first escape/avoidance session.

Testing for chronic failure to escape. Seven days later, Ss were again placed in the shuttlebox and given 10 further escape/avoidance trials. Again, each S failed to escape shock on every trial (although one S avoided shock once, on the fifth trial). By this time, each S was failing to make any escape movements and was remaining silent during shock on every trial. Previous work has shown that when a dog remains silent and fails to make escape movements during shock, this reliably predicts that the dog will continue to fail to escape and avoid.

Treatment. The attempt at behavioral modification consisted of two distinct phases: all Ss received Phase I; if Phase I succeeded, as it did with one of the four dogs, no further treatment was given, and "recovery" (see Recovery section below) was begun. The other three Ss received Phase II following Phase I.

Phase I: no barrier, calling. At intervals ranging from 4 to 25 days following the demonstration that the interference was chronic, Ss were again placed in the shuttlebox. The escape/avoidance contingencies used previously remained in effect during Phase I and II trials. The barrier dividing the two sides of the shuttlebox (formerly set at shoulder height) was removed. Thus in order to escape or avoid, S had only to step over the remaining 5-in. high divider. In addition, E opened the observation window on the side of the shuttlebox opposite the side S was on and called to S ("Here, boy") during shock and during the CS-UCS interval. The rationale for such treatment was to encourage S to make the appropriate response on its own, thus exposing itself to the response-reinforcement contingency. One S responded to this treatment and began to escape and avoid. The remaining Ss then received Phase II.

Phase II: forced escape/avoidance exposure. Phase II began when it was clear that Phase I would not produce escape and avoidance in the remaining three Ss since they remained silent and motionless during Phase I. The S was removed from the shuttlebox, and two long leashes were tied around its neck. The *S* was put back into the shuttlebox, and escape/avoidance trials continued. The end of each leash was brought out at opposite ends of the shuttlebox. Thus, two *E*s were able to drag *S* back and forth across the shuttlebox by pulling one of the leashes. Phase II consisted of pulling *S* across to the safe side on each trial during shock or during the CS-UCS interval. A maximum of 25 Phase II trials per day were given. The rationale for Phase II was to force *S* to expose himself to the response-reinforcement contingency. Such "directive therapy" continued until *S* began to respond without being pulled by *E*.

Recovery. Following Phase II (for three dogs) and Phase I (for the other dog), each *S* received further escape/avoidance trials. The barrier height was gradually increased over the course of 15 trials until shoulder height had been reached. Ten further escape/avoidance trials were then given. The last five of these recovery trials (with the barrier at shoulder height) were administered from 5 to 10 days following the first five trials with the barrier at this height. This tested the durability of the recovery.

Results

Figure 20.1 presents the results of this study. It is clear that the procedures employed in Phases I and II of treatment were wholly successful in breaking up the maladaptive failure to escape and avoid shock. With the single exception of one *S* on one trial, the dogs had not escaped or avoided the intense shock prior to treatment. This is indicated by the mean percentage of escape or avoidance responses present at or near zero during the pretreatment phase. Following Phase I (no barrier, calling) and Phase II (forced escape/avoidance exposure) of treatment, posttreatment recovery trials without forcing or calling were given to determine the effectiveness of the treatment. All *S*s escaped or avoided on every recovery trial.

The behavior of one *S* was successfully modified by Phase I of treatment. After sporadic failures to escape shock during this phase, it began to escape and avoid reliably after 20 Phase I trials. With the barrier increased to shoulder height, it continued to avoid reliably. The other three dogs all responded to treatment in a fashion similar to one another: after failing to respond to Phase I, each of these dogs began to respond on its own after differing numbers of Phase II trials on which it had to be pulled to safety. One of the Phase II *S*s required 20 forced exposures to escape and avoid in Phase II before it began to respond

Figure 20.1   Mean Percentage of Escape Plus Avoidance Responses Before
Treatment and During Posttreatment Recovery Trials

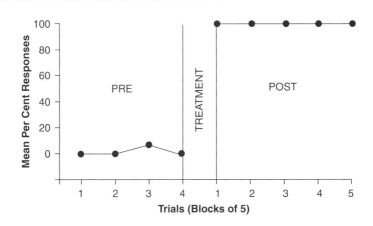

without being pulled; the other two required 35 and 50 such trials. During the course of Phase II trials, progressively less forceful pulls were required before S crossed to the safe side. With the barrier increased to shoulder height following Phase II, each S escaped and avoided efficiently. At this stage, the dogs responded like normal dogs at or near asymptotic avoidance performance.

Discussion

The chronic failure of dogs to escape shock can be eliminated by physically compelling them to engage repeatedly in the response which terminates shock. Solomon, Kamin, and Wynne (1953) also attenuated maladaptive behavior in dogs by forcing them to expose themselves to the experimental contingencies. They reported that dogs continued to make avoidance responses long after shock was no longer present in the situation. A glass barrier, which prevented the dogs from making the response and forced them to "reality test," attenuated the persistent responding somewhat. Such "directive therapy" also is similar to Maier and Klee's (1945) report that abnormal positional fixations in rats were eliminated by forcing the rat to respond to the nonfixated side, and to Masserman's (1943, pp. 76–77) report that "neurotic" feeding inhibition could be overcome by forcing the cat into close proximity with food.

Seligman and Maier (1967) suggested that during its initial experience with inescapable shock, S learns that its responses are independent of shock termination. They further suggested that this learning not only reduces the probability of response initiation to escape shock, but also inhibits the formation of the response-relief association if S does make an escape or avoidance response in the shuttlebox. That the dogs escaped and avoided at all after being forcibly exposed to the response-relief contingency confirmed the suggestion that they had initially learned that their responses were independent of shock termination and that this learning was contravened by forcible exposure to the contingency. The finding that so many forced exposures to the contingency were required before they responded on their own (before they "caught on") confirmed the suggestion that the initial learning inhibited the formation of a response-relief association when the dog made a relief-producing response.

The perception of degree of control over the events in one's life seems to be an important determinant of the behavior of human beings. Lefcourt (1966) has summarized extensive evidence which supports this view. Cromwell, Rosenthal, Shakow, and Kahn (1961), for example, reported that schizophrenics perceive reinforcement to be externally controlled (reinforcement occurs independently of their responses) to a greater extent than normals. Such evidence, along with the animal data cited above, suggests that lack of control over reinforcement may be of widespread importance in the development of psychopathology in both humans and infrahumans.

In conclusion, one might speculate that experience with traumatic events in which the individual can do nothing to eliminate or mitigate the trauma results in passive responding to future aversive events in humans. The findings of Seligman and Maier (1967) suggest that an individual might be immunized against the debilitating effects of uncontrollable trauma by having had prior experience with instrumental control over the traumatic events. Finally, the findings suggest that the pathological behavior resulting from inescapable trauma might be alleviated by repeated exposure of the individual to the trauma under conditions in which his responses were instrumental in obtaining relief. It has been demonstrated that normal escape/avoidance behavior can be produced in "passive" dogs by forcibly exposing them to relief-producing responses.

Note

1. This research was supported by grants to R. L. Solomon from the National Science Foundation (GB-2428) and the National Institute of Mental Health (MH-04202). The authors are grateful to him for his advice in the

conduct and reporting of this experiment. The authors also thank J. P. Brady and J. Mecklenburger for their critical readings of the manuscript.

References

Bettelheim, B. *The informed heart.* New York: Free Press of Glencoe, 1960.

Blueler, E. *Dementia praecox or the group of schizophrenics.* New York: International Universities Press, 1950.

Carlson, N. J., & Black, A. H. Traumatic avoidance learning: The effect of preventing escape responses. *Canadian Journal of Psychology,* 1960, 14, 21–28.

Cofer, C. N., & Appley, M. A. *Motivation: Theory and research.* New York: Wiley, 1964.

Cromwell, R., Rosenthal, D., Shakow, D., & Kahn, T. Reaction time, locus of control, choice behavior and descriptions of parental behavior in schizophrenic and normal subjects. *Journal of Personality,* 1961, 29, 36–380.

Lefcourt, H. M. Internal versus external control of reinforcement: A review. *Psychological Bulletin,* 1966, 65, 206–224.

Liddell, H. S. *Emotional hazards in animals and man.* Springfield, IL: Charles C. Thomas, 1956.

MacDonald, A. Effect of adaptation to the unconditioned stimulus upon the formation of conditional avoidance responses. *Journal of Experimental Psychology,* 1946, 36, 11–12.

Maier, N., & Klee, J. Studies of abnormal behavior in the rat: XVII. Guidance versus trial and error in the alteration of habits and fixations. *Journal of Psychology,* 1945, 19, 133–163.

Maier, N. R. F. *Frustration: The study of behavior without a goal.* New York: McGraw-Hill, 1949.

Masserman, J. H. *Behavior and neurosis.* Chicago: University of Chicago Press, 1943.

Mowrer, O. H. *Learning theory and behavior.* New York: Wiley, 1960.

Overmier, J. B., & Seligman, M. E. P. Effects of inescapable shock upon subsequent escape and avoidance responding. *Journal of Comparative and Physiological Psychology,* 1967, 63, 28–33.

Richter, C. On the phenomenon of sudden death in animals and man. *Psychosomatic Medicine,* 1957, 19, 191–198.

Seligman, M. E. P., & Maier, S. F. Failure to escape traumatic shock. *Journal of Experimental Psychology,* 1967, 74, 1–9.

Solomon, R. L., Kamin, L., & Wynne, L. C. Traumatic avoidance learning: The outcomes of several extinction procedures with dogs. *Journal of Abnormal and Social Psychology,* 1953, 48, 291–302.

Solomon, R. L., & Wynne, L. C. Traumatic avoidance learning: Acquisition in normal dogs. *Psychological Monographs,* 1953, 67 (4, Whole No. 354).

Wallace, A. F. C. Mazeway disintegration: The individual's perception of sociocultural disorganization. *Human Organization,* 1957, 16, 23–27.

Questions for Reflection

Let's look back at the letters and readings in **Part V, What Factors Influence Student Motivation?** Consider the following questions as you begin formulating your own ideas about how to apply theories of development into planned instructional practice.

1. How does what Kohn and Dweck have to say about praise sit with you? Does the research that they cite seem consistent with your own experience and what you have internalized about positive reinforcement in the form of praise or tangible reinforcers? Imagine a conversation between Alfie Kohn and B. F. Skinner. What kinds of evidence might each provide to bolster their arguments?

2. How might Maslow respond to Kohn and Dweck's assertions about praise? Does saying, "Good job" satisfy the kinds of complex psychological and emotional needs that Maslow describes in his hierarchy? To what degree can these kinds of verbal responses really promote self-actualization?

3. What school policies or classroom conditions might lead to students with disabilities and/or English-language learners developing what Seligman describes as "learned helplessness"? How might students without these challenges come to experience learned helplessness?

4. Think about Carol Dweck's ideas about what teachers really need to know about motivating students. How do her ideas help to inform teachers about making the kinds of connections with students that result in the most powerful learning? In what ways are her views consistent with those of Skinner, Kohn, and Seligman?

❖ YOUR OWN IDEAS

What ideas seem most important to you as you reflect about teaching and learning in real classrooms? What do you think is most important for new teachers to consider? What further questions did the authors raise for you in Part V that have not been adequately answered?

_____

_____

_____

_____

_____

_____

_____

_____

_____

_____

_____

_____

_____

_____

_____

Suggested Readings

Ames, C. (1992). Classrooms: Goals, structures, and student motivation. *Journal of Educational Psychology, 84,* 261–271.

Deci, E. L., Koestner, R., & Ryan, R. M. (1999). A meta-analytic review of experiments examining the effects of extrinsic rewards on intrinsic motivation. *Psychological Bulletin, 125,* 627–668.

Dweck, C. (2000). *Self-theories: Their role in motivation, personality, and development.* Philadelphia: Routledge.

Kohn, A. (1993). *Punished by rewards: The trouble with gold stars, incentive plans, A's, praise, and other bribes.* Boston: Houghton Mifflin.

Lepper, M. R., & Greene, D. (1978). *The hidden costs of rewards: New perspectives on the psychology of human motivation.* Hillsdale, NJ: Lawrence Erlbaum.

Maslow, A. H. (1970). *Motivation and personality* (2nd ed.). New York: Harper & Row.

Seligman, M. E. P. (1975). *Helplessness: On depression, development, and death.* San Francisco: Freeman.

Weiner, B. (1979). A theory of motivation for some classroom experiences. *Journal of Educational Psychology, 71,* 3–25.

Weiner, B. (1986). *An attributional theory of motivation and emotion.* New York: Springer.

PART VI

What Do Good Assessments Look Like?

21

Dear Professor Marlowe:

It has been a long time, but I want you to know that I'm alive and well. Still at Martin Luther King Elementary. Still teaching grade three. Still doing my best to offer students the most effective constructivist lessons that I can. Still trying hard to differentiate instruction. Still trying to apply all the things that we learned about great teaching and learning in your class. But, I have noticed some changes. The kids are a lot more ethnically and culturally diverse. When I came to MLK 6 years ago, the kids were mostly poor black kids. Now, there are growing Latino and Asian neighborhoods on the Westside and the population of my classroom reflects the changing community. I can remember talking about the standards movement in your class and the skepticism that you had about high-stakes testing. To be perfectly honest with you, I wasn't really concerned that much at that time. But, let me tell you, I have changed my mind. We are getting slammed. Standards and statewide assessments are impacting us in a big way and it seems that everything we do is driven by tests. I feel like I've been rolled over by this giant snowball and its getting bigger and bigger and moving faster and faster. So fast that I can hardly see where we are going. I know one thing for sure though, this snowball is flattening what I thought was the right kind of approach especially when it comes to individualizing learning. I do not see any end in sight. How can I put the standards and testing hysteria in perspective? How can I find the time to teach the way I know is best? It's getting in my way and I'm not happy about it. When I go to my fellow teachers and the principal they say, "Get used to it. This is the way it is."

Sue D'Amico

❖ HOW WOULD YOU RESPOND?

If so many people complain about standardized tests, why do schools continue to give them? Who decides what items should be on a standardized test? Who uses the results of these tests and for what purposes? In what ways is the use of standardized tests a self-maintaining process? Keep these questions in mind as you read "Standardized Testing and Its Victims" by Alfie Kohn. What questions do you have about standardized testing? How might you extend the discussion of these ideas in class? Finally, how would you respond to Sue D'Amico?

❖ STANDARDIZED TESTING AND ITS VICTIMS

Alfie Kohn

Standardized testing has swelled and mutated, like a creature in one of those old horror movies, to the point that it now threatens to swallow our schools whole. (Of course, on "The Late, Late Show," no one ever insists that the monster is really doing us a favor by making its victims more "accountable.") But let's put aside metaphors and even opinions for a moment so that we can review some indisputable facts on the subject.

Fact 1. *Our children are tested to an extent that is unprecedented in our history and unparalleled anywhere else in the world.* While previous generations of American students have had to sit through tests, never have the tests been given so frequently, and never have they played such a prominent role in schooling. The current situation is also unusual from an international perspective: Few countries use standardized tests for children below high school age—or multiple-choice tests for students of any age.

Fact 2. *Noninstructional factors explain most of the variance among test scores when schools or districts are compared.* A study of math results on the 1992 National Assessment of Educational Progress found that the combination of four such variables (number of parents living at home, parents' educational background, type of community, and poverty rate) accounted for a whopping 89 percent of the differences in state scores. To the best of my knowledge, all such analyses of state tests have found comparable results, with the numbers varying only slightly as a function of which socioeconomic variables were considered.

Fact 3. *Norm-referenced tests were never intended to measure the quality of learning or teaching.* The Stanford, Metropolitan, and California Achievement Tests (SAT, MAT, and CAT), as well as the Iowa and Comprehensive Tests of Basic Skills (ITBS and CTBS), are designed so that only about half the test-takers will respond correctly to most items. The main objective of these tests is to rank, not to rate; to spread out the scores, not to gauge the quality of a given student or school.

Fact 4. *Standardized-test scores often measure superficial thinking.* In a study published in the Journal of Educational Psychology, elementary school students were classified as "actively" engaged in learning if they asked questions of themselves while they read and tried to connect what they were doing to past learning; and as "superficially" engaged if they just copied down answers, guessed a lot, and skipped the hard parts. It turned out that high scores on both the CTBS and the MAT were more likely to be found among students who exhibited the superficial approach to learning. Similar findings have emerged from studies of middle school students (also using the CTBS) and high school students (using the other SAT, the college-admission exam). To be sure, there are plenty of students who think deeply and score well on tests—and plenty of students who do neither. But, as a rule, it appears that standardized-test results are positively correlated with a shallow approach to learning.

Fact 5. *Virtually all specialists condemn the practice of giving standardized tests to children younger than 8 or 9 years old.* I say "virtually" to cover myself here, but, in fact, I have yet to find a single reputable scholar in the field of early-childhood education who endorses such testing for young children.

Fact 6. *Virtually all relevant experts and organizations condemn the practice of basing important decisions, such as graduation or promotion, on the results of a single test.* The National Research Council takes this position, as do most other professional groups (such as the American Educational Research Association and the American Psychological Association), the generally pro-testing American Federation of Teachers, and even the companies that manufacture and sell the exams. Yet just such high-stakes testing is currently taking place, or scheduled to be introduced soon, in more than half the states.

Fact 7. *The time, energy, and money that are being devoted to preparing students for standardized tests have to come from somewhere.* Schools across the country are cutting back or even eliminating programs in the arts, recess for young children, electives for high schoolers, class meetings (and other activities intended to promote social and moral learning), discussions about current events (since that material will not appear on the test), the use of literature in the early grades (if the tests are focused narrowly on decoding skills), and entire subject areas such as science (if the tests cover only language arts and math). Anyone who doubts the scope and significance of what is being sacrificed in the desperate quest to raise scores has not been inside a school lately.

Fact 8. *Many educators are leaving the field because of what is being done to schools in the name of "accountability" and "tougher standards."* I have no hard numbers here, but there is more than enough anecdotal evidence—corroborated by administrators, teacher-educators, and other observers across the country, and supported by several state surveys that quantify the extent of disenchantment with testing—to warrant classifying this as a fact. Prospective teachers are rethinking whether they want to begin a career in which high test scores matter most, and in which they will be pressured to produce these scores. Similarly, as *The New York Times* reported in its lead story of Sept. 3, 2000, "a growing number of schools are rudderless, struggling to replace a graying corps of principals at a time when the pressure to raise test scores and other new demands have made an already difficult job an increasingly thankless one." It also seems clear that most of the people who are quitting, or seriously thinking about doing so, are not mediocre performers who are afraid of being held accountable. Rather, they are among the very best educators, frustrated by the difficulty of doing high-quality teaching in the current climate.

Faced with inconvenient facts such as these, the leading fall-back position for defenders of standardized testing runs as follows: Even if it's true that suburban schools are being dumbed down by the tests, inner-city schools are often horrendous to begin with. There, at least, standards are finally being raised as a result of high-stakes testing.

Let's assume this argument is made in good faith, rather than as a cover for pursuing a standards-and-testing agenda for other reasons. Moreover, let's immediately concede the major premise here, that low-income minority students have been badly served for years. The problem is that the cure is in many ways worse than the disease—and not only because of the preceding eight facts, which remain both stubbornly true and painfully relevant to testing in the inner city. As Sen. Paul Wellstone, D-Minn., put it in a speech delivered last spring: "Making students accountable for test scores works well on a bumper sticker, and it allows many politicians to look good by saying that they will not tolerate failure. But it represents a hollow promise. Far from improving education, high-stakes testing marks a major retreat from fairness, from accuracy, from quality, and from equity." Here's why.

- *The tests may be biased.* For decades, critics have complained that many standardized tests are unfair because the questions require a set of knowledge and skills more likely to be possessed by children from a privileged background. The discriminatory effect is particularly pronounced with norm-referenced tests, where the imperative to spread out the scores often produces questions that tap knowledge gained outside of school. This, as W. James Popham argues, provides a powerful advantage to students whose parents are affluent and well-educated. It's more than a little ironic to rely on biased tests to "close the gap" between rich and poor.

- *Guess who can afford better test preparation.* When the stakes rise, people seek help anywhere they can find it, and companies eager to profit from this desperation by selling test-prep materials and services have begun to appear on the scene, most recently tailoring their products to state exams. Naturally, affluent families, schools, and districts are better able to afford such products, and the most effective versions of such products, thereby exacerbating the inequity of such testing. Moreover, when poorer schools do manage to scrape together the money to buy these materials, it's often at the expense of books and other educational resources that they really need.

- *The quality of instruction declines most for those who have least.* Standardized tests tend to measure the temporary acquisition of facts and skills, including the skill of test-taking itself, more than genuine understanding. To that extent, the fact that such tests are more likely to be used and emphasized in schools with higher percentages of minority students (a fact that has been empirically verified) predictably results in poorer-quality teaching in such schools. The use of a high-stakes strategy only underscores the preoccupation with these tests and, as a result, accelerates a reliance on direct-instruction techniques and endless practice tests. "Skills-based instruction, the type to which most children of color are subjected, tends to foster low-level uniformity and subvert academic potential," as Dorothy Strickland, an African-American professor at Rutgers University, has remarked.

Again, there's no denying that many schools serving low-income children of color were second-rate to begin with. Now, however, some of these schools, in Chicago, Houston, Baltimore, and elsewhere, are arguably becoming third-rate as testing pressures lead to a more systematic use of low-level, drill-and-skill teaching, often in the context of packaged programs purchased by school districts. Thus, when someone emphasizes the importance of "higher expectations" for minority children, we might reply, "Higher expectations to do what? Bubble-in more ovals correctly on a bad test—or pursue engaging projects that promote sophisticated thinking?" The movement driven by "tougher standards," "accountability," and similar slogans arguably lowers meaningful expectations insofar as it relies on standardized testing as the primary measure of achievement. The more that poor children fill in worksheets on command (in an effort to raise their test scores), the further they fall behind affluent kids who are more likely to get lessons that help them understand ideas. If the drilling does result in higher scores, the proper response is not celebration, but outrage: The test results may well have improved at the expense of real learning.

- *Standards aren't the main ingredient that's in low supply.* Anyone who is serious about addressing the inequities of American education would naturally want to investigate differences in available resources. A good argument could be made that the fairest allocation strategy, which is only common sense in some countries, is to provide not merely equal amounts across schools and districts, but more for the most challenging student populations. This does happen in some states—by no means all—but, even when it does, the money is commonly offered as a short-term grant (hardly sufficient to compensate for years of inadequate funding) and is often earmarked for test preparation rather than for higher-quality teaching. Worse, high-stakes testing systems may provide more money to those already successful (for example, in the form of bonuses for good scores) and less to those whose need is greatest.

Many public officials, along with like-minded journalists and other observers, are apt to minimize the matter of resources and assume that everything deficient about education for poor and minority children can be remedied by more forceful demands that we "raise the bar." The implication here would seem to be that teachers and students could be doing a better job but have, for some reason, chosen not to do so and need only be bribed or threatened into improvement. (In fact, this is the tacit assumption behind all incentive systems.) The focus among policymakers has been on standards of outcome rather than standards of opportunity.

To make matters worse, some supporters of high-stakes testing have not just ignored, but contemptuously dismissed, the relevance of barriers to achievement in certain neighborhoods. Explanations about very real obstacles such as racism, poverty, fear of crime, low teacher salaries, inadequate facilities, and language barriers are sometimes written off as mere "excuses." This is at once naive and callous, and, like any other example of minimizing the relevance of structural constraints, ultimately serves the interests of those fortunate enough not to face them.

- *Those allegedly being helped will be driven out.* When rewards and punishments are applied to educators, those who teach low-scoring populations are the most likely to be branded as failures and may decide to leave the profession. Minority and low-income students are disproportionately affected by the incessant pressure on teachers to raise scores. But when high stakes are applied to the students themselves, there is little doubt about who is most likely to be denied diplomas as a consequence of failing an exit exam—or who will simply give up and drop out in anticipation of such an outcome. If states persist in making a student's fate rest on a single test, the likely result over the next few years will be nothing short of catastrophic. Unless we act to stop this, we will be facing a scenario that might be described without exaggeration as an educational ethnic cleansing.

Let's be charitable and assume that the ethnic aspect of this perfectly predictable consequence is unintentional. Still, it is hard to deny that high-stakes testing, even when the tests aren't norm-referenced, is ultimately about sorting. Someone unfamiliar with the relevant psychological research (and with reality) might insist that raising the bar will "motivate" more students to succeed. But perform the following thought experiment: Imagine that almost all the students in a given state met the standards and passed the tests. What would be the reaction from most politicians, businesspeople, and pundits? Would they now concede that our public schools are terrific—or would they take this result as prima facie evidence that the standards were too low and the tests were too easy? As Deborah Meier and others have observed, the phrase "high standards" by definition means standards that everyone won't be able to meet.

The tests are just the means by which this game is played. It is a game that a lot of kids—predominantly kids of color—simply cannot win. Invoking these very kids to justify a top-down, heavy-handed, corporate-style, test-driven version of school reform requires a stunning degree of audacity. To take the cause of equity seriously is to work for the elimination of tracking, for more equitable funding, and for the universal implementation of more sophisticated approaches to pedagogy (as opposed to heavily scripted direct-instruction programs). But standardized testing, while bad news across the board, is especially hurtful to students who need our help the most.

22

Professor Canestrari:

Take a look at this quiz. My cooperating teacher insists on these kinds of tests to assess student achievement in our seventh-grade geography class. All I can think of is traxoline, that term that Judith Lanier coined about the kind of busywork students get in social studies classes. Traxoline, traxoline, and more traxoline.

Matching—Put the letter of the correct answer in the space before each matching item.

___1. Great Barrier Reef   a. separates Australia from Indonesia

___2. Rabbits   b. covered by woodlands

___3. Murray River   c. world's largest coral reef

___4. Cape York Peninsula   d. longest river in Australia

___5. Timor Sea   e. a menace to sheep ranchers

First, how do I convince my cooperating teacher that this is altogether useless? He doesn't seem to see that his tests are a mirror image of the kind of teaching and learning that's taking place. Any advice? Oh and by the way, the homework looks a lot like this but in the form of recall questions like "How long was the fence that sheep ranchers built to keep rabbits away from their flocks?"

Tom Kiefer

❖ HOW WOULD YOU RESPOND?

Are exams important? Why? As a teacher, how will you go about preparing exams? What kinds of responses will convince you that students have mastered the content material? Do you think the matching exam Tom Kiefer writes about above is a useful way of assessing student learning? Keep these questions in mind as you read "Teaching to the (Authentic) Test" by Grant Wiggins. What questions do you have about testing? How might you extend the discussion of these ideas in class? Finally, how would you respond to Tom Kiefer?

❖ TEACHING TO THE (AUTHENTIC) TEST

Grant Wiggins

Testing can once again serve teaching and learning if tests clarify and set intellectual standards.

Practical alternatives and sound arguments now exist to make testing once again serve teaching and learning. Ironically, we *should* "teach to the test." The catch is to design and then teach to *standard-setting* tests so that practicing for and taking the tests actually enhances rather than impedes education, and so that a criterion-referenced diploma makes externally mandated tests unobtrusive—even unnecessary.

Setting Standards

If tests determine what teachers actually teach and what students will study for—and they do—when the road to reform is a straight but steep one: test those capacities and habits we think are essential, and test them in context. Make them replicate, within reason, the challenges at the heart of each academic discipline. Let them be—authentic.

What are the actual performances that we want students to be good at, that represent model challenges? Design them by department, by school, and by district—and worry about a fair, efficient, and objective method of grading them as a *secondary* problem. Do we judge our students to be deficient in writing, speaking, listening, artistic creation, research, thoughtful analysis, problem posing, and problem solving?

Let the tests ask them to write, speak, listen, create, do original research, analyze, pose and solve problems.

Rather than seeing tests as after-the-fact devices for checking up on what students have learned, we should see them as instructional: the central vehicle for clarifying and setting intellectual standards. The recital, debate, play or game (and the criteria by which they are judged)—the "performance"—is not a checkup, it is the heart of the matter; all coaches *happily* teach to it. We should design academic tests to be similarly standard setting, not merely standardized.

Reform of testing depends, however, on teachers' recognizing that standardized testing evolved and proliferated because the school transcript became untrustworthy. An "A" in "English" means only that some adult thought the student's work was excellent. Compared to what or whom? As determined by what criteria? In reference to what specific subject matter? The high school diploma, by remaining tied to no standard other than credit accrual and seat time, provides no useful information about what students have studied or what they can actually do with what was studied.

To regain control over both testing and instruction, schools need to rethink their diploma requirements and grades. They need a clear set of appropriate and objective criteria, enabling both students *and outsiders* to know what counts, what is essential—what a school's standards really are. Until we specify what students must directly demonstrate to earn a diploma, they will continue to pass by meeting the de facto "standard" of being doubtful and persistent—irrespective of the quality of their work. And standardized testmakers will continue to succeed in hawking simplistic norm-referenced tests to districts for lack of a better accountability scheme.

Exhibitions of Mastery

> *The diploma should be awarded upon a successful final demonstration of mastery for graduation—an "Exhibition" . . . As the diploma is awarded when earned, the school's program proceeds with no strict age grading and with no system of "credit earned" by time spent in class. The emphasis is on the students' demonstration that they can do important things.*

> —From the Prospectus of
> the Coalition of Essential Schools

The "exhibition of mastery," proposed by Ted Sizer in *Horace's Compromise* (1984) and a cornerstone of the "Essential School," is one attempt to grapple with these issues. The intent of the exhibitions project is to help schools and districts design more authentic, engaging, revealing, and trustworthy "tests" of a student's intellectual ability.

The reference to engagement is not incidental. The exhibition of mastery was initially proposed as an antidote to student passivity and boredom, not merely as a more valid form of assessment. The idea is to capture the interest value of an authentic test of one's ability, such as is often provided in schools by literary magazines, portfolios, recitals, games, or debates. Thus, "any exhibition of mastery should be the students' opportunity to show off what they know and are able to do rather than a trial by question."[1]

The exhibition of mastery, as the name implies, is meant to be more than a better test. Like the thesis and oral exam in graduate school, it indicates whether a student has *earned* a diploma, is ready to leave high school.[2] The school is designed "backwards" around these standard-setting tests to endure that teachers and students alike understand their obligations and how their own efforts fit in a larger context. Teachers "teach to the test" because the test is essential—and teacher designed.

But why institute a radically new form of assessment? Why not just improve conventional teaching and course-related tests? As the "Study of High Schools" documented, a major cause of the high school's inadequacies is the absence of direct teaching of the essential skills of inquiry and expression. Even in "demanding" schools, students often fail to learn how to learn. The culprit is discipline-based curriculums that lead to content-based teaching and testing the essential (cross-disciplinary) habits and skills of reading, writing, questioning, speaking and listening fall through the cracks of typical content-focused syllabi and course credits, as indicated, for example, when teachers say "I teach English, not reading."

A required final public exhibition of know-how ensures that those essentials are taught and learned. The final exit-level exhibition reveals whether a would-be graduate can demonstrate control over the skills of inquiry and expression and control over an intellectual topic that approximates the expert's ability to use knowledge effectively and imaginatively. A final exhibition provides students with an occasion to make clear, if only perhaps symbolically, that they are ready to graduate.

An exhibition challenges students to show off not merely their knowledge but their initiative, not merely their problem solving but their problem posing, not just their learning on cue, but their ability to judge and learn how to learn on an open-ended problem, often of their own design. The experience this typically focuses on the essential skills of "inquiry and expression"—a synthesis that requires questioning, problem posing, problem solving, independent research, the creation of a product or performance, and a *public* demonstration of mastery. Significantly, there is often a component calling for self-reflection and analysis of what one has undergone and learned.

Thus, a *final exhibition* is a misnomer in an important sense. Many Coalition schools provide a semester, or yearlong course, an adult adviser, and a committee to ensure that a student has adequate guidance, evaluation, and incentive (see Figure 22.1 for an example of a final exhibition from a Coalition school). The exhibition of mastery is as much a process as a final product, if not more so. The process of choosing topics, advisers, and committees and refining one's ideas and skills is a yearlong exercise in understanding and internalizing standards.

A similar approach to a diploma at the college level has been used successfully at Alverno College, Milwaukee, Wisconsin, for over a decade.[3] Assessment is a central experience, with coursework a means to a set of known ends students must achieve mastery in the following eight general areas, with their progress in each area being charted on a multistaged scale:

1. effective community ability,

2. analytic capability,

3. problem-solving skills,

4. valuing in a decision-making context,

5. effective social interaction,

6. taking responsibility for the global environment,

7. effective citizenship,

8. aesthetic responsiveness.

Performances: Better Classroom Tests

Course-specific texts also have glaring weaknesses, not only because they are often too low level and content heavy. They are rarely

Figure 22.1   An Example of a Final Exhibition

All seniors must complete a portfolio, a study project on U.S. history, and 15 oral and written presentations before a R.O.P.E. committee composed of staff, students and an outside adult. Nine of the presentations are based on the materials, in the portfolio and the project; the remaining six are developed for presentation before the committee. All seniors must enroll in a yearlong course designed to help them meet these requirements.

The eight-part *portfolio*, developed in the first semester, is intended to be "a reflection and analysis of the senior's own life and times." The requirements include:

- a written autobiography,
- a reflection on work (including a resume),
- an essay on ethics,
- a written summary of coursework in science,
- an artistic product or a written report on art (including an essay on artistic standards used in judging artwork).

The *project* is a research paper on a topic of the student's choosing in American history. The student is orally questioned on the paper in the presentations before the committee during the second semester.

The *presentations* include oral tests on the previous work, as well as six additional presentations, on the essential subject areas and "personal proficiency" (life skills, setting and realizing personal goals, etc.). The presentations before the committee usually last an hour, with most students averaging about 6 separate appearances to complete all 15.

A diploma is awarded to those students passing 12 of the 15 presentations and meeting district requirements in math, government, reading, and English.

NOTE: This summary is paraphrased from both the R.O.P.E. Student Handbook and an earlier draft of Archbald and Newmann's (1988) *Beyond Standardized Testing.*

designed to be authentic tests of intellectual ability, as with standardized tests, teacher-designed finals are usually intended to be quickly read and scored.

It seems wise, then, to talk about a move toward more intellectual performances in course-bound testing as a way of stressing the need to make tests more central, authentic, and engaging—as in the arts and athletics. (The term *exhibitions* would be reserved for those culminating graduation-level exercises designed to assess ability in the essentials underlying all coursework required for graduation.)

Designing performances implies a very different approach to standard setting than is implied by typical criterion-referenced tests or outcome-based views of mastery, though the instincts behind the designs are similar. Performances would ideally *embody* and *evoke* desired outcomes in authentic contexts. Too often, specifying only outcomes leads to tests that atomize and decontextualize knowledge: the test-maker designs a set of isolated pat exercises designed to elicit each desired outcome. Genuine tests of ability rarely provide such blatant cues and simple recall; they require us to have a repertoire, the judgment and skill to "put it all together" in one central challenge, repeatedly tried. (Imagine the assessment of music ability in a series of little exercises tried once, rather than through practice and performance of a complete piece in recitals.)

In sum, the goals behind the exhibition of mastery and the performance are to design standard-setting tests that provide more direct evidence of a student's intellectual ability; design tests that are thus able to stand by themselves as objective results; design more authentic intellectual challenges at the heart of a discipline, and design tests that are more likely to engage students and motivate them to raise their own intellectual standards to do well on them. (See Figure 22.2 for an example of a performance that illustrates and illuminates these design standards.)

Toward More Authentic Tests

Exhibitions and performances sound fine on a schoolwide basis, you say, but districtwide or statewide? Isn't that too costly and cumbersome? I contend that the supposed impracticality and/or expense of designing such texts on a wide scale is a habit of thinking, not a fact. The United States is the only major country that relies so heavily on norm-referenced, short-answer tests instead of performance- and/or classroom-based assessment on a national level. In addition, a national committee on assessment in Great Britain has called for an exemplary system requiring flexible, criterion-referenced, and performance-based tests.[4] Many of the tests would be created by classroom teachers, who would be part of the standardizing process through "moderating" meetings to compare and balance results on their own and national tests.

In the U.S., more authentic skill assessment can now be focused on various districts and states due, in part, to the work in writing assessment by the National Writing Project and its state off-shoots (such as the California CAP writing test), and the American Council on the Teaching of Foreign Languages in the assessment of foreign language proficiency. Some states, such as Connecticut, have already designed and piloted performance-based assessment using ACTFL tests and

Figure 22.2   An Example of a Test of Performance

An Oral History Project for 9th Graders

To the student:

You must complete an oral history based on interviews and written sources and then present your findings orally in class. The choice of subject matter is up to you. Some examples of possible topics include: your family, running a small business, substance abuse, a labor union, teenage parents, and recent immigrants.

Create three workable hypotheses based on your preliminary investigations and four questions you will ask to test out each hypothesis.

Criteria for Evaluation of Oral History Project

To the teacher:

Did student investigate three hypotheses?

Did student describe at least one change over time?

Did student demonstrate that he or she had done background research?

Were the four people selected for the interviews appropriate sources?

Did student prepare at least four questions in advance, related to each hypothesis?

Were those questions leading or biased?

Were follow-up questions asked where possible, based on answers?

Did student note important differences between "fact" and "opinion" in answers?

Did student use evidence to prove the ultimate best hypothesis?

Did student exhibit organization in writing and presentation to class?

NOTE: This example is courtesy of Albin Moser, Hope High School, Providence, Rhode Island.

criteria. In addition, they have piloted hands-on tests in graphics, small engines, and science. Vermont has proposed a statewide assessment system that would be portfolio based and teacher assessed.

We already have a national example in science: the 1987 NAEP pilot "Higher-Order Thinking Science Test," which includes some (though too few) hands-on experiments. One example:

Students are given a sample of three different materials and an open box. The samples differ in size, shape and weight. The students are asked to determine whether the box would weigh the most (and least) if it were completely filled with material A, B, or C. There are a variety of possible approaches . . . NAEP administrators used detailed check-lists to record each student's procedures and strategies.[5]

NAEP borrowed most of its experiments from the British Assessment of Performance Unit tasks, which have been used (and reliably scored) in Great Britain for a decade in reading, speaking, listening, math, and science.

Genuine tests *can* be widely implemented if we can overcome inertia and fatalism about current forms of standardized testing. Authentic, performance-based testing is a reality, not a romantic vision. There is also ample room for more intelligent design and use of conventional norm-referenced standardized tests.[6]

The state of Connecticut has developed a "Common Core of Learning," which lists objectives and criteria in all essential domains. Performance-based tests, built around criteria specified by experts in each field and involving tests administered by trained observers, are to be designed to honor those aims.

There are even standardized assessments worth noting. ACT has developed a wide-ranging multimedia test of "general education knowledge and skills" called COMP, designed for colleges but easily adaptable to the high school level. The test uses art reproduction and audiotapes of new programs, for example, in testing writing and listening skills. On other items, students draft letters on different topics. There is even allowance for the student to respond orally on tape to a few test questions. The test takes six hours to administer, covers all the essential skills of inquiry and expression, and includes a 54-question self-assessment about one's patterns of activity related to each competency.

In sum, authentic tests have four basic characteristics in common. First, they are designed to be truly representative of performance in the field, only then are the problems of scoring reliability and logistics of testing considered. Second, far greater attention is paid to the teaching and learning of the *criteria* to be used in the assessment. Third, self-assessment plays a much greater role than in conventional testing.[7] And, fourth, the students are often expected to present their work and defend themselves publicly and orally to ensure that their apparent mastery is genuine. (See Figure 22.3 for a more thorough list of characteristics of authentic tests.)

Toward a Performance-Based Diploma

The diploma by exhibition implies radically different standard for graduation. Instead of seat time or the mere accrual of Carnegie units, the diploma is performance based and criterion referenced. We may

Figure 22.3   Characteristics of Authentic Tests

A. Structure and Logistics

1. Are more appropriately public; involve an audience, a panel, and so on.
2. Do not rely on unrealistic and arbitrary time constraints.
3. Offer known, not secret, questions or tasks.
4. Are more like portfolios or a *season* of games (not one-shot).
5. Require some collaboration with others.
6. Recur—and are *worth* practicing for; rehearsing, and retaking.
7. Make assessment and feedback to students so central that school schedules, structures, and policies are modified to support them.

B. Intellectual Design Features

1. Are "essential"—not needlessly intrusive, arbitrary, or contrived to "shake out" a grade.
2. Are "enabling"-constructed to point the student toward more sophisticated use of the skills or knowledge.
3. Are contextualized, complex intellectual challenges, not "atomized" tasks, corresponding to isolated "outcomes."
4. Involve the student's own research or use of knowledge, for which "content" is a means.
5. Assess student habits and repertoires, not mere recall or plug-in skills.
6. Are *representative* challenges—designed to emphasize depth more than breadth.
7. Are engaging and educational.
8. Involve somewhat ambiguous ("ill-structured") tasks or problems.

C. Grading and Scoring Standards

1. Involve criteria that assess essentials, not easily counted (but relatively unimportant) errors.
2. Are not graded on a "curve" but in reference to performance standards (criterion-referenced, not norm-referenced).
3. Involve demystified criteria of success that appear to *students* as inherent in successful activity.
4. Make self-assessment a part of the assessment.
5. Use a multifaceted scoring system instead of one aggregate grade.
6. Exhibit harmony with shared schoolwide aims—a *standard*.

D. Fairness and Equality

1. Ferret out and identify (perhaps hidden) strengths.
2. Strike a *constantly* examined balance between honoring achievement and native skill or fortunate prior training.
3. Minimize needless, unfair, and demoralizing comparisons.
4. Allow appropriate room for student learning styles; aptitudes, and interests.
5. Can be—should be—attempted by *all* students, with the test "scaffolded up," not "dumbed down," as necessary.
6. Reverse typical test-design procedures: they make "accountability" serve student learning (Attention is primarily paid to "face" and "ecological" validity of tests).

not be ready for the demise of age grading and social promotion; but if the harm done by standardized testing is to be undone, we need to redesign schools "backwards" around graduation-level standards of performance.

The performances and exhibitions should be designed prior to instruction, thus setting the school's standards in functional, not merely abstract and idealized, terms. Seeing them as add-ons to the traditional curriculum is to miss the point. How must the school be redesigned to support exhibitions or any form of exit-level standards? This should be the question behind "restructuring" and the source of vigorous debate among faculties and school board members. Designing and institutionalizing exhibitions would better ensure, in other words, that the school had clear, coherent, and effective standards. Knowing the desired student abilities and work standards, as embodied in culminating performances and scoring criteria, would force key issues of policy: how will time, space, personnel, and other resources be best spent to ensure that diploma standards are met?

To talk with disdain of "teaching to the test" is to misunderstand how we learn. The test is the point of leverage—for learning and for reform. The issue is the integrity of the test: the genuineness, effectiveness, and aptness of the challenge. The finals (and the criteria by which they are graded) set the standards of acceptable work in a course and a school—irrespective of noble language in school district reports or teacher intentions as reflected in syllabi. Legitimate and effective assessment is as simple(!) as ensuring that tests, grades, diploma requirements, and the structures and policies of the schools practice what we preach as essential. If we so honor our professed aims, the problems associated with standardized testing will take care of themselves.

Notes

1. From *Horace's Compromise* (Sizer, 1984), p. 68.

2. This (final) exhibition is patterned after the 18th century model of a public display of one's ability to engage in disputation "candidates for degrees expected to be academically tested at Commencement itself. Bachelor of Arts candidates prepared theses or topics on which they would be quizzed, and candidates for the Master of Arts submitted questions they were ready to defend. Titles of theses and questions were printed in advance and handed out at Commencement, and visitors often took the opportunity of challenging the candidates on their knowledge" (from the Harvard University Commencement program).

3. See the booklet *Assessment at Alverno College,* available from the college. For a history and an analysis of Alverno's program (as well as a general discussion of competency-based higher education), see *On Competency* (Grant, Elbow et al., 1979).

4. *National Curriculum Task Group on Assessment and Testing: A Report.* Available from the Department of Education and Science. This is a landmark document, outlining in readable prose a plan for intelligent and humane assessment.

5. From *Learning By Doing* (Educational Testing Service, 1987).

6. See the excellent article by Dan Koretz of the RAND Corporation in the Summer 1998 issue of *American Educator,* which sums up the current controversy about norm-referenced state testing (the "Lake Wobegon effect" of each state being above average) and provides a useful set of guidelines for assessing assessment.

7. At Alverno, self-assessment is often the first level of proficiency. Thus, in the speaking requirement, students must give a five-minute videotaped talk—with the first evaluations given on the student's self-assessment after watching the videotape.

References

Alverno College Faculty. (1979/1985). *Assessment at Alverno College,* Rev. ed. Milwaukee, WI, Alverno College.

Archbald, D., and F. Newmann. (1988). *Beyond Standardized Testing Authentic Academtc Achievement in the Secondary School.* Reston, VA, NASSP Publications.

Department of Education and Science and the Welsh Office. (1988). *National Curriculum Task Force on Assessment and Testing A Report.* London, Her Majesty's Stationery Office, Department of Education and Science, England and Wales. A brief "Digest for Schools" is also available.

Educational Testing Service. (1987). *Learning By Doing: A Manual for Teaching and Assessing Higher-Order Thinking in Science and Mathematics.* A report on the NAEP pilot of performance-based assessment. A summary of the NAEP pilot of performance-based assessment. Princeton, NJ ETS. The full report: *A Pilot Study of Higher-Order Thinking Skills Assessment Techniques in Science and Mathematics.* ETS Report #17-HOS-80.

Grant, G., P. Elbow, et al. (1979). *On Competence: A Critical Analysis of Competence-Based Reforms in Higher Education.* San Francisco: Jossey-Bass.

Koretz, D. (Summer 1988). "Arriving in Lake Wobegon: Are Standardized Tests Exaggerating Achievement and Distorting Instruction?" *American Educator* 12, 2.

Steer, T. (1984). *Horace's Compromise: The Dilemma of the American High School,* Updated ed. Boston: Houghton-Mifflin.

Wiggins, G. (In press). "A True Test Toward Authentic and Equitable Forms of Assessment." *Phi Delta Kappan.*

Recommended Readings

Alverno College Faculty. (1984). *Analysis and Communication at Alverno: An Approach to Critical Thinking.* Milwaukee, WI, Alverno College.

Berk, R. A., ed. (1986). *Performance Assessment Methods and Applications.* Baltimore, MD: Johns Hopkins University Press.

Bloom, B., G. Madaus, and J. T. Hastings. (1981). *Evaluation to Improve Learning.* New York: McGraw-Hill.

Brooks, G. (1987). *Speaking and Listening Assessment at Age 15.* Great Britain: The Assessment of Performance Unit (APU), Department of Education and Science. APU material exists on the results of performance-based assessments in language, history, math, science, and history in primary and secondary schools.

Elbow, P. (1986). "Trying to Teach While Thinking About the End" and "Evaluating Students More Accurately." In *Embracing Contraries: Explorations in Teaching and Learning.* New York: Oxford University Press. The former chapter originally published in Grant, Elbow, et al. (1979).

Higgs, T., ed. (1984). *Teaching for Proficiency: the Organizing Principle.* Lincolnwood, IL: National Textbook Company and ACTFL.

Sizer, T. (1986). "Changing Schools and Testing: An Uneasy Proposal." In *The Redesign of Testing for the 21st Century.* 1985 EIS Invitational Conference Proceedings. Princeton, NJ: ETS.

Slam, R., et al. (1986). *Using Student Team Learning,* 3rd ed. Baltimore: The Johns Hopkins Team Learning Project Press.

Snow, R. (1988). "Progress in Measurement, Cognitive Science, and Technology That Can Change the Relation Between Instruction and Assessment." In *Assessment in the Service of Learning.* 1987 ETS Invitational Conference Proceedings. Princeton, NJ: ETS.

Spandel, Y. (1981). *Classroom Applications of Writing Assessment: A Teacher's Handbook.* Portland, OR: Northwest Regional Educational Laboratory.

Stiggins, R. (1987). "Design and Development of Performance Assessments." *Educational Measurement Issues and Practices* 6, 3, 33–42. An Instructional Model (ITEMS), published by National Council on Measurement to Education (NCME). Comes with an Instructor's Guide.

Stiggins, R. (January 1988). "Revitalizing Classroom Assessment." *Phi Delta Kappan* 69, 5.

Wiggins, G. (Winter 1987). "Creating a Thought-Provoking Curriculum." *American Educator* 11, 4.

Wiggins, G. (Winter 1988). "Rational Numbers: Scoring and Grading That Helps Rather than Hurts Learning." *American Educator* 12, 4.

23

Dear Professor Marlowe:

How are you? Are you still keeping students a little off balance with your cognitive dissonance tricks? I hope so. Those dilemmas always made us think. Well, I just wanted to touch base and tell you about where I've landed since graduation. I'm soooo . . . excited! I got a job teaching high school math in my home state. Yea . . . me. The kids are great. The school is pretty overcrowded but I have my own room. I like most of the teachers that I've met so far. I attended my first official math department meeting the other day and it went well except there was lots of talk about grades. What is the minimum number of grades we should accumulate? What percentage of the final grade should homework, tests, and quizzes count for? How should final grades be computed? No one even mentioned maybe factoring in effort. I really didn't hear anything that sounded like an alternative approach. One of the math teachers was pretty vocal about giving daily quizzes and weekly tests as his prescription for success. Quote: "At the end of the quarter, I just average all the grades and the student gets what he gets. If he is a fraction of a point away from passing, well, that's the way it is." I don't mind telling you, I'm a little afraid of that teacher. Incidentally, the department chair is requiring that we submit our grade book to her every week so that she can inspect it. Does this make sense? It just seems that these teachers are more interested in using grades as cops. What do I do?

Jamie Nolan

❖ HOW WOULD YOU RESPOND?

How would you respond to teachers who average a series of 20 grades to determine a student's final grade? What factors should be considered when determining a grade for a quarter or a semester? Should the same factors be used in elementary and secondary settings? Should effort be factored into the equation? Should a score be the only measure of student success? Can students participate in arriving at their own grades?

Keep these questions in mind as you read "Competitive Grading Sabotages Good Teaching" by John D. Krumboltz and Christine J. Yeh. What questions do you have about grades and grading? How might you extend the discussion of these ideas in class? Finally, how would you respond to Jamie Nolan?

❖ COMPETITIVE GRADING SABOTAGES GOOD TEACHING

John D. Krumboltz and Christine J. Yeh

Professor Jones took great pride in the bell-shaped curve generated from students' scores on his final exam. He was able to assign grades of A, B, C, D, and F with precision, simply by marking off segments of that normal curve. He told a colleague, "One semester I experimented with a new method of teaching in which I used more examples and explained the material more clearly. It was a disaster! My normal curve was hopelessly skewed. Too many students received high scores. So now I am deliberately more ambiguous in my lectures, I use fewer examples, and I am gratified to find that my exams produce normally distributed scores once again."

In other words, Professor Jones intentionally taught in a way that inhibited student learning. He chose this approach because of the need to assign grades. Clearly, competitive grading can redefine and distort the underlying purpose of education, which is to help every student learn.

To date, arguments against the current grading system have focused on ways in which competitive grading victimizes students, but teachers are negatively affected as well. Assigning competitive grades affects teachers' behavior in five basic ways: 1) it turns teachers into students' opponents, 2) it justifies inadequate teaching methods and styles, 3) it trivializes course content, 4) it encourages methods of evaluation that misdirect and inhibit student learning, and 5) it rewards teachers for punishing students.

Teachers Become Opponents

Many educators justify a differential grading system as a means of sorting students according to their performance. Unfortunately, sorting and ranking students inevitably creates a contentious relationship between students and their teachers. Imagine the following scenario.

Ms. Smith, an 11th-grade English teacher, has a pile of student papers to grade. The topics vary tremendously, and she must assign a letter grade to each paper. Since everyone cannot receive the same grade, Ms. Smith must find reasons to give some papers lower grades than others. As she reads the papers, she looks for flaws—awkward sentences, factual errors, incorrect interpretations—and marks each one in red ink. She concentrates on the negative, carefully counting errors. If a student complains about his or her grade, those errors will be her defense. But what about the student? Is he or she encouraged to write more or look for ways to improve the paper? More likely, the student will feel discouraged, defeated, and humiliated.

Now imagine the same scenario with one difference: no grades are expected or allowed. Ms. Smith's sole purpose is to motivate all the students to learn and to improve their work. Does she read and respond to the papers differently? Most certainly. Now she points out the strengths of the writing—the apt phrase, the persuasive argument, the clever use of alliteration. She considers and appreciates students' ideas and their individual learning styles. She is constantly looking for improvement.

To assign grades, teachers must become critics whose focus is negative, always seeking errors and finding fault with students' work. Moreover, students must be compared with one another, because there is no accepted standard for a given letter grade. A performance that earns an A in one classroom could earn a C in another classroom because of differences in the teachers' standards or in the composition of the two classes.

When judging the relative merit of students' performances takes precedence over improving their skills, few students can feel good about their accomplishments. Only one student can be the best; the rest are clearly identified as less able. Comparative grading ensures that, unlike children in Lake Wobegon, half of the students will be below average.

It could be argued that, despite the drawbacks, grading is necessary in order to sort people. Colleges demand high school grades, for example, to help them decide which applicants to admit. But high schools should never compromise their central mission in order to satisfy the demands of colleges for student rankings.

What would colleges do if high schools refused to employ a competitive grading system? Colleges would find some other method of deciding whom they wished to admit. High schools have no responsibility to serve colleges by performing the sorting function for them. Since mandatory sorting undermines student learning, colleges have no right to demand competitive grades from high schools. High schools cannot serve two masters.

Grading Justifies Inadequate Methods of Teaching

When students fail to achieve course objectives, whose responsibility is it—the teachers' or the students'? Current grading practices put the onus squarely on the students. Teachers can use the most slipshod of teaching methods, discover that many students do not understand the material, and then assign grades accordingly. Current grading practices do not encourage teachers to help students improve, because only the students are blamed when they fail to learn.

If every student achieved all the objectives of a given course, every student would earn an A—an unacceptable state of affairs in the current view. Thus teachers are reinforced for using methods that ensure that some students will not succeed. For example, instruction is often provided in a unidirectional manner, as in a lecture, and interaction between the lecturer and the students is discouraged. Moreover, teachers often create conditions that inhibit students from challenging them or asking questions. Most people find it difficult to sit and listen to someone else talk for long periods of time. Those students who can tolerate that situation best will tend to receive higher grades.

In developing examinations, many teachers tend to focus on objective information that cannot be disputed. By emphasizing the memorization of facts, however, such teachers discourage debate, inhibit the expression of opinion, minimize teamwork and cooperation, and force students to listen passively—the very worst way to learn. An emphasis on memorization deprives students of opportunities to ponder their ideas critically or to discuss their ideas publicly. Students have to remember the facts only long enough to pass the next exam.

Meanwhile, teachers find it easy to dispense, and then test for, factual information. Unidirectional teaching gives them a safety net. If students are unable to demonstrate comprehension of the material covered in lectures, they are presumed to have been inattentive and thus are blamed for their poor performance.

Teachers who rush to cover all the material in a course syllabus are really trying to cover their behinds. If a student fails to understand the material, such a teacher can say, "I did my job. I covered it in class."

Grades Trivialize Course Content

Which of the following questions is more challenging to a student?

- When was the Declaration of Independence signed?
- Would you have signed the Declaration of Independence if you had lived in 1776? Why or why not?

The answer seems clear. The first question requires students to memorize a date. The second question requires them to think—to imagine themselves in another time and place and then to justify an action that would profoundly affect their own lives and the lives of others. However, many teachers might hesitate to include such thought-provoking questions on a test. Grading students' responses would be time-consuming and laborious, requiring subjective judgments that would be hard to justify to students and their parents.

If assigning grades were not required, teachers might opt for the second question. Thus course content is determined, at least partly, by the need to grade students. Teachers would be liberated to teach toward more consequential goals if they were not obligated to assign grades.

Grading Inhibits Constructive Evaluation

Evaluation of student performance is essential, but it should serve to promote student learning. Ideally, the evaluation process would help students discover how to improve their achievement of important goals. Grading defeats this purpose by discouraging the vast majority of students, who receive below-average grades, and by not challenging students who could improve on what they have already learned. Constructive evaluation encourages students to exert maximum effort by emphasizing their strengths, identifying concrete ways for them to improve, and providing them with positive reinforcement for progress.

Mandatory grading encourages teachers to evaluate their students in ways that do not promote critical thinking and long-term retention. For example, teachers of large classes may assign grades based on students' ability to memorize facts. Tests based on factual information are simple and quick to score, but they do not foster critical thinking.

Pressure to perform well often causes students to attend only to "material that will be on the final." Their behavior in preparing for a test depends on the nature of the test. If they believe that the test will require knowledge of isolated facts, most students will try to memorize isolated facts (which will quickly be forgotten). Students develop learning styles that they expect to yield good grades. They quickly learn that the operational definition of a course objective is "what appears on the final exam."

Teachers Can Take Pride in Failure

Some teachers feel proud when a high percentage of their students fail. They want others to believe that a high failure rate signifies a difficult course and an intelligent teacher. To a large extent, they succeed.

There is a common assumption that taking a "tough" course is more prestigious than taking a "Mickey Mouse" course. Some teachers believe that giving students low grades adds luster to their own reputations. Such teachers may choose to include excessively difficult material in their courses simply to enhance their own self-importance.

One way of guaranteeing a high failure rate is to present material that is too difficult for most of the class to comprehend. But the inclusion of material for this purpose stands education on its head. Teachers deserve shame, not praise, if their students fail to achieve.

Teachers who take pride in giving low grades blame the students, not themselves, when course material is not mastered as quickly as it is presented. They expect every student to learn the same material in the same amount of time. The few students who master the material are "proof" that this expectation is realistic. Although the system is rigged so that some students fail, the teacher can always point to the few high achievers and say, "They understood. Why didn't you?" The students who fail are blamed undeservedly, and the teachers who fail them are esteemed undeservedly—but the real culprit is the grading system.

Competitive grades turn educational priorities on their head. Classes in which most of the students master the material are perceived as unchallenging. High grades are often dismissed as "grade inflation," not as a sign that the teacher and the students have successfully achieved their mutual objectives. Meanwhile, prestige is accorded to teachers who are unable to help most of their students learn the material. The situation is ridiculous.

Teachers and students are all victims of a competitive grading system. Competitive grading creates a conflict of interest for teachers: improving students' learning versus judging the relative merit of their academic performance. As long as teachers are forced to make comparative judgments, they cannot focus single-mindedly on the improvement of students' learning. Indeed, under the competitive grading system, teachers are not required to help every student learn, but they are required to judge every student. Judgment is mandatory; improvement is optional.

Teachers may not realize how much of their job frustration stems from this inherent conflict. By definition, half of all students must receive below-average grades. Student reactions to negative evaluations range from passive resistance to active rebellion. The resultant hostile interactions between students and teachers leave many teachers feeling apprehensive much of the time.

Competitive grading deemphasizes learning in favor of judging. Learning becomes a secondary goal of education. Clearly, then, the need to grade students undermines the motive—to help students learn—that brought most of us into the profession.

24

Dear Professor Canestrari:

Got a question for you. We are spending lots of time testing kids' reading ability in my kindergarten class and we are using the Developmental Reading Ability (DRA) assessment that produces a grade-level equivalency score. Well, I have this little girl in my class, Serena. She is a great kid . . . very precocious and I know that she can read. So, I bring Serena in and instead of starting with the recommended Level A, which is nothing more than, "I see the cat," I decide to start at Level C, which I'm guessing might be more appropriate for Serena. Of course, Serena reads the passage beautifully and scores 100% on the comprehension. So, I move up to the next level and the next and the next and Serena, who now feels that she ought to help me along with this whole thing, says to me, "You know Ms. Gardiner, I'm already reading chapter books at home." "I know, I know, Serena," I say. OK, I think to myself, let's try Level M, the lion and the mouse story. Serena proceeds to read the story with all the interpretation and emotion of an accomplished actress. She reads in a tiny squeaky voice, "I am a mouse." She reads the lion part with a huff and a puff and growl. I say, "You know what Serena, you are unbelievable!" What do I do with Serena, Dr. Canestrari? I mean the Curriculum Director has imposed the same basal readers on all the elementary schools in the district. And you know what's coming . . . monthly tests and reports on levels of student reading comprehension. Incidentally, the Curriculum Director offers a three-credit course on differentiated instruction. What irony. Can you believe that?

Nancy Gardiner

❖ HOW WOULD YOU RESPOND?

If students seem to be progressing at different rates, should they still be assessed in the same way, against the same standards? Is it important to group students according to ability? What should teachers do when some students are clearly exceeding the standard?

Keep these questions in mind as you read "Letter to a State Test Scorer" by Stephen Kramer. What questions do you have about classroom assessment? How might you extend the discussion of these ideas in class? Finally, how would you respond to Nancy Gardiner?

❖ LETTER TO A STATE TEST SCORER (FROM A SCIENCE TEACHER WHO KNOWS HIS 5TH GRADERS WELL)

Stephen Kramer

"*Not everything that can be counted counts . . . and not everything that counts can be counted.*"

—Albert Einstein

Dear Washington State Science Test Scorer:

I've been thinking about you this summer. I know that one of these days you'll be opening a box of test booklets my students worked on last spring. For three hours, approximately one hour per day, my 5th graders read and answered multiple-choice, short answer, and longer-response questions designed to measure their knowledge of Washington state's Essential Academic Learning Requirements for science.

Now it's your turn. You've been hired and trained to score my students' papers with a checklist/rubric. When you are finished, there will be 26 numbers—one for each pupil—that indicate how proficient my students are in science. This year the test is being piloted. Once it's finalized, however, annual science scores for my school will be published every autumn in our local newspaper, along with scores in reading, math, writing, and listening. People in both Washington state and in Washington, D.C., will make judgments about our school based on those scores and any increases or decreases they show in the next few years.

The funny thing is, I could have told you who was going to do well and who was going to struggle before my class had even sharpened their No. 2 pencils. The test, like many assessments we're being asked to give elementary students these days, contained many open-ended items requiring students to think, analyze, and write at cognitive levels at the upper limit of their developmental abilities. I love posing such questions to students. They're at the heart of any good science lesson, and we use them in classroom discussions to learn about science and to learn from each other. But there's a different dynamic at work when such items are given to 10- and 11-year-olds in test booklets. Under those conditions—when students work in isolation and aren't allowed to ask questions or clarify their thoughts through discussion-student performance is highly correlated with factors such as IQ, general background knowledge, attention span, and writing ability.

There are stories behind the names on the test booklets I'm sending you—things I think you should know. If I could sit at your side while you evaluate my students' work, here are some things I'd say:

I realize you'll have to give Vitaly a failing score. Except for the name on the cover, his test book is completely blank. But I hope you don't think he doesn't care or didn't try. Vitaly's family recently immigrated to the United States. He didn't attend school much before he came to this country. Vitaly is excited about learning to read, and he's making good progress. However, he's just now entering what English-as-a-second-language teachers call the "speech immersion stage" of language development—meaning that he's beginning to try out short phrases in English conversation. A couple of weeks ago, when I was checking with Vitaly about his lunch, I asked whether he knew what a peanut butter and jelly sandwich was. He smiled and shook his head "no." According to the rules of the federal No Child Left Behind Act of 2001, I had to give Vitaly the science test along with the rest of my class. After he wrote his name on the cover, I kneeled by his desk and we looked at the first page together. I asked him if he understood any of the questions. He wrinkled his brow, stared at the page for a long moment, and then shook his head "no." At that point, I patted his shoulder and smiled to let him know it was OK. Then I closed the test booklet and put it away: Vitaly now knows what a peanut butter and jelly sandwich is; we haven't been able to communicate much yet about the scientific method.

But I wish you could see the smile on Vitaly's face when he runs across the field behind our school with an insect net in his hands. And last spring, when we were doing a lab using baking soda to compare the acid content of various liquids, you should have seen how carefully he measured fruit juices with his syringe. Maybe Vitaly will grow up to become a veterinarian or a medical researcher.

Lindsey left quite a few of the essay-type questions unanswered. Reading has never been easy for her, and she sometimes goes off on a tangent when she has to follow written instructions on her own. But you should see Lindsey during our class discussions—when I'm explaining how metamorphic rocks are formed or how diabetes affects people. She's like a sponge, soaking up information—and she remembers what she hears. That's the *way* she learns. Lindsey doesn't say much, but when she raises her hand, I frequently hear a question or a comment that's full of insight. Last fall, our class built rubber-band-powered go-carts. When other students became exasperated by the technical problems of finding ways to increase wheel diameter or rubber-band-engine power, Lindsey was the one with the ideas and persistence who got things going again. She's also an excellent facilitator, a person who can help three other squabbling students get back on task. I believe Lindsey has a future as a mechanical engineer.

Logan's test booklet has some excellent answers—and some questions you may think that he skipped. Actually, it's not Logan's style to skip anything. You see, whether I give Logan an art project or a writing assignment, he needs lots of time to process and think things through before he can even make the first mark on his paper. Before I understood this: I sometimes tried to keep him moving along at the pace of his classmates. I quickly found that made both of us unhappy. I eventually discovered that if I let Logan work at his own pace, he would often complete a piece of artwork or writing that was so creative, detailed, and thoughtful that it would give me goose bumps. Even though the instructions in the science booklet said that Logan could have taken as much time as he needed, he was overwhelmed by the number of items on the test. Remember, he's only been an 11-year-old for a month! Although he left many items blank, I'll bet some of his answers are as thoughtful as any you'll see. I'm guessing that Logan will grow up to become a biological illustrator, or perhaps a children's science-book author/artist.

I know that the science test I gave was just the pilot. I also know that a committee has yet to evaluate the results and establish a cutoff point that will identify which students pass and which don't. But this emphasis on testing has a downside. I keep thinking about recent in-service trainings I've attended on teaching reading, writing, and math. The people in charge were all good presenters. They were enthusiastic and had the interests of students at heart. But as I left the trainings, I was saddened by the fact that in each one I'd heard about how the activities I was learning would improve my students' scores on state-mandated tests. I didn't hear, in any of them, how the activities would help my students develop a greater love of reading, writing, or math.

I could tell you stories about Michael, Jennifer, Richard, and every other child in my class—but I hope you understand my point. Evaluating students is a complex task. The science tests I just gave— and others like them—can turn out to be more like sieves than measuring cups. Some of the most important things we do in the classroom end up leaking through the holes. A well-constructed test can give teachers important information about what students know and where to focus instructional time. It's just that I'd hate for anyone to think that a single number represents what the 5th graders in our school know about science. It's a lot more complicated than that.

Questions for Reflection

L et's look back at the letters and readings in **Part VI, What Do Good Assessments Look Like?** Consider the following questions as you begin formulating your own ideas about how to apply theories of development into planned instructional practice.

1. What connections do you see between motivation and assessment? How might the type of assessment a teacher relies on affect student motivation? What kinds of assessment do you think B. F. Skinner would support?

2. Do assessments of student learning have to be rigorous to be worthwhile? Should assessments, ideally, be something that makes students nervous? How are high-stakes assessments (e.g., those that require a passing score to graduate or advance a grade) inconsistent with the research concerning motivation you read about in Part V?

3. How does competition for grades (or for teacher approval) influence learning and motivation? How do you think Grant Wiggins would resolve the difficulties that Krumboltz and Yeh ascribe to the use of grades? How should students be assessed if they are to work together in the kinds of groups that Aronson describes? Should teachers give grades to an entire group, or try to figure out the individual contribution of each group member?

4. Think about Kramer's "Letter to a State Test Scorer." How do his ideas help to inform teachers about making the kinds of connections with students that result in the most powerful learning? In what ways are his views consistent with those of Wiggins, Kohn, and Krumboltz and Yeh?

❖ YOUR OWN IDEAS

What ideas seem most important to you as you reflect about teaching and learning in real classrooms? What do you think is most important for new teachers to consider? What further questions did the authors raise for you in Part VI that have not been adequately answered?

_____

_____

_____

_____

_____

_____

_____

_____

_____

_____

_____

_____

_____

_____

Suggested Readings

Bracey, G. (1998). *Put to the test: An educator's and consumer's guide to standardizes testing*. Bloomington, IN: Phi Delta Kappan.

Brooks, J. G., & Brooks, M. G. (1993). *In search of understanding: The case for constructivist classrooms*. Alexandria, VA: Association for Supervision and Curriculum Development.

Kohn, A. (2000). *The care against standardized testing: Raising the scores, ruining the schools*. Portsmouth, NH: Heinemann.

Johnson, D. W., & Johnson, R. T. (2002). *Meaningful assessment: A meaningful and cooperative process*. Boston: Allyn & Bacon.

Meier, D. (2000). *Will standards save public education?* Boston: Beacon.

Neill, M., Bursh, P., Schaeffer, B., Thall, C., Yohe, M., & Zappardino, P. (1995). *Implementing performance assessments: A guide to classroom, school and system reform*. Cambridge, MA: Fair Test.

Popham, W. J. (2002). *Classroom assessment: What teachers need to know* (3rd ed.). Boston: Allyn & Bacon.

Taylor, K., & Walton, S. (1998). *Children at the center: A workshop approach to standardized test preparation*. Portsmouth, NH: Heinemann.

Wiggins, G. (1991). Standards, not standardization: Evoking quality student work. *Educational Leadership, 48*(5), 18–25.

Index

About the Editors

Bruce A. Marlowe earned his PhD in educational psychology from The Catholic University of America in Washington, DC, where he also completed 2 years of postdoctoral training in neuropsychological assessment. He is the coauthor (with Marilyn Page) of *Creating and Sustaining the Constructivist Classroom* (Corwin Press) and of a six-part video series titled *Creating the Constructivist Classroom* (The Video of Journal Education). He is also the coeditor (with Alan Canestrari) of *Educational Foundations: An Anthology of Critical Readings* (Sage, 2004). He has taught at the elementary, secondary, and university levels and is currently Associate Professor of educational psychology and special education at Roger Williams University.

Alan S. Canestrari, EdD, Boston University, is a veteran social studies practitioner and Assistant Professor of Education, Roger Williams University. He has had a long career in public schools and universities as a history teacher, a department chair, an adjunct professor at Rhode Island College, and a mentor in the Brown University Masters of Teaching Program. He was the RI Social Studies Teacher of the Year in 1992. He is the coeditor (with Bruce Marlowe) of *Educational Foundations: An Anthology of Critical Readings* (Sage, 2004).

Bruce and Alan have both taught courses in psychology; neither is satisfied with any of the educational psychology texts currently available on the market. Both authors can be reached by mail at Roger Williams University, School of Education, One Old Ferry Road, Bristol, Rhode Island 02809 and also by telephone and e-mail: Bruce A. Marlowe at (401) 254-3078, bmarlowe@rwu.edu; Alan S. Canestrari at (401) 254-3749, acanestrari@rwu.edu.